INSANITY BEYOND UNDERSTANDING

Bajeerao Patil

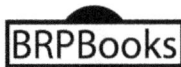

BRPBooks

MEDIA PA

Copyright

Design & Layout by Prem Puthur
Printed in the United States of America
ISBN 978-0-9895698-2-8
Published by BRPBooks
307 Woodridge Lane
Media
PA 19063

This book is for Dipti, Adwaita, Aditya, Arohi, my mother, and my late father.

Author's Note

The names and other identifying characteristics of the persons included in this book have been changed to conceal their identities.

Acknowledgements

It would have been impossible to write this book without the help of my best friend, Sandy Membrino. I do not have enough words to express my gratitude to her. I am also thankful to Sandy's entire family, including her sisters Donna Sue, Sally, and Shelly, and their beloved father, Mr. Harry Jones.

I am thankful to my guide and philosopher Prem Puthur, and my friends, Richard Bergamesco and Anthony Guarino, for their encouragement. Special thanks to J. Watts for being tireless in helping me in my endeavor. I am also grateful to Mr. Mohanrao Patil and Mr. B. G. Kolse Patil for their encouragement.

Most of all, I am thankful to my numerous patients. Without them, not a single word of this book would have been written. Their pain, their miseries, their heartache, and their suffering, has taught me more than any college education ever could. I am also thankful to them for allowing me to read my book to them during group sessions, discussing it with me, and providing me with valuable suggestions and encouragement.

Finally, I owe a debt of gratitude to my father-in-law Mr. Shankar Talekar for his patience, for staying awake night after night reading the manuscript, and for providing me with genuine suggestions; and to Nancie-Marie Beck, Darya Crockett, and Lacey Louwagie for their expertise, proofreading, and assistance in publishing my book.

Prelude

Insanity—Beyond Understanding highlights the selfish behavior, distorted thinking, and "my way or the highway" attitude of people who are addicted to mood-altering substances. This book aims at creating a general awareness about addictive behavior, the devastating consequences of using mood-altering chemicals, and how they turn normal human beings into beasts. It shows their inability to follow simple rules for living in harmony, their illogical thinking, and how logic does not make any sense to them. Through their dialogues, readers will get insight into their resistance to change. I want readers to see how impulsive behavior can cause a series of problems and destroy human beings. I want readers to experience the horrible world of addicts, what happens behind closed doors, and how innocent children get crushed and their hopes for living a normal life are shattered. I want readers to experience other people's pain, sufferings, and hopelessness, and at the same time, enjoy reading simple dialogues.

Through my work in the field of addiction, I've found that most addicts believe the world revolves around them. They think their problems are the biggest in the world. They refuse to be happy. They secretly cling to misery. They depend on others to make them happy. They firmly believe that they cannot live without sex. Drugs and sex ruin them.

Where sex is concerned, addicts behave like King David from the scriptures. When King David saw Bathsheba taking a bath, he lusted after her and ordered her to come to his palace. He desired her so badly he forgot that there would be repercussions. He was blinded by his lust. He made her pregnant by committing adultery and started scheming to conceal the identity of the child. He sent for her husband, Uriah, who was at the battlefield at that time. When Uriah arrived, King David told him to go in the house and spend time with Bathsheba, but Uriah refused to do so, stating that it was not fair for him to enjoy married life while his companions were in a battle. This became a cause of worry for King David. So he sent Uriah back to the battlefield and instructed the commander to abandon him at the front to be killed. King David, though an acclaimed warrior, did not know how to maintain his character and dignity. He did not know how to command respect nor enjoy his power. He misused his power and let his sexual lust take over his best judgment.

I've found that sex and drugs have destroyed the characters of those I've met. These addicts do not know how to be high on life, but they do know how to be high on drugs. Sex and drugs are the only two things they live for. As addiction progresses, sex takes second place. Always looking for excitement, immediate gratification becomes their sole goal. For that one kick, they recklessly give up their right to enjoy life. They stop living and start dying with slow poison. They become slaves to mood-altering chemicals.

Apparently, they don't exercise any control over their sensual gratification to avoid future complications. It is said that one should not allow oneself to be too hungry, too angry, too lonely, or too tired. This reminds me of the story of Esau, son of Rebecca and Isaac, twin brother of Jacob. Their mother loved Jacob, but their father loved Esau. Esau was a skillful hunter, and he brought meat that appealed to the old man's taste. One day, Esau returned from an unsuccessful hunting trip. He was hungry. He saw that Jacob was boiling pottage; he would not deny himself, but needed to at once gratify his appetite. He asked for a serving. Jacob asked if he would sell his right as the firstborn son in exchange for a bowl of food. Esau agreed, selling his birthright to Jacob for that now-infamous bowl of pottage. As the firstborn, Esau had a right to be his father's heir. However, his reckless decision to satisfy his appetite cost him future glory. He made an impulsive decision, for he was "too hungry."

The characters within this book also act impulsively, and they easily forget the consequences that come from using of mood-altering chemicals. They lack maturity. They behave like children. They want what they want, how they want, and when they want. They live in the past or in the future, but never in the present. When they need to step up and do something about their situation, they shy away. They refuse to walk a few miles to help themselves, but they expect others to walk extra miles for them. They are averse to hard work, want an easy way out, and look out for short cuts. Eventually, others get tired of them and stop entertaining them, then they start getting angry, and feeling miserable and rejected.

When the time comes to seek help, they postpone taking a first step. They become masters of procrastination. They get their priorities mixed up. They worry constantly, but do nothing to improve their lives. They generally refuse to take responsibility for their own behavior and blame the world for their situation. For them, it is easy to point fingers at others. They experience more pain than others do, but they don't seem to learn from their pain. The sad thing is that a firsthand experience of a rough life doesn't help them grow. If they used it, they could come out on the other side stronger, more capable people.

Once in a recovery situation, they frequently focus on developing a relationship with a "higher power." At the same time, they fail to understand that without developing a relationship with themselves, they cannot develop a relationship with anyone, including a "higher power." They desperately want others to accept them, but they refuse to accept themselves. Most of them are frequently in and out of treatment programs. They are known as "frequent flyers" in the recovery world. In the process, they acquire enough knowledge and information, but they lack a plan of action. They know the lingo and language of recovery very well. But they don't follow through, so the never-ending cycle continues. They simply remain the masters at lip service.

There are those who are victims of their circumstances. They struggle to overcome their situation. Some of them get frustrated and give up. I know staying in recovery is easier said than done. The few who make it work very hard to stop the cycle. No matter what, they don't give up, it is said that a winner is not the one who wins, but the one who doesn't give up. I salute those who make it. They are my heroes and heroines.

The world has become so materialistic that it is difficult for many of us to keep up. We look for shortcuts and quick fixes, even though we know there are none. The change in family structure from close, extended families to individual nuclear families to single parent families has impacted society adversely. Many children grow up without good role models as they are shunted from foster care to orphanages to the home of distant relatives and then back to foster care again. Many grow up on the streets after running away and never even complete eighth grade, let alone high school or job training. A disproportionate number are physically, emotionally, and sexually abused and don't know where to turn for help. The result, all too often, is a belief that this is normal, causing them to inflict the same damage on their own children.

Further contributing to the problem is society's failure to recognize and take responsibility for these situations and the constant under-funding—and at times, misuse of available funding. Too much emphasis is often placed on paperwork rather than on teaching individuals necessary life skills and adequately staffing the agencies and groups who try to make a difference in these lives. If we are ever going to stop this circle, then we, as a society, must take responsibility. We must fund education, job training, and family support systems for everyone, and we need to do so quickly, before we lose another generation to the tragedy of addiction.

Contents

John's Hostility 1
Kareena—The Master of Profanity 17
Hitching a Ride from a Perfect Stranger 29
You Indian Bum 37
Marcus—A Bad Man 50
Mathew's Oral Sex Scandal 55
Veronica's Pseudo Altruism 65
Bill's Typical Jail Mentality 73
Identity Crisis The Double Trouble 85
Adam Feels He's Treated Like a Dog 91
Beaver's Lecherous Father 95
Beaver is Back to His Sliminess 117
Irene's Mental Masturbation 120
Maria Swings at Dee 127
Fredrick—Spits Right Back 135
Lusty Fredrick 141
I Don't Want Your Fucking Counseling 148
Frank With a Sparkle and Craig With His Pants
Down 158
Cherry and Frank—What a Contrast 178
Cherry Blames the Program for Her Pregnancy 184
Ruby and Roger 194
Kathy's Brother is Quacko 202
Sex Ruined Albert 207
Cat is a Fuck Baby 232
Brenda, Rhonda and Wanda—The Innocent Victims of
Incest 237

Michael's Dilemma 247
Kevin Turns into a Beast 255
My Way or the Highway 266
Peter Objects to Staff eating Crabs 285
Brian's Unknown Paradise 291
Jill Contemplates Leaving but Peter is Gone 304
The Height of Impatience 309
Fatal Attraction 325
Chester—Mother's Little Doll 332
Gloria's Confounding Story 346
Bob Turns Homosexual 359
Tracey is Going to be Suicidal Tomorrow 373
A Crack head 393
Lust Mistaken For Love 408
Is This Fate? 416

Chapter 1

John's Hostility

It's 7:45 on Monday morning, and I'm in my office at the rehab center. I come in early so I can complete my work and then go to my evening job at the other rehabilitation center. I hear the front door open, and I smile to myself. Here comes Salina, our administrative assistant. She is always early. Next I hear the back door opening and the jingle of keys—it's Dawn, our substance abuse technician. The clients love her, and she loves them back. She has the heart of a giant. Eboni, our nurse, and Alana, my cotherapist, enter together giggling. It's nice to hear their laughter. "Good morning, Christopher," they chorus together. I wave. Scott, the director, and Stanley, our case manager, are the last to arrive. So everyone is here and we start a new week.

* * *

There is a knock on my office door at eight in the morning. "Who is it?"

"It's Dawn." A hefty woman stands at my door with a broad smile. The smile is her trademark, as if she has patented it.

"Come in, please."

"This is your new client." Handsome, but disheveled and bruised, a man in his early thirties stands behind her. "This is Christopher, your therapist. You can speak with him about your problems," Dawn tells him, then leaves us alone.

I wave him to a chair. He sits across from me, spreading his legs as if sitting on a couch. "Hi. I'm John." He has a husky voice.

"How may I help you, John?"

"I want to call my girlfriend," he says hoarsely.

"Why?"

He gives me a very long stare. I continue, "John, when did you speak with her last?"

"Last night." He continues to stare and then adds, "After I got here."

"You are allowed to make one call every evening after 5 p.m.,"

I tell him.

"No," he says rigidly, "I want to call her now."

"John, I'm afraid you won't be able to call her now."

"Why not?" he shouts.

"The policy of this program allows you to make one call after 5 p.m. every day," I explain calmly.

"Fuck your policy," he snaps.

"Look, John, we are meeting for the first time. We need to discuss your issues and plan how we can work together."

"I don't care." He slaps my desk. "I'm telling you, I need to make that call now."

By this time, I sense he is going to be very difficult. He is demanding and focused on immediate gratification. He also appears stubborn and hostile. I don't want to be judgmental; however, I can't help thinking that he's like a child intent on getting his way.

"I'm sorry, John. I cannot let you make a call unless, and until, you convince me otherwise."

"So, I can't make a call now ?" he asks again, looking fierce.

"No," I answer gently.

He sits there gazing at me.

"John, would you like to talk to me about your issues?"

"Sure—you are pissing me off."

"John, do you want to know anything about the treatment process or about me?"

"Fuck you." He slams my office door on his way out.

* * *

Later in group, I notice John sitting on a couch staring at the floor. I greet the group. "Good morning."

"Good morning," they reciprocate in chorus—except John, who is constantly shifting his sides.

I continue, "I am Christopher; I work here as a therapist. I conduct group sessions between 11:00 a.m. to noon, Monday to Friday. All groups are mandatory. If you are sick and don't want to attend group, you can do so, provided you obtain permission from Ebony, the nurse. If you don't obtain the permission and fail to attend the group, there will be consequences, which include no phone calls, no store run, and if necessary, other privileges will be denied to you. Please be informed that no one is allowed to eat or drink in the community room. A sexual relationship of any kind with your peers is strictly forbidden. We discourage all intimate relationships between clients. Verbal or physical threats to peers or staff will not be tolerated. If you are involved in any kind of misconduct, your name will be written on the communication board in the staff office, along with the corresponding consequences to your misconduct. You can read the handbook about the rules and regulations of this program. A copy is available in the staff office. Your main focus needs to be on your own recovery. I encourage all of you to share your thoughts and feelings without any reservations. You are not allowed to cross talk while group sessions are in progress.

If anyone wants to share or ask a question while another person is sharing, I ask that you raise your hand and obtain permission to speak. Please do not resort to disrespecting the staff or your peers. This is our group, so it is our collective responsibility to make it an interesting, learning experience. Thanks for listening. Now, let's start on my left."

One woman begins: "I'm an addict; my name is Stephanie." She is disheveled, overweight, and anxious looking. She's in her early forties.

"Hi Stephanie," the others respond.

"I'm doing well today," she continues. "I had a good night's sleep, and I'm very happy because my mother sent me one hundred dollars yesterday. That's all I have to share."

"Thanks for sharing," we all say together.

"I am a recovering addict; my name is Marcus."

"Hi, Marcus." We welcome a well-built man in his early forties.

"I don't like to call myself an addict. I prefer to call myself a recovering addict, even if I have only one day clean," he explains.

"Thanks for allowing me to share."

"You're welcome," we say together. "Thanks for sharing."

"I'm Kareena. I'm thirty-three and homeless. I drink alcohol, and smoke marijuana, and crack. I don't want to be here," Kareena grumbles.

"Why not?" I ask.

"I want to get high," she answers flatly.

"I am Sandra. My friend kicked me out. I have no place to live—that's why I am here. I am pregnant. I want to go back home."

In this manner, everyone introduces himself or herself as their turn comes.

"I'm John. I have nothing to share." He lifts his head up slightly and glances at me.

"Thanks for not sharing." I hope injecting some humor will make him feel comfortable.

Everyone laughs except him. He glares at me. *I sense that he is looking for trouble and seems ready to bark, but he wants to be coerced into it. I am afraid that at this point in time, any confrontation about his behavior would be counter productive so I better leave him alone and not look for trouble.*

"Okay. What are we going to discuss today?" I ask.

"You were going to continue our discussion on suffering that we didn't finish the other day," Marcus reminds me.

"Well," I begin, "as I told you earlier, most of the time we suffer emotionally because we want to suffer. Emotional suffering is optional. It is a matter of making appropriate decisions. Any questions, any doubts?"

"No, that's wrong ; it's untrue," John rushes in aggressively.

"Why do you say that?" I ask softly.

"I am not suffering because I want to suffer!" he shouts. After a pause, he continues, "I suffer because no one understands me. Even my girlfriend rejects me."

"John, you don't need to suffer because someone rejects you. The most wonderful relationship you can ever have is with yourself, and it's called self-love. Do you think you should suffer because someone rejects you?"

"No." He shifts in his seat. "But that is easier said than done."

"Let me explain. We are born to be happy. We are not born to suffer. However, if anyone wants to do so, he or she is free to suffer. We can program ourselves not to suffer emotionally. First, we need to deprogram ourselves. We need to unlearn what we have learned in the past that makes us suffer emotionally. I know it's difficult, but it's not impossible." I glance at him; he appears preoccupied, constantly shifting in his seat. He seems anxious to say something back. Instead of letting him speak, I continue. "It is just a matter of being open-minded and willing to unlearn in order to learn new behaviors. Some people refer to learning these new behaviors as an 'awakening.'"

"That's bullshit!" he cries. "If we could just 'reprogram' ourselves, why do we suffer?"

"Because we choose to suffer," Marcus interjects.

"I don't want anyone else to answer; it's his group, let him answer!" He glares at me.

"Well, John, let me make it clear that this is a group session." I speak slowly, keeping him in my view. "Everyone is allowed to share his or her thoughts and feelings. Once you put across your question or share your problem, thoughts, or feelings with the group members, you cannot have a person of only your choice respond. Any group member can do so by raising his or her hand. And John, you need to mind your language. You cannot use "shit," the f-word, or other words of that nature. Am I making myself clear?"

"That's the way I am," he rages, "and I don't want anyone else to speak on your behalf. If you don't know the answer, just say so!" He doesn't take his eyes off me.

"John." I look at him closely. "If you are adamant that you want only me to answer your questions, I can do it when we meet for a one-on-one session. This is a group session, and you cannot choose who will answer your question. We must involve all the members of the group." John shifts his sides again. I continue explaining, "One cannot explain all the suffering in the world. As Anthony de Mello, my spiritual guru, would say, 'there is always a better way of living besides emotionally depending on another human being.'"

Early the following morning, I hear John shouting, "Kareena, give me that literature! I was reading it, and I'm not finished."

"But you weren't reading it when I picked it up." Kareena gives him a hard look. "It is not yours. It belongs to the community."

He angrily steps forward and attempts to snatch the pamphlet from her hand. She is about to plunge into action and at that very moment, I enter the community room. They stop their battle abruptly. However, the incident becomes the focus of discussion, and John walks out of group.

After group, he comes to see me. He appears sullen and depressed. "I am sorry for walking out of the community room, but I feel I have every right to express my personal rights and feelings, don't I?"

"Yes, you do," I reply, "but you need to learn to express your rights and feelings more appropriately. You have every right to protect yourself when something seems unfair. But you need to be assertive and not aggressive."

"What's the use of being assertive when nothing is going right?"

"It helps to decrease the frequency of passive collapse or hostile blow-ups," I explain. "Just because nothing is going right doesn't mean you have the right to be aggressive."

"I wasn't doing anything wrong."

"John, you were hostile and aggressive, verbally as well as physically. You attempted to snatch that literature from Kareena's hand."

"I was just standing up for my own rights," he says defensively.

I glance at him. "You were conscious of your rights, but you were conveniently ignoring her rights. You have to stand up for your own rights without violating the rights of others."

"Just being assertive doesn't help. I think nowadays we have to fight for our rights."

"John, you have to understand that every right comes with responsibilities. However, if you learn to be assertive, you'll be able to express yourself effectively," I tell him carefully, keeping in mind that he has severe anger issues and I don't want to anger him further.

"Do you think we are all treated equally?" he asks unexpectedly.

"No," I reply.

"So, shouldn't we fight when we are not treated equally?" He leans forward.

"I am not talking about fighting. I am talking about being assertive. You have to object when being exploited and mistreated in an assertive way and not in an aggressive manner."

"What if others mistake my assertiveness for aggressiveness?"

"John, if you are assertive, you are assertive. You don't have to look for validation of your feelings and thoughts from others."

He smiles. *During our conversation, I learn that John is thirty years old and a father of three children, ages eight, six, and three. Currently, they are living with his parents. He was raped by a neighbor when he was barely five years old. He is separated from his wife, with whom he used to get high. He has a new girlfriend. He started using marijuana at age seventeen to fit in with the crowd from his neighborhood. Later, he went on to abuse alcohol, cocaine, heroin, and other opiates. He has been in and out of several treatments facilities. This is his seventh long-term rehabilitation program. He is very impulsive and has severe anger issues. He has been convicted twice—once for possession with intent to deliver and the other time for aggravated assault. He has served significant jail time. Although he was brought up a Catholic, he is now practicing Islam. He converted to Islam while in jail, thinking that he would get better protection in jail if he were Muslim. In the course of my work, I have met several clients who converted to Islam just like John—while in jail. But I still don't know whether it is true that they converted to Islam thinking they would be better protected while in jail. Most of them denied it, stating that wasn't the reason for their conversion. They had converted to Islam because Islam is the only true religion, they would say. However, John had stated that he became Muslim while in jail because guards don't dare touch you, nor will the other inmates go after you if you are Muslim.*

* * *

There are continual complaints about John's erratic behavior. He isn't getting along with any of his peers except Bill, who says that John is like a son to him. When the staff tries to talk to him to calm him down, he disrespects them and refuses to follow any directions given. He does not exercise any control over his impulsive behavior and appears to think that getting angry is his birth right. He is so consumed by his anger that he is unable to see how his out-bursts cause him inner turmoil, anxiety, discomfort and disturb his peace of mind. I hope one day he wakes up and gets a grip over his anger and stops this self-destructive behavior that is keeping him sick.

I call him into my office and request that he take a seat. He grudgingly pulls the chair toward the window and begins reaching for the shutters. He opens them and chilling air comes in. I look at him, a little amused by this action. He turns his back toward the window, leans forward in his chair and asks, "What did I do now ?"

I take a careful look at him and am about to say something, but he cuts in with a touch of annoyance and irritation in his voice, "What are you looking for? Signs of resentment? Stress? Anger?"

"None of these," I say slowly.

"Then what do you want to know, Christopher?" he stares at me and puts a lot of emphasis on my name.

"John, why are you having so much difficulty getting along with your peers and staff ?"

"What are you talking about?" He frowns. "I don't have

any difficulty getting along with anyone here. Who the hell is telling you that? These mother-fuckers like to watch what I am doing and then talk about me behind my back." He shifts his weight.

"John, who are you talking about?"

"You know who I am talking about. That fucking Stanley, the case manager. He is a liar. The only thing he does is lie about clients and nothing else."

"Why are you calling him names?"

"I know he is the one who is lying to you about me." He bangs on my desk with his fist.

"John, Stanley did not say a single word about you to me. You are unnecessarily accusing him."

"But I don't like him."

"Just because you don't like him you talk ill of him?" I stare at him.

He grumbles, "But he told me that he will throw me out of this program."

"Why did he say that?"

"I don't know." He shrugs his shoulders. "Maybe because he is a liar."

"John, will you please stop calling him names?"

"I'm sorry but this is how I lash out when my orbit gets ruined."

"What do you mean by your orbit?"

"Everyone has an orbit. I'm talking about my comfort zone. They are fucking getting into my comfort zone. They want to disturb my peace of mind and make me mad." He stands and again reaches for the window shutters. "It's fucking too cold in here," he mutters while shutting them down. He sits down and picks up a stapler on my desk and starts playing with it. I tell him to stop playing with it. He stops, picks up the wasted stapler pins, and holds them in his hand. He seems to be unaware that I am observing him minutely. *I*

rely on the data that I collect myself by 8John's Hostilityobserv-
ing my clients and how they handle certain situations and their
interactions with others while in treatment. The data I get from
other sources including the clients themselves also plays a vital
part in helping them. However, I have experienced that most of
the time the data I receive from clients is biased because it is only
based on their own perceptions. Mostly, what I hear from them
is their side of the story; they knowingly or unknowingly delete
the other side of the story.

"John, can I say something ?" I ask him slowly.

"I guess," he pauses. "Yes, you can."

"John, it seems you have a tendency to blame others and you don't take any responsibility for your behavior."

He moves forward in his chair. "That's a fucking stupid statement you're making. I'm not blaming anyone. They are all full of shit and that's their problem, not mine. How can you ask me to own any responsibility? That's fucking crap you're talking."

"John, you need to have a close look at yourself."

"Why?" he questions gutturally.

"Because you seem to be unaware of your issues."

"Give me an example." He looks at me intently.

"You have serious anger issues."

"Everyone has anger issues," he replies without any noticeable change in his expression.

"So you agree that you have anger issues?"

"Yes," he hesitates.

"Then let's talk about your anger issues."

"Christopher, I'll exhaust you if I start telling you about my anger issues my remorse and regrets."

"I get paid to listen, so go ahead and tell me."

Suddenly, we hear the call for a smoke break. He stands and hurriedly utters, "I'll be right back. They're going for a smoke," and he is out the door.

Instead of feeling angry when he leaves abruptly, I feel rather relieved, because I get some time to reflect on what I have come to know so far about him.

Within fifteen minutes or so, he comes back and sits in a different chair this time. "I like this chair better than that one." He points to the chair he was sitting in earlier. "Because this is softer and more comfortable than that one," he pauses, looks at me carefully, takes a deep breath, and resumes, "you won't believe it but it is true that my anger issues started off when I was an infant. I would get angry for being fed milk that was too cold for my belly. At the time, I never know it would grow with me and would haunt me like this. As far as remorse goes, I've developed a crazy, crazy theory. It is called 'Hunter never mourns for the deer.' Regrets are something that we all live with. I am sure even you have some regrets, don't you?" He looks at me, then continues, "I have many. I regret that I use drugs. I regret that I did not complete my studies. I am a very smart dude, but my anger has ruined me. I even get angry with you when you tell me to learn to manage my anger. I am like 'what the fuck is he talking about? How the fuck can you learn to manage anger that started in the crib?

"Oh, yeah, when I was ten I almost killed a kid from my neighborhood for talking about my dad. I banged his head on a water fountain till I broke his front teeth and his mouth was flooded with the blood. I do regret that with great remorse. My mother's mother used to say cruel things to me. I made her very angry when I became Muslim. She called me a cult member— "The Terrorist." Do I regret converting to Islam? No, I don't. But I do regret not clinging to the den of Islam. I regret having beautiful babies with a junkie. I feel remorse for everyone I robbed on my stick up mission. That angered me a lot." He pauses, takes a deep breath, shifts his sides, then resumes, "I used to go to the train tracks with my whacked out friends from all over the neighborhood and put large stones and bricks on the tracks. When the train came by, you could imagine what happened. If not, I'll tell you that this was the reason why Amtrak and transit cops are deployed at the train yards so widely. We also threw rocks at passing trains." His eyes sparkle. "Once I found my father's .44 Magnum six-shooter under his bed. I was playing with it and I accidentally cocked out the hammer. Take a wild, stupid little guess who walks in?" He looks at me and waits for an answer.

I take a wild stupid guess as directed. "Your father."

"No," he shakes his head in a "no" motion like a bull. "You are not fucking good at guessing," he tells me. "My mother walks in." He suddenly stands and turns around with an action of holding a gun in both his hands. "I am holding a gun in my hand, unaware it's loaded. My mother is scared to death, crying, trying to negotiate the gun out of my hands. I was having a great time but as she got closer inching toward me," he bends and acts as if he is keeping the gun down, "I put the gun down." He sits back in his chair and continues, "And when she felt that she was safe she beat the hell out of me. But let me tell you, when I was pointing the gun at her and saw her sobbing, crying, and pleading, I felt powerful and enjoyed every moment of it. Just for a kick I wanted to do something crazy. It thrilled me. After that I became real crazy. I started doing real crazy things just for the thrill. I would randomly pick fights by punching someone for no reason at all. This is a sick game called 'Pass the Pain'. It is a game where you find a target out of nowhere and hit it. I was a squad member, we used to jump people on their way to work or wherever..."

I interrupt him, "What do you mean by jump people?"

"You fucking don't know what jumping means?" He laughs, then continues, "Attack man, attack. When you attack others it is called jumping. We used to attack people on major public transits and bus stops. No kid, homosexual, or animal was safe from beat down. Once we captured a stray cat and set her on fire. It was real fun to watch her dancing all over the place. This went on until I turned sixteen. I regret all these things now. I want these things to be in my past and also want to get a handle over my anger. But the problem is I don't know how to." He stops and takes a deep breath.

I look at him closely. "John, are you sure you want to learn to handle your anger effectively?"

He nods. "Yes. I'm willing to do anything. You can put me to the test." I hear some urgency in his voice.

"I want you to stand up now."

"What? You want me to stand up?" He repeats.

"Yes."

He stands up reluctantly.

"Now I want you to leave my office and come to see me tomorrow sharp at 8 a.m."

He stands still.

"John," I said, "see you tomorrow at eight in the morning. Bye for now."

He drags his feet out of my office.

Next day, around 8:30 in the morning, he comes into my office.

"Good morning, John," I greet him.

"I am very pissed off with you," he retorts.

"Why?"

"You treated me like shit yesterday." He pulls a chair, sits, and the next thing he does is pull another chair with his right leg and puts his feet on it. I shake my head in a "no" motion, indicating that he can't put his feet on the chair. He reluctantly takes them off the chair.

"Did I?" I ask.

"Yes, you did. You fucking asked me to stand up and then

asked me to leave. I am a grown ass man and I like to be treated like one."

"John, your own reaction to what I did made you upset and not what I did."

"No. You kicked me out of your office and that made me angry."

"When you said that you were willing to do anything to learn to handle your anger effectively I just asked you to leave my office and told you that I will see you the next day."

"But the way you said it made me angry."

"John, you know what you are doing ?"

"No."

"You are justifying your anger."

"How ?" He growls.

"One time you say 'what I did to you made you angry' and the next, 'the way I said it' was what made you angry. You think every time people should say what you want to hear?"

"Why not?"

"You tell me why should they?"

"Because that is a reasonable thing to do."

"John, I agree with you but there are very few people in the world who are reasonable. Let me ask you, how often have you been reasonable to others? Why go that far? How often have you been reasonable to me?"

He shifts in his seat and says haltingly, "I know, I have been unreasonable to you most of the time."

"So does that give me a right to be angry with you?"

"Yes, it does."

"No it doesn't. How will being angry with you for your being unreasonable to me help me to have peace of mind? I might feel justified and get momentary pleasure and feel powerful, but at the end I will have regret and remorse. So what's the earthly use of getting angry?"

He nods. "Now I see your point. I wish I could learn soon

to think like you do." He slouches in the chair.

"John! Yesterday I wanted to see how you would react to an unexpected situation and I wanted to make a point that it is our expectations and reactions to what happens that makes us angry and not the incident itself. If you keep your expectations and reactions under check you will be less angry and not be hostile to others as you always have been. You have to learn to think before you react."

"I always react violently and expect people to be respectful, but now I promise you that I'll think before reacting and will not be mad even when my expectations are not met."

"Are you sure?" I doubt his sincerity.

"Yes." He smiles.

Chapter 2

Kareena—The Master of Profanity

Early morning, Kareena storms into my office, and I greet her: "Good morning, Kareena."

"What the fuck's so good about this morning ?"

"What's the problem? Are you all right?" I am bewildered.

"No!" she growls.

"What's wrong ?" She looks the other way. "I want to be with my father."

"If I remember correctly, isn't your father dead?" I take a long look at her.

"I want to die, too," she replies, averting her eyes.

Kareena has been in treatment for the last four days. She has difficulty getting along with others. She is verbally aggressive and full of profanity. She finds fault with everyone and everything around her. She is depressed and cannot take "no" for an answer. Kareena has three children by three different men. Two of them are in the custody of their respective fathers and one is with her sister. Now she is missing her father who died ten years ago.

"Why?" I ask.

"I want to be with him," she says. "I miss him."

"Don't you miss your children?" I scan her face.

"No," she responds coldly. "I don't give a fuck about them. I miss my father."

"When did your father die?" I continue looking at her.

"Ten years ago.

" She looks down at the floor.

"And you still miss him?"

"I sure do."

"How is it that you miss your father who died ten years ago, and you have no love for your own children?"

"I never loved my children from the beginning," she answers.

"Why?" The thought crosses my mind that this is insane.

"I don't know," she responds wearily.

"Then why did you have them?"

"I don't know!" She sighs.

"Kareena, don't you want to be a responsible mother?"

"No, I am better off without them."

"But they are your own flesh and blood."

"So what? Who cares?" She shrugs.

"Kareena, that doesn't sound right. You seem to be very selfish."

"I'm fucked up," she responds. "I have always been like that. I'm being honest."

"It doesn't matter."

"It matters to me," she says. "I'm not dishonest like other people."

"Kareena, you can't say that you are honest and be dishonest about other things. You are either honest or dishonest. You have been using your father's death as an excuse to get high. You told me several lies on the day of your admission. Your information did not add up. And worse still, you have been such an irresponsible mother."

"I don't want to be a responsible mother! I tell you that all the time. Why do you keep harping on it?" She glares at me.

"So what are your plans now ?"

"I'm going to kill myself.

"She appears full of smoke and toothless. However, I still

take a careful look at her. "When?"

"The moment I'm out of here."

"How ?" I try to size her up.

"I'll jump in front of a bus," she says listlessly.

"Kareena, I want to help you but I need you to cooperate with me. I want you to think positively and stop thinking about killing yourself. You need help and I am sure if you cooperate with me, we will be able to find some way out."

"But I don't want to live." She averts her eyes.

"Please, do me a favor," I suggest. "Go to your room and rest for a while. You might start feeling better. Time heals everything."

"If I go to my room, I'll hang myself.

" She still avoids looking at me.

"Kareena, if you don't listen and keep talking about killing yourself I will have to call 911 and commit you."

"I want to be transferred to another hospital."

Suddenly she comes up with a new idea. "Or I'll kill myself.

"Since you are not listening," I bring out the suicide prevention contract and tell her, "you need to sign this suicide prevention contract for me."

"Heck no, I am not signing any fucking contract," she says, pushing my hand away.

"Kareena, I told you that I want to help you...

"She cuts me off, "I told you that I don't need any fucking help from you. I just want to be transferred to another hospital."

"But if you don't cooperate with me I don't think I will be able to help you in any way."

"Cooperate? My foot!" She stamps her right foot.

At this point, I started feeling impatient, hopeless, and irritable. For a moment I thought of telling her 'Go kill yourself. I can't help you since you don't want to be helped.' But then some sense prevailed over me that I wasn't thinking right.

My job was to help her and I needed to be patient with her.

I look at her, still feeling some desperation and finding myself lost in the situation. I close my eyes and think for a moment and it works. I feel some kindness for her in my heart. I feel relieved so I open my eyes and speak to her slowly. "Kareena, if you sign these papers I will be able to go and speak with my supervisor and see whether we can transfer you to another hospital." I place the papers in front of her.

"Okay, give me that fucking pen," she says, leaning across the table, pointing at the pen in my hand and I hand it to her and she reluctantly signs the contract.

I go to my office door and instruct Dawn who sits in the hallway to monitor clients' activities to stay at my door until I came back.

Then I go speak with Scott, my supervisor for further instructions.

"But she just signed a Suicide Prevention Contract," he reasons.

"She really didn't know what she was signing," I try to explain the situation a little more.

"What does she want?" he asks impatiently.

"She wants to be transferred to a hospital in her neighborhood," I reply.

"She has no choice of the hospital, and I'm short of staff."

"I can keep her in my office while you make some arrangements," I suggest.

"That will work.

"I go back to my office and ask Kareena to stay while arrangements are made for her to go to the Emergency Room. She agrees. "Kareena, tell me something more about yourself."

"What else do you want to know ?" She pauses a few seconds, then continues. "I was a whore, and I like being a bitch."

"Kareena, don't you want to give up your old behaviors?"

"No. " She shakes her head angrily.

"Why not?"

"I'm a fucking bitch, and I love being a fucked-up bitch. Do you have a problem with that?" She glares at me.

"Why would I have any problem with it?" I respond calmly.

"Do you want to know more? I used to make about one thousand dollars a day. Do you want to know how ?" And without waiting for my answer she repeats, "Do you want to know how ?"

"Yes," I reply.

"By sucking dicks."

"What did you do with that money?"

"My mother said I could stay with her if I paid her three hundred dollars a week, and I gave the remaining money to my father."

"Did your parents know about your prostitution?" I look straight at her.

"My father did," she answers, "but he didn't give a fuck about what I was doing."

"Do you have any savings?" I ask.

"No, I spent all my money on drugs."

"Kareena, what is your source of income now ?"

"Prostitution," she responds indifferently. She continues, "When my baby was small, I would call my mom to baby-sit. I was living on the third floor of an apartment building, and a dealer was living on the first floor. One day my mother was looking after my baby, and I went to see the dealer. He asked, 'What do you need?'"

'Drugs,' I said. 'I don't have any money, but I promise to give you double the moment I receive my money.'"

'Don't worry about it,' he said, 'you can help me in another way.'" "How ?' I asked.

"'Satisfy me.' He pointed to his crotch. I satisfied him by giving him a blowjob that day, and after that, I satisfied him every day. I'm a dirty bitch. I slashed five or six guys in the past with a knife."

"Why did you slash them?" I am horrified.

"Because they couldn't get hard enough," she laughs.

"Did anybody die?" I ask, maintaining eye contact with her.

"No," she replies. "Nobody died. I just slashed them slightly on their necks. I didn't intend to kill them."

"I don't understand why you slashed those men. Did you think it was taking too long and you were losing money?"

"No," she responds. "I threw their money in their face."

"Do you have a particular choice in customers?" I ask.

"I sleep only with black and Hispanic males," she replies.

"How about white males?"

"No," she says. "I don't sleep with them; they are no good in bed."

"Oh, I see."

"When am I going to another hospital?" She suddenly remembers why she is still in my office.

"I'm not sure. After someone comes to escort you, you might be able to go to another hospital. I have to go lead a group session and you cannot be left alone here, so why don't you join us there?" I suggest.

Surprisingly, she agrees and follows me to the community room.

"I don't want to share anything," she tells us when it's her turn.

"You may feel relieved if you share," John tells her. I think to myself, *Look who is talking? How easy it is to advice others what to do and what not to do.*

"You shut your fucking mouth!" she yells. "I didn't ask for your advice, did I?" She glares at him.

"That is very disrespectful," Stephanie jumps in.

"Who the fuck cares?" Kareena shouts again. She is glaring at Stephanie now. "If you want respect, then just leave me alone."

"You just want attention. We have better things to do. " Stephanie returns her glare.

"You fucking bitch! You better stay out of my life. " Kareena stands up, panting.

"Kareena, stop cursing and sit down!" I intervene.

"You are so fucked up!" She turns on me. "You are a useless therapist; you are no good. " She storms out of the community room and goes and stands next to Dawn in the hallway.

I continue as if nothing happened. "Some people are trained to be unhappy; they refuse to be happy.

"Suddenly she returns and stands in my face. "Are you talking about me?" she demands.

I ignore her and move aside.

She moves backward, and while settling on the couch, repeats, "Are you talking about me?"

"No, I am talking in general," I reply.

"No," she shouts vehemently, "you are not!"

"As I said, we were talking in general, but it applies to your behavior as well," I try to explain.

"You have no business talking about me," she warns.

"Kareena," I say slowly, "I can't help it if our general discussion applies to you. By the way, you did say that you love your miserable life and you don't want to be happy. Didn't you?"

"I did," she responds haltingly.

"Then what are you objecting to?"

"Fuck you all!" She marches toward the door and then stands, stock-still.

"Please don't allow her to come in again," Stephanie pleads.

"Who the fuck wants to come back here?" Kareena snaps.

"Kareena, if you are going out, then stay out with Dawn, because you are disturbing us. " I hold the door for her.

"Who the fuck wants to be here?" She slams the door behind her

I can see her through the glass door, acting restless and pacing

rapidly in the hallway. Later, she knocks at the door repeatedly and wants to come in, but we refuse. We don't want to feed into her negativity. Her goal is to get high. She wants that kick which brings her nothing but misery. I hope she becomes receptive to treatment and gets her act together someday.

After a couple of years, she is back in treatment at my evening job. She is much more messed up than before. The night shift staff who admitted her to the unit have left me a message that she is manic and that no paper work could be completed.

I see her the next day. She appears to be in a good mood. "Hey, how are you?" she asks. She looks at me carefully, then continues, "I think I know you."

"Yes, you do know me. I am Christopher."

"You are damn right! You are the one who kicked me out last time.

"I think of saying 'no, I didn't, you asked for the transfer to another hospital, so we transferred you.' Somehow, I curb my desire to speak my mind because I know it won't make any sense to her and I'll be wasting my time.

Late in the evening, the psych technician asks for the attention of all the clients on the unit and requests the return of the missing keys to the clients' refrigerator.

No one comes forward with any information for several hours. After a change of shift, another technician addresses the same issue with clients. He is assertive and confident. He says that if no one comes forward with information about the missing keys, the clients will not get any juice or snacks and he will make sure that the refrigerator is moved to another location and they will no longer have access to it. This works. After most of the clients go out to smoke; Kurt, a client in his early twenties approaches the technician and tells him that he had seen a female client leaning forward, picking up the keys, and putting them in her clothes. Kurt requests that his name is not mentioned to anyone because he does not want to be called a rat. The tech agrees. Kurt does not know the name of the client, so he describes her looks.

The tech tells me he has figured out who she is.

"Who?" I ask.

"Kareena, but I am not going to speak with her because she is psychotic and has anger issues.

"I nod.

He continues, "I have called in for security to go through her stuff. They will be here any moment."

"I know her. Let's go and talk to her. " I start walking toward her room.

He pulls me back. "I don't think it is a good idea."

"Don't worry," I say, moving forward. "Let's give it a try.

"He stops resisting and starts walking behind me. I knock on her door.

"Come in," she says.

We both enter her room. She is sitting on her bed with a porno magazine in her hand. Clients aren't permitted to have sexually explicit reading material but due to the carelessness of the admitting staff, she was able to sneak in the porno magazine.

"Hey Kareena. How are you?" I ask.

"I'm okay. " She puts the magazine away.

"Why are you in your room when all the other clients are out there smoking ?" I ask cautiously.

"I don't want to smoke. Do you have an objection to that?" She picks up her pocketbook, which is lying on her bed.

"Do you have any withdrawal symptoms?" I continue.

"Yes. Aches and pains, nausea, sweats and chills."

"Why don't you go to see the nurse?" I insist.

"I don't want to see anyone. " She turns her face away from me

The tech interjects, "Give back the keys, Kareena."

"What keys? I am not a thief. Are you accusing me of stealing ?" she snaps.

"I am not accusing," he says. "I know for sure you took them."

"I hope you know that I am protected by HIPPA laws. You will be in trouble for harassing me. " She clings tightly to her pocketbook.

"Give me those keys. " He insists.

"Fuck you. I don't have any keys."

"Kareena," I intervene, "by mistake, if you have picked up those keys, please return them to us."

"Why are you accusing me of stealing ?" She looks at me.

"I am not here to accuse. I know you are not a thief," I say.

"You are damn right.

"At that moment, the shift supervisor enters the room. Kareena looks at him and shouts, "Why are you ganging up against me? Get out of my room."

"Kareena," I say, "he is in charge of this place. Please don't be disrespectful to him."

"Okay," she says.

"We are going to check your stuff," the tech continues.

"Don't dare touch my stuff." She firmly clutches to her pocketbook.

"Can I look into your pocketbook?" The tech moves forward.

"No!" she shouts.

"If you don't want to cooperate you have to leave," the shift supervisor intervenes.

"I am not leaving! You do whatever you want to do. " She challenges him.

"I am going to get a female staff member to search your stuff." The tech turns to leave the room.

"Look here. " She empties her pocketbook on her bed. A weird variety of things such as chicken bones, holy water, stones, and baby powder is spread out all over her bed.

"I am going to get a female tech. " The tech leaves her room.

"Kareena," I say, "I don't think you want to be strip searched. Why don' t you tell us the truth?"

"I don't want to lie," she says. "I will give you the keys. " But she does not move.

"Kareena, you said you would give back those keys.

"She inserts her hand into her underwear, removes the keys, and hands them to me. I hurriedly grab them without thinking where they were lying. For the rest of the evening I can't seem to wash the thought of where those keys were lying off my hands.

The next day, she is accused of stealing from her peers and also using drugs in her room. She says, "I can't take it anymore. I am tired of this shit. I don't know what's wrong with these people. I want to leave."

The female technician looks into her belongings and finds a tube with a needle from an IV line wrapped in a black cloth

When asked about it, she said, "I saved it because the other hospital I was in before coming here left it in my arm. I want to sue them. I will talk to my boyfriend about finding me a lawyer.

" She removes a picture and hands it to me. I look at the picture of a disheveled man in his late fifties and give it back to her.

"Why are you stealing things from others?" I ask.

"I have the right to steal because they steal from me all the time. I got a sword. I got a sword, a real big one. One of these days I am going to use it because they are knocking me around." She laughs, then continues, "I hear voices. I hear you talking bullshit. They want me to go underground to get drugs. I won't do it. I know where to find drugs. They are everywhere. He is all alone. Naked and hungry."

"Kareena? Who are you talking about? Your boyfriend?"

"No. I am talking about Jesus Christ. They don't know he is back. He is born again. He is there. I talk to him all the time. I have met him personally and I am sure I will meet him again.

"Meanwhile, the shift supervisor gets on the phone with the psychiatrist, who orders an increase in anti-psychotic medication. She receives her increased dose of medication, and soon she starts feeling much better and seems somewhat stable mentally.

Two days later, she says, "I am tired of the shit here. I don't see any sunshine here. I don't like the darkness around me. I am leaving." The next thing you know she is collecting her belongings from her room and is out the door.

Chapter 3

Hitching a Ride from a Perfect Stranger

Sandra is forty-two and was molested by a close family member when she was a child. She has been abusing cocaine, alcohol, and pills for the past thirty-three years. Her mother had an affair with a neighbor. Not wanting Sandra to tell her father about it, her mother started her on pills to put her to sleep. Sandra is a perfect example of denial. She does not feel that she needs help. She won't allow herself to experience feelings of pain and sadness. She talks vaguely, and there is no consistency in what she says. She projects a cheerful persona and seeks validation and appreciation from others. There are times when her intelligence shines through. But she has poor judgment and very low self-esteem. She is diagnosed with bipolar disorder but she definitely has many more mental health issues. In the past, she entrusted some religious organization with the responsibility for placing the kids but she maintains that hey have been given away in adoption to that religious organizaion. She says that no one from her immediate family does drugs. They don't want anything to do with her. Her source of income is prostitution and Social Security.

Sandra and I are working together on her psychosocial assessent in my office. She is constantly shifting her sides. Her eyes are wandering around the office. "Sandra, why are you here?" I ask.

"I don't know," she answers wearily. "The man I was living

with kicked me out of his house. I'm pregnant. How can he kick out a pregnant woman like that? He can't do that. Can you call him and tell him to let me stay with him? I don't want to be here. I went to a crisis center and they found a lot of drugs in my system, so they sent me here."

"Are you willing to give life without drugs a shot?" I ask.

"No," she says. "I like getting high. I like when I put on makeup and stand on the road and guys stop and look at me and pick me up to have sex."

"So you enjoy that lifestyle, but what about the consequences?"

"I don't like being homeless, cops chasing me or those horrible withdrawal symptoms when I miss my next hit, but I still don't want to stop using. My boyfriend also loves getting high. We get high together."

"What does your boyfriend do for a living ?"

"He works for a construction company."

"Sandra, since you are here, I would suggest that you share your feelings and thoughts in group. It might help you get better insight into your problem."

"I don't have a problem with drugs. I'm all right with it. My friend should not have kicked me out of his house. I had no place to live, so I went to a crisis center. He should at least have considered that I am seven months pregnant. I have always been nice to im. He lacks compassion and discipline; don't you think so, Mr. Christopher?"

"Sandra, discipline starts with self. You have to stop running way from reality and learn to take responsibility for your own actions and behavior."

"Mr. Christopher, don't you think he was real inconsiderate? He should not have kicked me out of his house." She is harping on he same point again and again.

"Sandra, people are basically inconsiderate by nature. So what? That's how they want to be. It's not his behavior that is causing your anger, it's your protest against his behavior. Don't labor under the impression that when you treat people with kindness, courtesy, and consideration, they are going to reciprocate in kind. If they do, you can take it as a bonus. People will treat you the way they want. If you wish to be treated differently, you are free to wish it; that is your conditioning and programming. No one else has anything to do with it. Your basic problem is that you keep thinking in terms of 'should' and 'should not.' A 'should' is a demand, and knowingly or unknowingly, you are being demanding. Today, you are not in a position to handle 'shoulds' and 'should nots' effectively. Because when your expectations are not met you feel disappointed and miserable. So, if you don't change your thinking and your behavior, you will never be happy."

"But, Mr. Christopher, he kicked me out of his house and I am pregnant," she insists.

"Why did he kick you out?" *A thought crosses my mind that this has something to do with her boyfriend.*

"He didn't like my boyfriend coming to his house."

"Does your friend use drugs?"

"No," she answers. "He is seventy-eight years old. He drinks socially. He demands oral sex from me. He doesn't like me going out and hanging with other guys. He doesn't like my boyfriend."

"All right. Let's start by taking things one day at a time."

"I will be fine," she says optimistically, "once I get my own place to live."

* * *

Before the week is over, Sandra announces, "I'm leaving."

"Why?"

"I have enough money to take care of myself," she answers.

"What does money have to do with your leaving ?"

"I have five-hundred-and-thirty dollars," she says.

"That won't last you for more than a day or two."

"I also have a place to live." She is searching for something in her untidy pocketbook.

"But you told me that you are homeless." I insist.

"Yes," she replies, "but I am going to live with my friend."

"Which one?"

"The one I was living with before coming here," she answers.

"The seventy-eight-year-old?"

"Yes," she says.

"But you said he kicked you out of his house."

"That was because I invited my boyfriend to his house to have sex. But he told me last night that he loves me, and he'll allow me to stay with him if I stop messing with my boyfriend. I promised him that I would stop."

"Sandra, don't you understand that old man is exploiting you sexually?"

"No, he isn't."

"Didn't you tell me that he sits in front of the TV set undressed and starts counting his money and then tells you that he will give you money to go out, if you perform oral sex on him?

Isn't that sexual exploitation?"

"I don't mind it."

"What? You don't mind being sexually exploited?"

"I have known him for eight years," she explains.

"Are you telling me that since you've known him for eight years it's okay for him to exploit you?"

"My boyfriend has no place to live; he lives with someone else." She jumps from one subject to another.

"This is insane that neither you nor your boyfriend has a place to live and you still went ahead and got pregnant."

"I didn't want to get pregnant, but my boyfriend talked

me into it."

"In that case, he should be more responsible, be a man and take responsibility for the unborn child," I tell her.

"No," she says, "he said he can't."

"Is he the father of your other children too?"

"No." She shakes her head. "He is the father of one of them, and the other three had different fathers. I conceived them while I was tricking."

"Do you see them?"

"No. I gave them to a religious organization."

"Then why do you keep getting pregnant?"

"This time my boyfriend wanted me to get pregnant," she replies.

"Sandra, you are playing with an innocent life."

"I know, I know." She nods. "I just wanted to please him."

"At whose expense?"

"I can't keep this child. I don't like responsibility. I know I can't be a responsible mother. I like my freedom. I'm not going to hange his diapers and feed him. I've never done it, and I'm not going to. Can you call the hospital and get the number, so they can come and pick up the baby when it's born?"

"Don't worry about that now; you have two more months to go. Do you want to talk to your boyfriend about it?"

"No. I don't want him to see my child."

"Why? Are you mad at him?"

"No." She shakes her head vehemently. "I just don't want to bother him."

"That is ridiculous. This is a question of life and death for a baby, and you are saying you don't want to bother the guy who coerced you into pregnancy!"

"So you think I should stay here?" She looks at me quizically.

"Yes," I reply. "You need to stay in treatment because you

are responsible for two lives now."

"I need to call my friend then, and tell him that I'm not coming today."

"Sandra, you shouldn't even think of going there. We will help you into a long-term program where they accept pregnant women."

"Will you?" She leans forward excitedly.

"Yes."

"But, Mr. Christopher, if I don't call him now, then he will not let me live with him in the future."

"Don't worry about it; you will definitely have a better place to live," I reassure her.

"He says I have no problems, I don't need any help, and that he loves me." Her eyes sparkle.

"When did he tell you that?" I ask.

"Last night."

"Well, it's not true." I shake my head. "Neither he nor your boyfriend love you. They want your money and your body."

"I guess you're right." She looks at me sadly.

I feel bad for her and think of shouting at the top of my lungs 'What's wrong with you? Why are you letting these guys take advantage of you? Don't allow them to exploit you. Leave them and think of your own welfare.' But the next moment, I think she needs to stay in treatment a little longer to be ready to hear this, so I give up. I look at her kindly, take a deep breath and tell her, "Now first things first. Stop worrying about whether they love you or they don't. You have to first start loving yourself. So just hang in there, don't rush. Don't think of leaving ; it is cold and raining. You have to take care of your health for yourself as well as for your unborn child. I will see you on Monday. Have a good weekend."

Sandra leaves treatment that same night, stating that she is going to her friend's house and that she has enough money to take care of herself.

Four days later, she is back. She looks tired and worn-down.

"Mr. Christopher, I should have listened to you. I shouldn't have left here."

"What happened?"

"You were right." She looks down at the floor. "They don't love me."

"Did your friend ask you to leave his house again?"

"No." She avoids looking at me. "I didn't go to my friend's house. I stayed in a hotel with my boyfriend and spent all my money."

"Did you get high?"

"Yes, we got high together. We also made love. When I ran out of money, my boyfriend called a friend of his, and they decided I had to go. I have nowhere to go. So I am back here."

"Why did your boyfriend call his friend?"

"We were broke. He wanted me to give his friend a blowjob or money, but I refused. I was tired."

I think of saying, 'Your boyfriend appears to be a pimp and he sad thing is that you are wearing blinders and refusing to see his ulterior motives' but instead I say, "Good for you."

"People here love me." Her eyes shine up. "My boyfriend is no good. He made me spend my all money. I'm broke now. I will not make the same mistake again. I will complete the program this time."

"Good. Now, go and take a shower—you smell!" I tell her gently.

* * *

Sandra comes to my office early in the morning the fol-lowng Monday. She is dressed and made up, looking like she is ready, able, and willing to go tricking. She has on skin-tight jeans, a low-cut top, and is obviously not wearing a bra. She is wearing high-heel shoes. She smells like she has put on a bottle of dollar store perfume. She has too much of a bright red lipstick on her lips. She has on dark eye shadow, big gaudy earrings, and a necklace that might have come out of a bubble gum machine. She is carrying her meager belongings in a large, dirty, knock-off pocket-book. She declares, "I'm leaving."

"Now what?"

"I don't want to be here," she states flatly.

"Do you know what time it is?"

"No, I don't." She shrugs.

"It is six thirty in the morning," I tell her.

"So?"

"Why do you want to leave so early?"

"Because I don't want to be here. I want to be free, and I can do it on my own," she replies tartly. "I want to leave!"

"You said the same thing before," I remind her. "I think you are making a mistake. I advise you to reconsider."

"I am leaving. I need tokens to get on a bus. Do you have any?"

"No," I reply, "we don't give out tokens to clients who leave on heir own."

"No problem," she says airily. "I know how to hitch a ride."

She signs the AMA (Against Medical Advice) form stating that she has to manage her money and walks out of treatment. "You will always be in my prayers," she says standing in the door. Then, within a few minutes of her leaving our premises I see her hitching ride with a heavyset guy after a brief talk with him. I am surprised mainly because she evidently doesn't know how to stay sober, but she sure knows how to get a ride from a perfect stranger.

Chapter 4
You Indian Bum

Clara weighs about three hundred pounds. She wears a perpetually angry expression, and her eyes look like they are about to pop out of her head. When she is angry, she raises hell. She is hostile and fierce. It would not be an exaggeration to say that she is always furious and agitated. She finds it almost impossible to get along with the other clients or the staff; there are constant complaints about her behavior. She has a loud and filthy mouth and once she starts cursing, she does not know when to stop. She invades everyone's private space. She walks up to a person, sticks her face into theirs, and starts shouting and cursing. She does not take "no" for an answer. She is more than capable of injuring someone. She constantly lies and tries to split the staff. When she is desperate, she goes from one staff person to another complaining. She is attention-seeking, and she wants what she wants when she wants it.

Early in Clara's stay, Alana expresses her inability to handle her. Scott advises me to talk to the insurance company and request transfer. However, the reviewer declines our request for the lack of good clinical reasons to justify her transfer. Due to negligence neither, the psychiatrist's notes nor Alana's progress notes reflect Clara's aggressive behavior, and she does not display any suicidal or homicidal ideations. Scott does not like the reviewer's decision; however, he is left with no choice but to keep her. He transfers Clara to my caseload.

"I'm so glad to have you as my therapist," Clara blurts out during our first meeting. "I was tired of that other bitch. She said that I was not serious about my recovery and that the unit has an open-door policy. Who the fuck does she think she is? I'm going to report her to my insurance company. They are paying for me to stay here. I have been in many places, and I know my rights. Nobody else has ever told me that they have an open-door policy. She is racist. She doesn't know that if I report her, she will lose her job. She asked me personal, intimate questions about my sex life. I am not here to talk about my sex life. She's a bitch. I don't need to tell her about my family and my criminal history. Would she tell me anything about her personal life if I asked her? Bitch. I complained to the director and he listened to me; he transferred me to you."

"Clara, are you ready to complete the remaining paperwork now ?" I ask.

"What do you want to know ?"

"I want to know about your life, your issues, your goals, your likes and dislikes, your strengths and weaknesses," I reply.

She starts: "Okay, I'm thirty-nine years old, and I don't have any issues. I'm only here because I want to get section eight housing and a welfare card. My ICM (Intensive Case Manager) is going to help me with it. I wanted to make a call, but that bitch refused to let me use her phone and said that I had to talk to the case manager, what's-his-name, Stanley? Well, he is never available. He is always out."

"That's not true. He takes his lunch break between noon and one. The rest of the day he is always on the unit," I tell her.

"Can I call Patience, my ICM?" she asks, staring at the phone on my desk.

"No," I reply, "actually, you do have to talk to Stanley about it." When clients have to contact outside agencies such as the Department of Human Services, Welfare Office, Social

Security Office, court, probation officers, etc., they have to go through Stanley, our in-house case manager.

She immediately flounces out of my office to go see Stanley. She is back ten minutes later, her eyes shining. "Stanley is a nice man," she relates enthusiastically. "He did let me make a call. My ICM will be here tomorrow. He's going to speak to you about it."

* * *

The group is on the way to the park for our session when, about halfway there, she halts and flatly refuses to walk another step. She complains that she can't walk that far, that she has a bad back, that she has arthritis, that she can't breathe, and that it's too hot. We accommodate her and settle down onto a nice patch of lawn under some shady trees, but she refuses that also. She whines, "I am not going to sit on the grass, I'll get dirty." With a great deal of effort, we finally persuade her to continue into the park where we can sit on benches. However, by the time we get there, we only have a few minutes before we have to return to the unit. When John expresses his disappointment, she snaps at him: "Leave me alone if you don't want me to punch you in your face, you white trash." He looks at me, and I indicate by my expression to leave her alone. He shrugs and we continue our return journey.

Now she is showing her true colors. She calls the staff every bad name under the sun. She calls Stanley a cracker and alleges hat he is abusing her. "He asked me what kind of music I like. I didn't like it. He's trying to get personal. I find it very inappropriate," she complains.

On another occasion during group, instead of sharing her issues, she tells discontented Mathew that he has every right to leave the program, call his insurance company, and report this place for bad treatment.

"Clara, do not instigate or encourage him to leave. That is not our place," I tell her sternly.

"I thought you were better than that bitch, but you really are worse!" She storms out of group, slamming the door so hard the glass rattles.

She demands vistaril, a medication for her anxiety, from Eboni. She had stopped using that medication when she was transferred to my caseload. Now, every time she is angry, she wants to call Patience. I find it amusing that her ICM's name is Patience because it would be impossible to work with Clara without having a truckload of it.

One day, while standing in the hall, she suddenly points her finger at me and screams, "I don't like this man! I don't like the way he looks! I don't like the way he speaks! I'm scared of him! Every time I go to him and ask him to let me call my ICM, he tells me to go and talk to that frog, and that frog," she says referring, to Stanley, "doesn't like me. He has something against me. He wears the same pants and shirt for days on end. I know he was a drug user in his past. He may have stopped using, but he still behaves like a druggie. I am not staying here one more day; I am leaving!"

"Where will you go?" I ask quietly.

"I have an apartment," she answers. "My ICM has the key for me to my new apartment."

"That's not true, Clara." I pause, look at her, and continue, "Patience is trying to get you a place to live but hasn't gotten one yet."

"That's because of that cracker," she retorts. "He's trying to take more money by keeping me here even though I don't want to stay here. He's a robber. He is robbing my insurance company of their money. Can you get him to tell the truth to my insurance company, that I'm ready and that I do have a place to go?"

"He does tell the truth," I reply, "and the truth is that you don't have an apartment yet, and you will need to stay here a little longer."

"You fucking Indian bum!" she shouts at the top of her lungs.

"You look like a street dog, look at the way you dress. You don't look professional to me. You look like a monkey. You're a fucking snake-charmer." She storms down the hall. Sighing, I follow in her wake. Now she is shouting at Stanley that she is leaving.

"You can't," he says. "You have no place to go."

"You can't tell me when I can leave!" She stamps her foot.

"Stop abusing me. I know you don't like me; I am calling my ICM now!" She snatches the receiver off the desk, calls Patience, and orders her to come and get her. Patience arrives at the unit shortly and tries to calm Clara down, explaining that she will soon have a place to live. She also tells her to behave and respect the staff.

There are more incidents involving Clara. Whenever I confront her for disorderly behavior, she calls me an Indian bum; it as become her favorite slogan. One day, joking, I mention that I might file charges against her for ethnic harassment. That works; she stops for a while, but before long, she is back at it. She physically threatens the other clients and staff on a daily basis. She gets under everyone's skin. Her name is almost permanently on the board for disorderly behavior, but she doesn't care. She is a torture to the clients as well as the staff and is hostile almost every day.

Scott refuses to discharge her. "When I tried to transfer her, neither Alana's nor the psychiatrist's notes sufficiently documented her behavior. Now the situation is different; we have to keep her here until she gets housing. It's too late now for an administrative discharge."

She stops attending group and individual therapy sessions, roams up and down the hallway finding fault with people and things or pigging out on leftover food in the clients' kitchen instead.

I ask Stanley, "Why can't we discharge her to a shelter?"

He stands me in front of the census board. "Look," and he points to the half-empty board. It indicates that we are not getting any new admissions; business is down. I figure out that discharging her will not be a viable business decision. I get the answer to my question. I quietly walk away.

A few days later, when Clara spots Stanley in the hall-way she whines, "I've completed forty-five days. I'm leaving tomorrow."

"No, you are not." Stanley shakes his head. "You can't dicitate your discharge date. We are still working on your housing situation."

"You're lying," she snaps. "You aren't doing a thing for me; you are robbing my insurance company of their money by keeping me here. My ICM is doing everything for me, and I want to call her now."

"Calm down, Clara. Patience is on her way to take you to sign our apartment lease papers. If you don't stop shouting, you are not going anywhere."

She calms down. Stanley is on the phone doing reviews with the insurance company when Patience arrives, so I meet with them. Patience uses my phone to call the office where they are supposed to go and is told that the papers won't be ready for two more days. She explains the situation and tells Clara to hang in here.

"Why can't I live with my aunt until I get my apartment?" Clara asks Patience.

"Because," Patience replies, "your aunt doesn't want you at her house; don't you remember what happened when we went there the last time? She made it very clear that she doesn't want to see you anymore."

"I can't believe you are telling me to stay here for two

more days. I don't like this man." She whirls toward me. "Whenever I want to talk to him, he says 'not now' and tells me to go and talk to Stanley, and that guy is so rude he doesn't ever talk to me. This man didn't even ask me to sign my treatment plan. He just tells me 'be quick' and hands me a pen. Look at the way he looks at me. I don't want to see this man. I don't want to attend his group sessions. Are you sure it's only two more days?"

"That's what I think," Patience adds cautiously, "but it all depends. Then she turns to me and says, "Christopher, is it okay if she doesn't attend your groups?"

"It's fine. She hasn't been attending my groups anyway." I shrug.

"He's lying!" she shouts. "Can you take me to my aunt's?"

"No. I have to go to court with another client. I don't have time for you now," and Patience starts toward the door. However, before she is out, Clara stares at me and yells, "You Indian mother-fucker! I don't like him." For some strange reason she talks to me in a third person. "I'll slap him," and she starts walking toward me. It scares me, but I try to hide my fright.

"These are mine. Scott gave them to me," and she snatches a bag of donuts lying on the table. She loves to eat—she doesn't eat to live, she lives to eat. Scott gives her the leftover donuts every morning to placate her when she goes to his door and starts complaining. Patience leaves without saying another word.

She is no longer allowed to go to the cafeteria for meals because she once threatened the cook. "That cook is an ass-hole. I'll break his neck when I see him. He doesn't wash his hands when he serves food; he's dirty; he keeps scratching his balls—I've seen him doing it," she grumbles.

On Independence Day, although it's a holiday, I decide to work. To my surprise, I find Clara in a good mood. When she sees me, she says good morning and expresses her desire to go out with the other clients for the cookout. She hogs food as though she's never eaten before and never will eat again. I felt the permission was worth granting.

The next day, she attends my group. I start with the quote, "You reap what you sow," from the Bible.

"I can relate to that," Steve, who is close to discharge, volunteers. "I used drugs, and the results are devastating. My blood pressure is always sky-high, my diabetes has worsened, my sex life is ruined, and it is the result of my putting foreign substances into my body. Now I am learning that if I have a pleasant thought, I will feel pleasant. If I feed myself with negativity, I become negative, but if I practice a positive attitude, I will become a positive person. If I treat people with respect, others might start respecting me, too. If I shower love onto others, I might receive love back from them. Every behavior has a reaction. I have anger issues, but I'm getting better with them now. I think before I act.

"This has become possible because I am clean. I can think clearly now. When I'm under the influence of drugs, I stop thinking and become focused on my fix, my immediate gratification. Drugs and anger together ruined me. I know I have to stay clean, and I have to control my anger because drugs and anger are interrelated, at least for me. Thanks for allowing me to share."

"What is anger?" Clara asks.

"Anger is an emotion," I explain, "widely felt but often very poorly handled. We all feel anger. It is like any other emotion.

Anger alone has caused more destruction in the world than any ther emotion. It is a part of life however, and we need to understand it to reduce its negative impact on our mental and physical health. We have to learn to handle anger before it starts handling us. When we let anger take control of us, it consumes us. We have choice to be angry or not in any given situation. We don't do anyone a favor by reacting to a situation. However, we do ourselves a big favor by not reacting, because it helps us to stay in control. When you are angry, it affects your body chemistry, it turns your positive energy into negative energy, and you lose more than you gain."

"I don't think so. How do you explain my anger?" Clara demands.

I avoid answering her question directly, believing she will react indifferently to whatever I say. Instead, I cautiously continue, "When we are angry, we can't think. We become preoccupied and bsessed with whatever is on our mind. It blinds us. However, the ultimate decision to be angry or not to be angry, is ours."

"So, you are saying that I have a choice to be angry or not?" Clara asks.

"Yes," I answer.

"How ?" she growls.

"Let me explain this with the help of an incident we had the ther day." I pause to think for a few seconds, scan her face, and go on. "You called me an 'Indian motherfucker,' but I chose not to react. I had a selfish motive. By not reacting, I did myself a favor because it helped me maintain my cool. I decided not to add fuel to the fire. I didn't want to generate negative energy and cause myself stress and anxiety. I didn't want to subject myself to further turmoil."

She jumps up, shouting, "That's very inappropriate! You can't bring up an incident that happened between you and me. That is a breach of confidentiality. I will report you to my insurance company, you Indian bum."

"Clara, stop. We all heard it. You were very loud, you were standing in the hallway, and anyway, he's not talking about anyone's personal business," Marcus intervenes. "He's just trying to help us understand how to handle anger-producing situations, how not to lose our cool, how to be more effective when things might go wrong and cause further complications. You are the one who asked him a question, and now when he is trying to explain his answer, you are getting angry. I don't understand it. It seems hat you think you have a right to be mean just because you are an addict and your life is messed up, and that no one else has a right to express even their true feelings."

"Fuck you. I'm going to talk to Stanley and call Patience." She leaves, slamming the door behind her.

Stanley informs her that if she doesn't calm down and listen to him, she will not be allowed to make any calls. She relates all this when she comes back into the community room. She sits for a while and then gets up to leave again, but on her way out the door, he points a finger at me and shouts, "I'm going to get you!"

After she leaves, the whole group makes fun of me by singing, "One way or another, she's going to getch you, getch you, getch you, getch you."

Five minutes later, Selina sticks her head in the door. "What's up?" I ask.

"She's in the staff office on the phone and refuses to hang up. She is not supposed to be in there alone. Please ask her to leave."

"I'm in the middle of group, please ask Stanley to handle it."

"He just stepped off the unit." She holds the door open.

I step out and go into the staff room. "Clara, you can't be on he phone without permission. You know the rules!"

"Yes, I can be on the phone." She gives me a deadly look. "I'm calling Patience!"

"You can't barge into the staff office without permission. You have to get off that phone and leave this office, or else you will have to face the consequences," I warn her.

"I don't care," she snaps, continuing to dial. I leave her

there, tell Selina not to worry about it, and return to my group. Later, Clara claims that Selina hit her.

"She made that accusation because she was upset about you,"

Selina tells me when I come out after group. "You know she's a bitch she has a filthy mouth, and she is manipulative. She lies, and if I lose my job because of her, so help me, I'll pinch her head off and use it for a bowling ball!"

I smile; this woman would not swat a fly, and here she is threatening to kill a giant who has gotten under her skin. "Don't worry about it. You are not going to lose your job. Everyone knows hat she has issues so no one is going to believe her. "

Clara is now complaining to Stanley in the hallway. "He has no right to talk about what I said to him when I was angry. He can't use profanity. He used the same words I used. He is supposed to be a professional. I want to leave now. I can't stay in a place where the staff uses profanity. I want to call Patience."

"He can say whatever he wants to say," Stanley states emphatically. *Stanley is second in command; he becomes acting supervisor in absence of Scott. What I appreciate about Stanley is that he always stands by his staff; he takes any threats by clients very seriously. He warns them and tells them that if they do it again they will have to pack up their stuff and leave. For instance, when John had resorted to threatening staff and his peers, Stanley told him to stop making threats or he would have to pack up and leave. Since then, John started calling him a liar. Scott, on the other hand, does not say anything to clients when they resort to threatening.*

"No, he can't!" she shouts.

"Yes, he can!" he shouts back at full volume.

Startled, she yells again: "No, he can't."

Stanley takes a deep breath. "Look, Clara, this is our

program, and you cannot dictate what is or is not said. You have to stop vertually abusing staff and peers. Now, go to your room and relax."

"You can't tell me to go and relax. You've been abusing me from day one. I will not let you abuse me anymore." Now she is shouting at the top of her lungs, and her eyes look ready to pop out of their sockets. She looks menacing and fierce. I move forward and stand next to Stanley, fearing that she might attack him because he was confrontational.

"I want to call Patience," she says.

"She is already on her way over here," he informs her.

"I want to leave now!" she shouts.

"If that's what you want to do, go ahead." He shrugs.

"You asked me what kind of music I like, and then you said you like the same music as I do, and that is very inappropriate."

Sensing that she is being ignored, she whines, "Look at him! He is not even listening to me. You are paid to listen to me!"

"Clara," he says, "you need to stop shouting. Otherwise, pack up your stuff and get off the unit."

"No! I'm not going to listen. I'm packing my stuff. I'm leaving." She starts toward her room, but turns around halfway there and comes back. "Oh no, I'm not leaving. You want me to leave so you can tell my insurance company that I left AMA. I'm not doing it. I know your tricks."

"But that's what you want to do," he reminds her.

"No!" she shouts again. "I'm not leaving. You wear the same jeans every day, and you don't know how to talk to people. I'm not going to listen to you." She is now standing right in his face.

"Clara, you need to stop abusing us—you have been abusing us from your first day here. You have done it at every place you have ever been. This is our program. You don't dictate how to run it. I'm in charge today. You are not going to talk to any of my taff except me or your therapist." He instructs Eboni, Dawn, and Selina not to interact with her in any way, and they all disperse.

Clara has dragged a chair from the client kitchen and is now sitting outside my office. As soon as she sees me, she spits, "You stinky rat." I enter my office without responding. After a while, I come out of my office and she is still sitting there fuming. She mutters, "You fart." I walk to the staff room, and after completing my notes, I head back down the hall to my office.

She stands in the door behind me and hisses, "You monkey, I am going to report you." I ignore her, but she rambles on. "Don't you have a tongue? Can't you speak?" I close the door behind me.

"You can't close the door in my face, you Indian bum."

I leave work that day having not said another word to her. After I left, Patience came and spoke with her for a long time but still could not find her an apartment, leaving her with no choice but to put up with us for a few more days. Poor soul.

Chapter 5
Marcus—A Bad Man

Marcus is very disappointed because he has to continue to tolerate Clara, and he tells me so. "I understand your disappointment," I say. Marcus is forty-five. He was born in Puerto Rico and raised n the United States. He grew up in an area surrounded by drugs; at least fifteen people were selling drugs on all four corners. He and his three brothers used drugs together. He was sixteen when he first started using with them. He has two sons. One is sixteen, the other twelve. They live with their respective mothers; one in the States and the other in Puerto Rico. He claims that he has an excellent relationship with his sons even though he has not spoken with them for the past three-to-four years.

"In that case," I ask, "how can you say you have an excellent relationship with your children?"

"Well," he responds, looking away from me. "I had a good relationship with them while I was sober. In my active addiction, I kept myself away from them. I didn't want to influence them to start using drugs."

"I appreciate your concern. But you haven't been clean for more than ten days at a stretch, so when was the inactive period in your life?"

He sits dumbfounded.

I continue, "The absence of a father figure must be causing problems in their lives."

"You're right." He nods. "I've heard they aren't doing well

in school. But I can't do anything at this stage. I am helpless. I have my own issues!"

"That is why you need to straighten out your life. If you help yourself first, you will then be able to help them. You need to be a responsible father."

"I'm not an irresponsible father," he protests.

"That's not true," I tell him. "You have been using drugs your whole life. You are never present in their lives."

"But I call them," he insists.

"Marcus, just calling is not enough. A responsible father is the one who guides his children toward the right path of life. He is physically available and emotionally supportive. Your children should be able to talk to you and rest their heads on your shoulder when they need to."

Marcus has been abusing cocaine, marijuana, and heroin for years. He was using at least a bundle a day. He was working as a painter and committed several drug-related offenses while in his active addiction. He was arrested and convicted for possession of controlled substances and conspiracy seven times and was in jail for eight years. He is an expert at stealing gas from cars. He would find cars that were out of sight, and using a hose, he would siphon the tank. He used the stolen gas to drive his own car. He drove around and robbed people at knifepoint. He always carried a long knife and a gun. He robbed people who were trying to help him. He robbed people from just around the corner where he was living. Once he broke into his sister's house and told her not to move. Using a huge flashlight, he blinded her. When neighbors heard lots of noise and suspected that something was wrong, they called the cops; but his sister said, "Leave him alone, he's my brother. He lost his key, so he came through the window." Then there was Padua, real estate agent who trusted him and gave him a key to a house that they were remodeling. He stole stuff out of the place and sold it for a fraction of its worth to buy drugs. He admits, "I was a bad man."

"You wouldn't rob me, would you?" I ask jokingly.

"Oh no! I did that while in my active addiction. Now I am trying to go straight."

Marcus is handsome and has a well-built, athletic body. He has serious anger issues. Once he nearly slapped Fitler, a feminine male who touched his well-developed biceps. He has low self-esteem and also chronic relapse issues. He is working on the recovery process now. He is willing to learn, and he is open to the feedback that he receives from other clients and the treatment team. I am pleased with his progress.

There is a sudden unhealthy development. Veronica starts trying her best to seduce him. He seems unable to curb his desires and feelings. He is unable to stay away from her. He's in an early stage of his treatment, and I am concerned. I'm not sure how he will react if I try to address the matter. I decide to call him into my office for a one-on-one session. We discuss his progress and other related issues, including this new relationship. I tell him that it is healthy to have a sex partner, but not while in treatment. He needs o stay focused and learn to deal with his existing issues. I also reiterate that he has to be careful because of sexually transmitted diseases and that the program does not allow rehab romance.

"Yes, you're right." He nods. "I'm trying my best to stay away from her, but she won't leave me alone."

"Do you remember how Troy left treatment?" I ask.

"Yeah." He pauses. "He was caught kissing a female client who he wanted to have sex with, and when he was asked to refrain from indulging, he lost his cool and left."

"Exactly! Now, you have been doing very well. You should not jeopardize your recovery for momentary pleasure."

"Yes," he says. "I understand. But I don't know how to stay away from her."

"Well, just tell her frankly that you're not interested in her and that you want to concentrate on your treatment. You need to be focused and committed if you want to achieve your goals. What is our main goal here?"

"Learn to stay clean by staying focused, committed, and following directions."

Veronica was also counseled but her reaction wasn't good. She became verbally aggressive. It was expected. I will deal with her later.

For the next two days, Marcus avoids her. But he falls back again and they are spotted together several times. It appears they get together whenever they can. Their behavior was discussed in the treatment team meetings for the past two days; and we decide to put them on Contract stating that they will abide by rules and regulations of the program and failure to do so would render them to disciplinary action including termination of the treatment, which is known as administrative discharge.

Marcus and Veronica are both on Contract and are forbidden from any verbal or physical contact with each other. Marcus is not particularly bothered; Veronica, however, is unable to handle it. She is furious and demands that I remove her from the Contract, because she wants to be able to talk to Marcus freely but I explain that if being able to talk to Marcus is her goal, then she will never be off the Contract. It works; she stops griping.

Marcus starts taking his recovery very seriously. He spends considerable time with his roommate Mathew. He is trying to encourage Mathew to stay in treatment. He is off the Contract, but he hardly speaks to Veronica. He is learning to stop and think before reacting. He no longer experiences depression. He is getting along well with all the other clients. He is learning to be honest and open-minded. He shares his thoughts and feelings freely in groups. He is asking questions with a willingness to learn something new. He has become convinced that nothing can be grafted onto a closed mind. This time, he appears to be serious about his recovery.

Based on his behavior, it appears that he understands the Buddha's metaphor: The Gautama would tell his monks, scholars, and disciples not to agree with him out of respect, as that would not be learning. They had to be like a goldsmith who scrapes, cuts, heats, and then molds the gold.

Chapter 6

Mathew's Oral Sex Scandal

Mathew is fifty-five years old and single. He has been abusing cocaine daily and marijuana occasionally and has been in and out of twenty rehab programs. Due to an overdose he was in a coma for two-and-a-half weeks but returned to using as soon as he was released. He says that he does drugs because he has nothing else to do. He is unemployed and has nothing to look forward to. He has lost interest in life.

His father was a police officer and his mother was a home-maker. His parents were busy getting high, they had no time for him. He had many relatives including his paternal and maternal grandparents but he tells me, "I grew up on the street."

I am puzzled. "Why on the street when you had so many relatives around you?"

"I never had a close relationship with anyone. I always ran on the street."

"What about your siblings?" I ask.

"I have four siblings." He pauses. "But I did not have a good relationship with them, either. They had no religious background."

"What does a religious background have to do with personal relationships?"

"I was a Catholic," he answers. "I went to Catholic school. I was educated."

"How many years of schooling did you complete?"

"I completed eighth grade." He looks down at the floor.

"Do you have any children?"

"Yes." He is reluctant.

"How many?"

"I don't know," he responds wearily. "Six or seven or maybe five."

"Don't you know for sure?"

"No." He shakes his head.

"By how many mothers?"

"They all have different mothers." He shrugs. "I have no relationship with any of my children."

"What are their ages?"

"I don't know. The oldest may be thirty-two, the youngest twenty, and the others are all in between."

"Do you have a history of crime?"

"I was in jail for five years for robbery," he answers.

"How do you describe yourself sexually?"

"Heterosexual," he replies.

"How old were you when you first had sex?"

"I was twelve years old."

"Do you have any homosexual experience?"

"Yes." He hesitates. "While I was in jail. There was this old man, my celly, he wanted to have it, and I agreed. I didn't like it."

"Do you have any sexual problems?"

"Yes." He averts his eyes. "I don't get it up."

"How is using drugs helping your problem?"

"I don't know." He shrugs. "There is nothing else to do. I can't find a job."

"Mathew, if you get yourself together, you can look for a job.

What kind of work would you like to do?"

"Labor work."

"That shouldn't be difficult," I tell him, "if you are willing to work hard."

"But I'm on Social Security," he responds.

"Oh! I see. You want to work, but you don't want to give up your Social Security benefits?"

He hesitates. "But lots of people on Social Security have jobs."

"Forget about what others do," I say. "You are getting full social security benefits so you can't work a full time job. But you still may be able to work a certain amount a week."

"I don't know whether I want to do that," he says, avoiding eye ontact.

"Mathew, you need to decide what you really want to do: whether you want to work, or live on Social Security. But don't worry about it now, just take one day at a time, and everything will fall into place."

Later, in group, he shares, "I'm depressed. I feel lonely and hopeless and don't know why I'm alive. I had a horrible past, I have no future, and there is nothing in the present."

"We have to learn to live in the present," Marcus interjects. "Yesterday is history, tomorrow is a mystery, and today is a gift, a gift given by a power higher than us, and that's why it is called 'the present.' We have to learn to enjoy the present."

I am glad to hear this from Marcus. He is changing. He is being receptive. Whatever they learn here might not make a difference in everyone's life, but even if it makes a difference in one person's life, that is good enough. I remember the story of silver fish.

"A man is out on a morning walk when he sees another person in the beach, bending and rising again and again," I start. "He is curious and decides to find out what is going on. As he walks closer, he sees the man picking something up and throwing it into he sea. The man continues his walk, assuming the man is throwing pebbles. The next morning, he sees the same man in the same spot doing the same thing. This time, he decides to take a closer look, and to his surprise, finds that the man is throwing silver fish into the sea.

"'What are you doing ?' the man asks.

"'I am throwing silver fish back into the sea.'

"'But why?'

"'I am trying to save the life of a fish.'

"'What difference does it make?' the man said. 'There are millions of fish dying without water.'

"'I don't know whether it makes a difference to those millions or not, but it will definitely make a difference to this one,' and he holds the live fish in his hand ready to throw it back into the sea, hoping it will get caught in the undercurrent and be saved.

"The next morning, two figures could be seen bending and rising repeatedly. As the days go by, slowly, many more people are seen involved in this noble act of humanity."

I wasn't born with a philosophy. I am learning everything on this planet. My thinking and philosophy of life is greatly influenced by my spiritual guru whom I never met, Tony, the Catholic priest. He did make a difference in my life.

There is a saying: "You don't get to eat where you grow." My spiritual guru came from India. I had heard of him while I was in India, but I got to know him through his literature after I came to the States. His writings have become my Geeta, my Bible, my Koran. Name it what you want, it really doesn't matter. What does matter is whether I am really living what I appreciate so much. Am I living my thoughts, am I honest with my feelings?

Through his literature, I learned tolerance and the skills to master my emotions such as loneliness, anxiety, stress, and anger. Now, I understand the importance of looking within. My outlook toward life has changed drastically. I have learned to detach myself from my own emotions and also enjoy relationships with other human beings on a non-clinging basis. He freed me of my own emotional baggage. I have acquired clarity of thoughts and my emotional suffering has stopped. He opened my eyes to the reality of the world. He taught me how to live in the present and enjoy it. I am indebted to him forever. I do not have enough words to express my gratitude to him. Today, I am able to stand up to any emotional storm just because of him.

I may speak with a great deal of love for his writings and his philosophy, but if I am a zero when it comes to action, then what is he earthly use of my love for his literature and philosophy?

"Today is a new day, Mathew. It comes with new challenges, but it's up to us how effectively we handle them. Life is full of challenges, but as you know, every problem has a solution." I try to instill some hope in him.

Veronica chimes in: "My problems have no solutions. You haven't been in my shoes, and you can't possibly feel my pain, my loss."

"I don't need to be in your shoes to feel your pain," I respond. "I experience pain, feel sad and down, and experience the same emotions as you do. My body is flesh and blood just like yours. We are products of the same Creator. We all have problems. Sometimes their nature and intensity differ. You don't need to die to talk about death."

"We are called human beings," Marcus jumps in sarcastically, "but in reality we are inhuman. We just need to be human and feel the pain and the loss of others. We have lost sensitivity. We are turning into fucking beasts, always ready to pounce on others."

"Some people look for solutions, others look for problems," I explain. "If you live in the past or are caught up in the future, you are definitely missing the pleasure of enjoying the present, the truth. We have to learn to take care of the present moment. It automatically takes care of the next moment. By staying in the past or worrying about tomorrow, we spoil the beauty of the present moment. No one is sure about tomorrow. Tomorrow always comes in the form of today; tomorrow never has its own identity. You can make your tomorrow bright by leaving tomorrow alone. The best bet is to face the present moment with courage and a positive attitude."

"But my past was so dark, so gloomy," mumbles Mathew.

"There is no reason to carry the burden of the past darkness with you today," I tell him. "As I said earlier, today is a new day with new challenges, new experiences, and new solutions. Today brings you the freedom to enjoy life, to love yourself and others and be happy. Today you have the power and the strength you need to make your life work. You can move forward only if you are willing to let the past go. Let all the shackles be loosened."

It's a lovely March day, and the temperature is in the forties. We decide to go for a walk instead of conducting our usual in-house group. We are enjoying a walk on the road behind our facility. Mathew and I are walking together a bit ahead of the rest of the group. I decide to take a different route this time.

"This is not the same road we walked last time," he points ut.

"I know," I respond, "this time we shall explore another way." However, every other group member who had been on the walk before is wondering why we are changing routes.

"We are taking a new road," I say, loud enough for all to hear.

Eventually we reach a dead end and are unable to go any further. We are looking at nothing in particular, everything in general. We are free to watch and enjoy everything in sight. Beyond the dead end there is an expressway so we enjoy watching the speeding vehicles. Whenever we hear the urgent braking sounds, it makes our hearts beat faster than usual. Curiosity takes over our best judgment and we keep wondering whether there is an accident or what. Almost everyone, including those who have ever driven in their entire life, remark or share their expert views on how drivers should drive. Suddenly, we all have become experts on safe driving.

"Attention please! What is this?" I point to the dead end.

"A dead end," Mathew answers.

"Right." I nod. "It's a dead end. How do you relate it to your ddiction?"

"Addiction is also a dead end," he answers again.

"Okay, now we are standing at the dead end of the road, so what do we do?" I ask.

"Take a turn. Find another way," they respond together.

"Exactly!" I say. "That's the point, there is always a way out. There is always hope. There is always a morning after each night."

The weather is calm. The sky is cloudless. Even our minds are cloudless. The sun is clearly visible. No worries, no tension, all our problems have suddenly disappeared. We are engrossed in enjoying nature's beauty without any thoughts of past or future. No attachments. We are birds of the air. We are lilies of the field. We are like children with innocent eyes.

"I never really noticed sunlight," continues Mathew. "I never walked so freely. I was always high. I had forgotten that there is a sun in the sky. There was always darkness when I was using. I am eally enjoying today."

"What made this possible?" I ask.

He thinks for a while. "You."

"Not me," I correct him. "You made it possible by choosing not to use drugs."

Now he is in tears and looks vulnerable. He doesn't know what else to say.

I look at him closely. "Mathew, are you happy with your progress in the recovery process?"

"Yes, I am." He wipes his tears with his shirtsleeve. "I am doing well mentally and physically. I feel healthy now. I don't feel weak anymore." He pauses, then adds, "You know what? I was sexually aroused the other day! I felt very happy about it. I haven't had a hard-on in months or years. This was the first time in a long ime."

"Good for you." I smile.

He continues, "I was in the kitchen with Jackie, and I got hard.

I told her so, and she said 'wow'! And then she asked me if I was going to have sex with her."

"What did you say?"

"We were supposed to have sex last week," he answers, "somewhere in the building."

"Where in the building ?"

"I don't know," he replies. "Jackie wants ninety dollars just for blowjob, but I don't enjoy blowjobs."

"I see," I respond. "Do you think that would be harmful to our recovery process?"

"Yes."

"Then why are you planning this?"

"I don't know," he answers looking away from me. "I guess I thought it was a good idea."

"It's not. It will impact your recovery adversely."

"But Christopher, I'm curious. I was hard, after not being so, for so long ; you don't know how frustrated I feel due to lack of sex. I haven't felt like a man for so long. I feel depressed and sad. You know I have erectile dysfunction?"

"Yes, But that doesn't mean you have to make wrong decisions.

You need to be focused and committed to your recovery."

"I am focused, and I'm committed, too."

"No, you're not."

"Yes, I am!" he insists. "I never miss a single group. I love your groups."

"That's not the point, Mathew."

"I always share in group," he rushes on.

"That is also beside the point," I tell him. "Apparently, you aren't learning anything."

"Aw c'mon," he says defensively, "I'm not as depressed as I used to be. I know my goals I'm here to learn to stay clean, to get a place to live, and to get a job."

"Mathew, without commitment you cannot achieve your goals. You can't afford any indulgences if you desire to stay in a recovery process. The kind of indulgence that you are contemplating is going to be your biggest hurdle. I think you are losing focus. You are getting distracted."

"I'm not distracted!" he protests.

"Yes, you are," I assert, "and even if you are not distracted at his point in time, you soon will be. You are focused on immediate gratification, and that is disastrous. You are not seeing what I am seeing. Instead of working to stay in recovery, you are regressing."

"I just want to make love because I am curious," he repeats himself.

"Mathew, you have a whole life ahead of you to make love, but before that, you need to put your life back on track, try loving yourself."

Mathew is close to completing his sixty-day program. We decide that a recovery house with an Intensive Outpatient Program (IOP) will be the best aftercare option for him. Accordingly, Stanley starts working with Mathew to get him into a recovery house, but two days before discharge, Mathew changes his mind and says he wants to go back to where he was living before.

"Mathew, that is an unsafe place for you to live," I tell him.

"You should reconsider your decision."

"There is nothing unsafe about that place," he protests.

"The landlady is using drugs, and you had a sexual relationship with her."

"I don't like her," he says. "I'm not in love with her. I didn't have sexual intercourse with her, just oral."

"But you have claimed all along that you didn't want to

go back there, so why this sudden change now ?"

"No particular reason." He shrugs.

"Mathew, my guess is that you want to leave here, go and get high with her, and have sex."

"That's not what I intend to do! And I told you that I don't have sex with her."

"Okay, oral sex," I correct myself.

He smiles.

"Whatever it is, I don't think you are making the right decision. You have gotten high together, you had a sexual relationship with her, and on top of that, you don't even like her. So how will you maintain your sobriety in that place?" I stare at him.

"I have my tools," he replies. "I will use them."

"It's easier said than done. Mathew, I sincerely feel you should avoid going to a place where drugs are easily available and sex is involved. I don't see any recovery there; I see a clear path to relapse."

"I know you mean well," he says, "but I don't want to reconsider my decision. I will be in touch with you. I will let you know how I am doing. I have learned a lot from you."

I smile ruefully. I know what he's saying is crap but I decide not to say another word. He isn't willing to change his decision. He went to live with his landlady after his discharge, and I wished him all the best knowing very well that it wouldn't make any difference. Unfortunately, my skepticism proved true when I learned hat he had relapsed after just a few days.

Chapter 7

Veronica's Pseudo Altruism

Veronica is forty-two. She has been using alcohol and cocaine since she was fifteen, and she is currently homeless. She has a history of multiple treatment attempts and relapse. On many occasions, she was asked to leave treatment facilities for unacceptable behavior. She was in several abusive relationships and has three teenage children who live with her parents.

While she is in my office for a prescheduled session, I ask her, "Veronica, what do you do for a living ?"

"Do I need to tell you that?" she retorts.

I shrug. "If you don't want me to know, it's all right with me."

She hesitates. "Prostitution."

"How do you describe yourself ?" I ask.

"Intelligent and altruistic."

"What do you mean by that?"

"I'm interested in the welfare of others," she explains. "And I know how to handle men. I can easily get them to do things for me."

Veronica is an intelligent woman, but she is also manipulative. She says she is altruistic, but she is not. She is self-centered. For Veronica, the world revolves around her; everything begins with her and ends with her. She is the center of the solar system. She rationalizes all her acts. Her game is intellectualization. She fakes 'panic attacks.' She is lazy. She does not like to get up in the morning. She says, "I am a nocturnal animal. I love sleeping during the day and staying awake at night, and that's what I have been doing my whole life. I did my business at night." I understood what she meant by business. She has difficulty follow-ing directions. She does not like to be told what to do. She doesn't take responsibility for her own behavior. She blames others for everything.

Her parents are retired. Her dad is seventy-two, and her mom sixty-seven. Her mother looks after her children. But still, she talks nothing but ill of her mother. Veronica once asked her father, "Daddy, how could you live with such a miserable woman?" "I love your mother," was his reply.

While in a one on one session, Veronica whines, "I hate my other because she keeps saying that she can't go on vacation because of my children. That is an utter lie. My children are grown. Their diapers don't need changing. They can be left on their own. So what's the big deal about it? My mother makes a fuss over it because she is such a miserable woman. She just wants to remind me that she is doing me a favor. She wants to glorify herself. I pity her."

"Veronica," I say cautiously, "I think you are avoiding your own issues."

After a long pause, she reluctantly admits, "I know, I do have issues."

"Veronica, I'm glad that you are acknowledging that you have issues. But what are you doing to learn to handle them effectively?"

"I'm being honest," she replies.

"Honesty is the best policy," I agree, "but just being honest isn't enough. Recovery calls for more than honesty."

"But acknowledgement is the first step," she rationalizes.

"That's right. But you show no inclination to change. Are you learning anything new ?"

She just looks at me with a blank stare.

Veronica lacks open-mindedness. She clings to her past, loves misery, and refuses to be happy. She dwells in a house where negativity reigns. She is a perfect example of someone who sees a glass half-empty instead of half-full. Point to a full moon, and she will see only your finger. It seems that she hasn't hit rock bottom yet. I think she needs to suffer a little more before she can come awake.

During group, we are discussing the importance of attitude.

"Attitude is everything," Bill begins.

"I don't think attitude is that important. Even people with so-called 'positive attitudes' are miserable and whiners." Veronica shakes her head.

"You say that because you are so negative. A person with a positive attitude can't be a whiner. He may have genuine concerns, and everyone has a right to express his/her disappointment or concerns," Bill reasons.

"You shut your fucking mouth," Veronica snaps. "You don't now what you're talking about!"

"Veronica, mind your language," I intervene.

"I'm sorry for being nasty." She avoids looking at Bill.

"You always say you're sorry, but then you do the same thing again. I've noticed it is your pattern," Bill asserts.

"Damn it!" she shouts. "You are all getting on my nerves!"

"All right, calm down," I say. "Let me tell you a story about how attitude matters.

"The Creator was considering creating human beings on this planet. He decided to send a couple from another planet for reproduction. He short-listed two couples, selected a window, and instructed these two couples to look down on earth using the same window and position, and report back what they saw. The fiirst couple reported that they saw mud everywhere and nothing else. They said, 'It is filthy.'

"Then the second couple went and looked through the same window. They said, 'Wow! It is so beautiful! We saw the lotus, the king of the flowers.'

"The essence of the story is that the second couple had an optimistic attitude. So they were selected for reproduction and sent to the planet called earth."

"I love your stories; can you tell us one more please?" Marcus requests.

"They aren't my stories," I explain. "These stories have been told millions of times in the past; and they will be told as many times in the future. By the way, how much time is left?"

"Twenty minutes," he replies.

"Well," I begin, "this story is about twins who were born to very loving and caring parents. They loved both their kids equally. They named them Fillmore and Seemore. Fillmore grew up with a negative attitude; he even disliked his name, thinking that something was missing in him, and that's why he had been named Fillmore. His twin brother grew up with a positive attitude. He always saw the positive side of every event that happened in his life.

Eventually, Fillmore's negativity became a cause for concern, and his parents were unable to make a decision about buying gifts for the boys' upcoming birthday because of it. They were worried about Fillmore's reaction. They decided to seek help from a psychologist, who, after listening carefully to what they had to say, advised them to buy Fillmore whatever he wanted for his birthday, and present Seemore with a box of horse manure. Fillmore asked or a laptop, and they gave him one even though it was out of their budget. Seemore was presented a box filled with horse manure.

"The parents expected that Fillmore would be very happy with his gift, so they checked in on him first. To their dismay, they found Fillmore sitting at the end of his bed, very disappointed and gloomy. His parents asked him the reason for his unhappiness, and he stated that he wanted a Mitsubishi, not a Compaq Presario. In truth, they had bought the most expensive one at that point in time.

"They left Fillmore alone and went to see how Seemore was doing with his gift, expecting a real scene. To their surprise, he was busy digging deep into that manure and happily searching for something. 'What are you looking for?' his parents asked.

"'I'm looking for a pony. Since there is manure, there has to be pony in there somewhere.'" After a pause, I say, "So, in conclusion, we always see what we want to see."

"That is so stupid," Veronica snorts. "Seemore has no brain.

Looking for a pony in a box of manure? I have never heard of anything more absurd than that."

"It's just a story," Marcus interrupts. "You have to try and get the essence out of every story."

"Essence my foot," she snaps.

* * *

After a couple of days in my office, Veronica tells me, "My triggers are anger, loneliness, frustration, money, places, things, neighborhoods, relationships, and depression. However, my main trigger is nasty people, people who have attitude piss me off, and I end up getting high because of them."

"How could you better deal with your triggers?" I ask.

"Those nasty people just need to change their attitude," she answers.

I look at her. "You can't change the people around you, but you can change the people you are around."

"I don't have to put up with their nastiness," she repeats.

"If that's the case, then you need to work on changing your attitude," I suggest. "It's easier for us to change our attitude than to try and change the attitude of someone else."

"People like Bill and John make me angry," she says.

"No one can make you angry without your permission," I tell her. "You give them the power to make you angry."

"How ?" She stares at me.

I explain, "I remember a beautiful story from the East. I am sure this story will answer your 'how'. The story is about a master, his student, and a woman with a nasty attitude. The master and his student were wandering. Their mission was to preach peace and instill love in the hearts of people. He was an enlightened master, a mystic. His student had recently joined him in his mission. They were living from moment to moment and begging for their sustenance. They knocked on many doors; some were opened and then slammed in their face. Other people just politely refused.

"They were exhausted and hungry. They saw the house of a seemingly wealthy family, and they knocked, hoping to get some food. However, they received nothing but curses. The lady of the house called them every name under the sun. The master was in front, so she directed her verbal abuse at him. He did not respond, and they continued on their journey. As he was moving quietly away, his student asked, 'Master, why did you let that woman take you for granted? You need to say something back to her; you have to put her in her place.' The master didn't respond and kept walking.

"They walked a few miles further, and the student brought the subject up again. 'Master, I can't understand how you can be such a coward that you don't have the courage to get even with a single woman!' The master ignored him and kept on the journey. They walked a few more miles, and the student asked for the third time about the master's behavior. The master, tired of the nagging, finally responded: 'Let it go. It happened hours ago. It's not worth dwelling upon.'

"'Your behavior is beyond my understanding," continued the student. 'I feel like you can't even stand up for your own rights. What can you teach me? I don't want to be a coward like you. I want to be a courageous person.'

"The master was carrying the begging bowl, and he showed

the bowl to his student, asking, 'Who does this begging bowl belong to?'

"'It belongs to you,' his student responded.

"'Here, take this as a gift,' and he offered the bowl to his student, who accepted it. 'Now who owns the bowl?'

"'Now it belongs to me,' the student answered.

"'Now give it back to me please,' the master requested.

"And the student offered the begging bowl to the master.

"'No, thank you, I don't want it,' the master responded.

"'Now I understand!' the student said with excitement. 'That woman was full of poison. She wanted to vent her anger, so she ented it on you. However, you refused to feed into her emotional poison by refusing to react to her outburst.'

"'Excellent,' the master said appreciatively. 'You are bright, and you are willing to listen and learn. I am glad to have you as my disciple. You can always refuse to be angry or unhappy. You always have a choice. If I were to react to her outburst, I would have given her the power to make me angry and unhappy. But, I refused to do so. I want to be my own master. I want to rule my own emotions. No one can control them but me.'

"'Thank you, Master.' his student looked at him admiringly. 'This is the greatest wisdom I have ever had. You explained it so well.'

"The master smiled. 'If you listen from your heart and don't rush to conclusions, you will understand it on your own; you will never impatiently seek explanations. If you listen, things will automatically be revealed, and you will be enlightened on your own without the help of a master.'

"Veronica, do you understand the essence of the story?" I ask.

"I don't think things ever work like that," she answers.

"Do you know what your problem is?" I look at her.

"Bill," she replies.

"Beside Bill," I insist.

"No," she answers. "I don't know."

"Your problem is that you are a pessimist. You only see the negative side of life. You need to develop a positive attitude. You need to look at the bright side of life."

"I'm tired. I want to go back to my room and rest." She bounces out of her chair and out the door.

Chapter 8
Bill's Typical Jail Mentality

Bill is forty-four, homeless, and diagnosed with bipolar disorder and hepatitis C. He has been using heroin, cocaine, and sedatives for many years, although he was clean for nine years while in jail, he still lacks knowledge of recovery process. He served jail terms totaling twenty-one years. His criminal record includes three counts of armed robberies, several DUIs, burglaries, simple assaults, and terroristic threats. Ironically, he believes in God and prays daily. His wife left him because he was in jail for several years. His current girlfriend of six years has been clean for seven months, but he coerced her into prostitution. Shamelessly, he lives on her money.

Bill is defiant, cunning, manipulative, has difficulty listening to authority figures, at times he shuts down completely, feels that others are scheming against him and they are out there to get him so he has to get them first. He fears the unknown, experiences lots of anxiety, schemes and conspires against others. Despite so many character defects in him, we still establish a good rapport. Whenever he is in my office, he cracks jokes and laughs whole-heartedly. Once, while in my office, he said, "I am going to do something to you that even Satan hasn't done to you yet." Then he suddenly rose and walked toward me. For a moment it scared me of death, but when he said, "The Satan hasn't left you yet, but I m going to leave you now." I was relieved. He left my office laughing. He got me good. I sometimes wonder whether he has a split personality.

When he is out with his peers, his personality changes drastically. He resorts to instigating others and gets busy conspiring. He gives Eboni, the nurse, a hard time.

He has too many ups and downs. He has difficulty following directions. He doesn't like to be told what to do. Apparently, he has big, inflated ego and false pride. He holds grudges against people. He hates two of his peers in particular. One is his roommate, Jack, because Jack knows him from the street and knows everything about Bill, and the other is Veronica. He feels that the staff treats her favorably and that she doesn't get sufficient consequences for her acts. He focuses more on her than his own issues. He feels severely depressed, immensely lonely, victimized and jealous. He does not understand that jealousy is keeping him sick.

One day during a one-on-one session, I say, "Bill, besides being compliant with your medication for depression, you need to develop a positive attitude if you want to get rid of your depression. Clinging to negativity is unhealthy; you have to learn to enjoy life as it comes, and you can do it only if you are willing to see the right side of life."

He retorts angrily, "I've been in jail half my life. It's easy for you to say this stuff, because you haven't been there."

"Bill, I know it is difficult, but you need to give it a try. By clinging to the past, you are refusing to enjoy the present. We have to enjoy every moment as if we are living for that moment alone. It's futile to dwell on the past. It will only bring you sad memories. Bygones are bygones. We have no control over the past. It is possible to live in the present. You need to let some things go." I glance at him. "Why do you want to dwell in a past that brings you nothing but misery?"

"I don't know." He shrugs.

"Bill, I want you to write down five advantages of dwelling in the past and show them to me tomorrow."

He sees me the next day and hands me a piece of paper. As expected, I see that he has written only one word. "Why did you write 'none'?" I ask.

"Because there are none," he responds, looking down.

"Good!" I say. "Now, can you think of ten disadvantages of dwelling in the past?"

He looks up and ticks them off on his fingers: "It causes unnecessary anxiety, takes focus away from the present, brings up painful memories, and causes tension, worry, depression, and stress." He pauses, seeming unable to add more disadvantages to his list.

"Excellent, well done!" I congratulate him.

"Also," he resumes, "it makes a person ineffective in his actions; it can cause anger, takes away positive energy, causes indecisiveness and inner conflicts."

"And it doesn't take us anywhere," I add.

He nods. "Right!"

"So tell me, what are the advantages of not dwelling in the past?" I ask.

"I don't know. I've been an addict for so long. It's not easy for me to forget my past."

"Bill, the advantage of not dwelling in the past is that it allows us to enjoy and live in the present. And, one can get rid of the disadvantages you mentioned a few minutes earlier."

He leaves all smiles, and I see John standing in my door, puffing and fuming. "I need to talk to you," he says, entering my ffice.

"What about?"

"Bill is crossing his fucking limits," he complains.

"Give me ten minutes, and I'll be with you." I try to resume writing my notes.

"No," he says impatiently, "I can't wait. I need to speak with you right now."

"John, you'll have to wait till I finish the job at hand."

"I told you, I need to speak with you right away," he insists.

"Please leave my office and come back in ten minutes."

He leaves my office, disappointed, but is back promptly. He settles in the chair opposite mine looking very serious. His pointed nose suddenly looks sharper, and to call it red does not do it justice; it looks red-hot. I give him time to calm down and then ask him what he's upset about.

"Bill says I'm not Muslim."

"Why is he saying that?" I ask.

"I don't know." He pauses for a few seconds, then adds, "I am Muslim. I follow Islam."

"If you are Muslim and you follow Islam, why do you need approval from Bill?"

"He has no right to talk about my faith."

"I know he shouldn't get into your business, but we have no control over the behavior of others. You have the right to follow any religion of your choice. Just ignore him," I suggest. "The matter doesn't seem to be worth getting upset over."

"What if someone says that to you?" he snaps.

"I wouldn't react," I reply.

"I don't take crap from others," he says, looking fierce.

"John, learn to stop, listen, and think before acting. There are always negative consequences of impulsive behavior."

"I don't care," he says.

"In that case, you are free to react any way you want."

"What are you going to do about Bill?" he demands.

"I will speak with him," I answer.

"You need to take action against him." He shifts his sides.

"I need to know his version of the story," I say calmly.

"I don't think that will help me," he says, appearing disappointed.

"What do you want me to do?"

"I don't know." He shrugs.

"John, since you don't know, you should leave it to me to andle it, and I'll get back to you when I've something to tell you."

I did not have to get back to him because they work out their differences on their own. Again they have become close buddies and hang around together most of the time. They have started going to the gym and working out regularly. Bill is no longer paranoid. He seems to be doing well displaying some maturity and patience. He appears to handle difficult situations better than before. When Jack allegedly left a plastic bag full of human feces under Bill's bedding on the day of Jack's discharge, Bill said, "He just didn't like me. That's why he did it. I don't want to sweat small stuff." He is less depressed and appears more energetic, apparently progressing in recovery. Then suddenly, an unfortunate episode happens. The gym director reports to Scott that Bill and John are not following the instructions given by the trainers, and they will not be allowed back. It's also reported that John acts out and Bill is the instigator.

Scott informs me that Bill and John have been denied gym privileges.

"But Scott," I reason, "going to gym is therapeutic, and Bill doesn't deserve such harsh consequences. I agree with you that John has been pumping up his body, threatening peers and being intimidating. I will speak with John and report back to you."

"It's not my decision," Scott responds. "It's the decision of the gym director, and it is not up for discussion anymore."

Scott makes decisions and conveys them to his employees via edicts. However, he agrees to let me find out what John and Bill have to say about the situation. We decide if they are willing to how improvement in their behavior, then he will speak with the gym director. He suggests that I speak with them immediately, and I agree.

I see John in the hallway. "John, I need to talk to you. Please ome to my office."

"Sure, what's up?" he questions as we walk down the hall.

"I am sorry to inform you that you won't be allowed back

to the gym because, apparently, you don't follow the trainer's directions."

"But I didn't do anything!" he protests.

"John, you weren't following instructions at the gym."

"That's fucking crap," he snaps. "They want me to do limited workouts. You see how big I am." He points to his newly built biceps. "I can easily work with the heavy weight, I am not going to listen to those cronies, fuck them." He puts his middle finger up in the air.

"John, you were supposed to be progressing in your recovery, but now it seems that you are regressing."

"Christopher, I'm very angry. I can't believe that they are making such a big deal about it just because I want to follow my own workout program."

"John, if you show improvement in your behavior, you'll be able to go back in a few days."

"Fuck it," he snaps. "Whenever I try to do something worthwhile, they always screw it up."

"John, don't blame it on others. It is the consequence of your own behavior. Let it go."

"I am working hard for my recovery, and they are fucking with me." He pauses, looks at me, and snaps, "And you are saying 'let it go'? That shit won't work with me."

"John, don't be immature. Be patient, and do what needs to be done, and everything will go back to normal."

"No one here fucking wants me to live a normal life. I am trying to take care of my health, and they are telling me that I cannot go to the gym, and you are saying everything will go back to normal. How the fuck will everything go back to normal? That's fucking crap. Don't try to bullshit me. I would be better off leaving this program."

"John—" I look directly at him. "You weren't going to a gym before coming here. So why can't you show some patience and improve your behavior? That will enable you to start your workouts again."

He appears to calm down. "Okay," he says sullenly.

"John, take it easy. Don't do anything that will hamper your recovery. Think before you act. Your impulsive behavior will always land you in trouble until you learn to think first and act second."

He nods and leaves my office.

I go to my morning group and start the session as usual, but then I notice that Bill is staring at me and appears very angry. The moment I meet his eyes, he says in a husky voice, "I have nothing to say today." I think that John has told him what we discussed in my ffice. I decide to lead the group in a discussion regarding honesty.

"Practicing honesty helps us enjoy life to the fullest extent. When we share honestly, we feel at ease; we experience serenity, calmness, and peace of mind. We want to seek the truth. Honesty helps us to walk the talk. It helps us to get out of our illusions. It makes life happier. We have less tension, fewer worries, and less fear of consequences. Honesty never puts us down. It eliminates the chain of lies. It helps us to communicate effectively and with positive energy. Honesty helps us to refrain from indulging in gossip—"

Bill cuts me off, snapping, "You are not an honest person."

"Why do you say that?" I ask.

"You know very well why!" he shouts. "Don't pretend to be innocent. I give you respect, nothing but respect, I never respected anybody as much as I respect you, and you backstabbed me." He glowers at me.

"How did I back-stab you, Bill?"

"I'm not allowed to go to the gym, and you didn't even tell me," he responds.

"Bill, who told you about the gym? I didn't say a single word about you. You are presuming that I said something about you. Of ourse, I am going to speak to you later—"

Before I can finish, he interrupts with, "I don't want to talk to you."

I continue, "We experience wholeness through honesty.

It keeps us away from self-deception. We attain deep trust in ourselves only through being honest. It helps us to build high self-esteem. We are all hypocrites only differing in degree. We say one thing and do another. There are billions of people in the world who say they love peace but still fight wars. There are billions who say they respect the dignity of others but only pay lip service to that ideal. We say honesty is the best policy, but do we practice it?" I pause, then continue, "No. Honesty requires courage. Honesty requires practice. Practice, practice, practice, and the ultimate result is peace of mind. If you practice honesty, a sound sleep is guaranteed." At the end of the session, I look at Bill, but he has turned away from me.

Though John has been in treatment for over a month, he still behaves immaturely. He acts out over trivial issues. His behavior is inappropriate in most situations. However, I am more concerned about Bill. I clearly see relapse in his behavior. Bill has taken this decision to heart. He has become very negative. Whenever we meet for a one-on-one session, he hardly speaks and if he does speak, he complains that he got a raw deal in life. It was true when he said he gave me nothing but respect. When he was happy, he was lively, too. He was learning to enjoy life on life's terms. It is not so easy to change behavior and old habits. It takes time. One has to be willing and open to change. Bill had shown some inclination toward change, but it took only one incident for him to resort to his old addictive behavior.

After about a month in treatment, Bill's primary care phycician recommends a biopsy to rule out cancer. Bill is anxiously waiting the results. He becomes very depressed, irritable, paranoid, and negative in his attitude.

"Bill, how are you doing ?" I inquire.

"Do you expect me to be happy and dancing when I have been biopsied?" he snaps.

"No, I don't," I respond.

"I'm really upset with the doctor for even suggesting it," he says.

"I am sure the doctor had a good medical reason for his decision."

"I don't care! They just want me to be more and more miserable."

"Bill, that's not true," I say calmly. "No one wants you to be miserable. We want you to be happy. But if you keep on worrying bout the future, it will bring misery and nothing else."

"You don't understand what I am going through!"

"I do know what you are going through. I sympathize with you, but you need to be positive in your attitude. Feeling depressed and anxious is not going to help. Why think negatively when no one knows the result of the biopsy? Why worry? Wait and see.

Worry won't solve the problem. Worry just causes more worry. It would be unfortunate if you were diagnosed with cancer, but if you are, you and your doctor will plan treatment. But it could be nothing. So just wait and see."

He looks at me before walking out of my office with no apparent change in his mood.

In group that day, I see Bill still looking depressed. When his turn comes to share, he grumbles, "I'm not allowed to feel anything. I can't be feeling depressed or sad, even my feelings are controlled by others."

I know he is referring to the talk we had earlier but I decide to let it go.

John jumps into the discussion: "Look I lost my wife, my kids, my house, and I went bankrupt. I know my losses. Nobody has been in my shoes." He looks at me. "It's easy for them to tell me what to do. They are being paid for it; but I know my emotional turmoil. My therapist is asking me to be appropriate and practital." He again glances at me. "If he were to lose his wife and kids, he wouldn't say this. How can I be practical when I have lost practically everything I had?"

"Everyone is paid for working. What's wrong with that?" I pause, take a careful look at him, then continue, "John, it's important for you to understand that your losses are the consequences of your behavior. Being angry with me will not help resolve your issues. In fact, this anger is causing you unnecessary stress that you really don't need right now. Are you familiar with Newton's theory that each and every action has an equal and opposite reaction? What do you expect when you continue using heroin?"

"I don't want to hear that crap," he retorts. "Are you or are you not going to help me with my losses?"

"You are laboring under a misperception," I reply. "Who told you that I am going to help you or anyone else here for that matter?"

"Then why are you here?" he shouts.

"I am here to do my part," I answer. "I will do my part, and you will have to do yours."

"So, you are not going to help us?"

"No," I reply. "You have to help yourself. If you are hungry, you have to find food. Then you have to eat and digest it. No one else can digest it for you. If you are sleepy, you have to sleep. No one else can sleep for you. Basically, it comes down to help comes to those who help themselves."

"You don't love anybody here," he snaps. "You just want to take big bucks. What do you care?"

"Good grief, John," I say. "Do you think we help people because we are in love with them?"

"Yes," say John and Danny together.

"You might be surprised to hear that we, human beings are never in love with anyone," I explain. "Actually, we love our own perception of that person. For that matter, we say we trust others, but in reality, we don't trust anyone; we trust our own idea of that person. We trust our judgment of that person, our opinion of that erson. We need to understand reality for reality's sake. This becomes possible only if we are willing and open to learn something new, something practical and healthy, physically and mentally. We have wrong ideas about love, about joy, about happiness, about relationships, and about everything else. We pretend everything. We are masters of pretending. We pretend for so long it becomes a art of our daily behavior. We get used to this behavior and knowingly, or unknowingly, we see this particular behavior as a part of our personality.

"Have you heard the story about the donkey?" I pause, look at the group and then continue, "A donkey finds the skin of a lion and decides to pretend he is a lion. He wears the newly found skin and starts scaring the villagers. This goes on for quite some time. He is acting wily, shrewd, subtle, and clever just like you and me. He is imitating a lion's behavior except the roaring. One day a herd of donkeys passes by, and this false lion hears their braying. He can't control his natural urge to respond in kind, forgetting that he is dressed and acting as a lion. He is unable to keep up with the pretense. And when the villagers hear him, they stone him to death."

John seems a bit calmer and less anxious, and I am relieved. I wish them all a happy weekend, and I tell Bill that everything will be all right and to just hang in there and stay focused.

Monday I am informed that Bill left on Saturday. He had acted out the entire day and left that evening. He never got the results of his biopsy. It remains a mystery to me and probably to him too. However, his relapse is no mystery. He chased his real cancer the day he left the program. Surprisingly, Bill's leaving changes John for the good. He starts taking his recovery seriously. He becomes more open and willing to learn and is more honest in his sharing.

Chapter 9

Identity Crisis The Double Trouble

Fitler is a twenty-five-year-old homeless male who has been abusing alcohol and cocaine for the past two years. He was so unfortunate in that his mother died a few minutes before he was born. Neither ever got to see each other. He had a rough child-hood. It wasn't easy for him growing up without a mother. He was in an orphanage for a while and occasionally lived with his grandmother. Things did not go well for him. He grew up with a lot of anxiety and insecurity. He still sucks on his thumb when he is upset. He stays preoccupied with sexual thoughts and behaves inappropriately. He wears heavy eye makeup and lipstick. He polishes his fingernails. He walks and talks like a female.

"Do you have any sexual abuse issues?" I ask in our first session.

"Not really."

"What do you mean by 'not really'?"

"I started having sex at age six—" He pauses, scans my face, and continues, "—with my older brother."

"Fitler, don't you realize that was child abuse as well as incest?"

"No," he says, "it wasn't child abuse. I liked it."

"Do you consider yourself male or female?" I ask.

"Male."

"Then why do you behave like a female?"

"I like it," he replies, playing with his fingernails.

"Do you consider yourself homosexual or bisexual?"

"I only sleep with men. And, well, I'm taking hormones to grow breasts."

"Aren't you making things a bit complicated?" I look at him.

"I don't know." He sighs.

"What is the highest grade you completed in school?"

"Twelfth grade," he replies proudly. "And my goal is to complete four years of college." He continues playing with his nails.

"How about staying clean?"

"I don't think it's a big deal," he responds carelessly. "I don't have a serious problem with drugs."

"Then what exactly is your problem?" I ask.

"Sex. I want to have sex all the time."

"You are sexually preoccupied," I state.

"I wouldn't say that," he protests. "I just like sex, that's all."

The next day in group, Fitler, caressing his budding breasts, crows, "My hormones are jumping."

"Stop it!" I say sternly.

"It's my body." He licks his lips and moves his hand all over his chest.

"So?" I stare at him.

"Why do you object to my touching my breasts?"

"It is disgusting," I reply.

"I feel sexy," he says, pressing them more firmly than ever.

"Stop touching yourself and behave!" I almost shout at him.

He immediately removes his hands from his chest and starts playing with the threads of his subtly torn jeans.

"I crave sex," he tells us. "Drugs are my secondary problem, just a by-product. I don't think I can live without sex."

"Fitler, craving for anything isn't good; it makes you feel anxious and stressed. That includes cravings for fun, enjoyment, satisfaction, peace, joy, or anything else, for that matter."

"I don't get it." He looks at me, confused.

I explain, "Peace of mind, for example. If you are constantly craving peace of mind, how can you be at peace?"

"Well, I never thought of it that way." He starts sucking on his thumb again.

"Can I ask you something ?" Bobby puts his hand up.

I nod.

"Do you know what I think of all day long ?"

"Sex," I reply.

"You are right about that." He grins. "But how did you now ?"

"Because we all do that." I smile back.

"You, too?" He looks at me, surprised.

"I have the same emotions and needs as you do," I reply.

"So, you mean there is nothing wrong with thinking about sex all the time?" He appears eager to know.

"No," I reply. "I don't mean that. What I mean, Bobby, is that thinking about sex is not a problem as long as you don't act on it. Being preoccupied with sexual thoughts all the time is unhealthy. You need to learn to divert your mind. Find activities that interest you. Stay busy."

"I've been busy my whole life using drugs," Adam cuts in, laughing.

"You have to stay busy doing something that is constructive. It's that simple," I state.

"People say sex is a good thing," Fitler jumps in, licking his lips and touching his private parts with both hands.

"Fitler, stop playing with your tools and say what you have to say," I tell him firmly. He stops.

"I was saying that people say sex is good," he repeats.

"I do think sex is a most enjoyable activity. It revitalizes us. Someone once said a boost in bed is equal to climbing one hundred steps. Sex involves both your mind and physical body. It is the best mental and physical exercise. However—"

Adam interjects, "Then why do people here make such a fuss bout it?"

"Look Adam," I reply, "everything has its appropriate time and place. You need to have the right partner, the right place, and the right time."

"I can understand the importance of the right partner," Bobby chimes in, "but I fail to understand what you mean by the right place and time."

"Bobby, one can't have sex in inappropriate places and at inappropriate times. For example, let's say you are married with school-age children, and you are having sex on the sofa in the living room when the children come home from school. Would that be an appropriate place and time?"

"I've been in that situation," Adam volunteers. "Once I was in bed with my girlfriend. My eight-year-old son was playing outside. He came in the house—we had left the bedroom door unlocked—and he saw us having sex. We were so embarrassed we couldn't look him in the eye for days."

"That kind of carelessness can cause serious relationship ssues," I say, "and leave a long-lasting negative impact on a child's growing mind."

"You're right about that." Adam nods. "my son and I still don't have a good relationship."

"The whole world is crazy," Marcus chips in. "They want nothing but sex."

"I often find that some of the most troubled people are overly sexual," I remark. "Sexual indulgence is one of the most common barriers to their recovery process. That is why I advise you to stay way from sexual indulgence and be focused and committed to our recovery process."

A few days later, I call Fitler to my office because there have been several complaints about his inappropriate behavior, including some plans for having a threesome. He comes in, again fondling his breasts. "I'm feeling sexy; my hormones are jumping."

"Cut that crap," I tell him.

"Don't you like it?" He licks his lips.

"Fitler, it's inappropriate to lick your lips like that. You need to be serious and realize that you need help."

"I need sex," he says.

"You are not here to have sex! You are here to work on your ssues!"

"It's hard for me to stay here without sex," he whines.

"Fitler, you need to stop thinking about sex, otherwise you will become a sex addict."

"I don't want to be a sex addict!" He gets a panicked look as though he will turn into a sex addict on the spot. "I'll tell you the truth: I like Adam, and we were talking about having sex last night."

"Is there anything more?" I ask.

"No that's it," he says, "nothing more."

"How about a threesome?"

"Jerome, my roommate, and I thought of having a threesome, but nothing materialized," he answers, avoiding eye contact.

"But Jerome isn't homosexual, is he?" I ask.

"He's straight." He pauses, then adds shyly, "but we agreed to give him a blowjob, and he was okay with it."

"Stop this nonsense and start working on getting your act together before any action is initiated against you," I warn him.

"Okay," he replies.

"I am giving you an assignment: write five hundred words stating the relationship between addictive behavior and sexual inappropriateness."

"Can I write three hundred?" he pleads.

"Okay, I'll accept that. When will you have it done?"

"In two days?"

"No," I say. "Write it tonight and give it to me tomorrow morning."

"No problem." He leaves my office.

The next day, while the clients were on their way back from breakfast Fitler ran away. Everyone who saw him running gave a different version and a different direction. I don't know whether he went north, south, east, or west, but he definitely went where the drugs were best. I hope nobody ever gives him any more assignments to write.

Chapter 10
Adam Feels He's Treated Like a Dog

While in group, Adam whines, "I'm not getting anything out of this program. This program has nothing to offer. The staff is full of crap. They're only concerned about their checks. They don't want to help anyone. They treat us like dogs. Have you seen anyone treating us like human beings?"

"You reap what you sow," quotes Marcus.

"Whatever," Adam retorts. "We have a right to be treated like human beings."

"I don't think we are treated like dogs. I believe I am getting fair treatment at the hands of the staff," John says.

"The staff here is partial. Some of the clients are favored over others," Adam continues, "because they listen and do whatever the staff tells them. I don't take crap from them."

"It's easy to forget that our own actions brought us here," Marcus interjects, "yet we are unwilling to follow the directions and advice given by our therapist and the staff."

"I don't need directions from others. I am perfectly capable of directing my own life," Adam boasts.

"You are in denial—" Maria looks at Adam, "because if you were capable, you wouldn't be here."

"I'm not here to take shit from you, Maria," he retorts. "You just take care of yourself!"

"This is an open forum. I have a right to state my opinion,"

Maria snaps back.

"Let me say something. You guys are making things personal. It is very important to remember the purpose of your being here. What brings you together?"

"Our common problem and the common goal of staying clean," Marcus answers.

"If what you are saying is true, then why are you guys fighting like cats and dogs?" I look at them, but nobody speaks up, so I continue, "You have to learn from adversity. You cannot expect good treatment from others. You can't demand respect, you have to command it. You have to learn to respect yourself first."

"Have you ever heard the expression that a closed mouth doesn't get fed?" Adam looks at me.

I nod. "Yes, I have. But why are you asking ?"

"Well, nowadays, if you don't demand respect, you won't get it," he responds.

"I disagree. The meaning of the expression is that if you don't ask for help, you won't get it. It's out of context here," I explain.

"No." He is adamant. "It's not out of context. You are saying the same thing : that you have to ask for anything you need."

"Adam, I was explaining the meaning of the expression. However, help is one thing and respect is another."

"But we are talking about asking," he insists.

"Adam, we need to stop this futile discussion, it is leading us nowhere and wasting time."

"Why do you say that now, Christopher? You always say that we learn from everything." He keeps looking at me.

"Yes," I reply, "we learn from everything, but only if we are willing and open to learning. Let me put it bluntly. You have never shown any inclination to learn anything new. You argue for the sake of argument, and you keep harping on the same things."

"You can't say that! I share more than anyone else, don't I?" he sks defensively.

I sigh. "You sure do, but you don't listen to what you say."

"I don't have to listen to what I say. I say it for others to listen, not me."

"Adam," I say slowly, "if you don't listen to what you are saying, you won't understand yourself. You have to practice your listening skills."

"I have been listening to people my entire life," he sputters, "but it didn't change my situation, so what difference will it make now ?"

"You aren't listening from the heart," Maria chimes in. "If you listen from your heart, things will change."

"That's so absurd," he snaps.

"That isn't absurd Adam," I intervene. "It is a very enlightened statement."

"You always appreciate whatever she says," he whines.

"That's probably because she says things which deserve to be appreciated," I tell him.

"That's why I feel you guys are partial," he grumbles. "I want to pack up my stuff and leave."

"It's all up to you. I have told you the advantages of staying in treatment and the negative consequences of leaving. However, almost everyday you talk of leaving. You seem to be looking for an excuse to leave. Some people work for their recovery and others work for relapse. You belong in the second category. You have been talking about leaving from day one. I am not allowed to ask you to leave treatment; otherwise, I would have, because you discourage others from staying."

"I haven't told anyone else to leave!"

"That's true," I admit. "You haven't told anyone to leave, but you badmouth the program, you say everything sucks here and that there aren't enough smoke breaks, and you continue to talk bout leaving day and night. How does that encourage anyone?"

"I don't know," he responds wearily. "But I can't stop smoking. I can't stop everything at once."

"That is the tragedy, Adam. What you should know, you don't know. Let me tell you again: stop talking about leaving and start working on your issues. That will help you to stay in recovery. You aren't here to smoke, are you? Don't waste your energy on unimportant issues; invest your energy into something worthwhile."

"He is just verbalizing his feelings." Beaver, a new client, comes to Adam's rescue out of the blue. "He does talk about leaving, but he doesn't leave. Isn't that worth appreciating ?"

I just look at him with no expression on my face.

Chapter 11
Beaver's Lecherous Father

The next day, Beaver enters my office looking grumpy. I smile at him. "Beaver, how are you doing ?"

"Good," he growls.

"We need to complete your psychosocial assessment, and I would appreciate your cooperation." I put the paperwork on my desk and pick up my pen. "To begin, how old are you?"

"Why?" He gives me a flat stare.

"How old are you?" I repeat.

"Forty-six," he replies reluctantly.

"What is your living situation?" I glance at him.

"Are you buying me a house?" he snaps.

"No," I reply.

He hesitates. "I'm homeless."

"What drugs are you currently using ? Please be specific."

"What difference does it make?" He pauses and looks at me angrily. "I use alcohol, cocaine, and marijuana."

"How old were you when you first started using drugs?"

"This is ridiculous," he grumbles. "I started using drugs at nine."

"Beaver, how many years of schooling did you complete?"

"Do you want to see my certificates?" He stares at me coldly. "Or are you planning to send me back to school?"

"Neither," I reply.

"Twelfth grade. Why do you want to know ?" He continues

staring at me.

"Don't worry about the reasons now," I say, allowing some impatience to creep into my voice.

He is tall and hefty and has a cold, stony, intimidating look. Every time I ask him a question, he looks at me with those cold eyes that penetrate straight through me. It's frightening. I scan his face, looking for some clue that will help me handle him more effectively. So far, he hasn't answered any question without asking a counter question.

"What is your weight?" This question comes near the end of the assessment; I don't know why I ask so far ahead. I guess I am either intimidated or subconsciously scared of him. I just don't know for sure what it is.

"Why?" He stares at me. "Do you want me to go on a diet? I weigh two-hundred-and-ninety pounds."

"How many children do you have?"

He pauses, then answers reluctantly, "Three. Are you going to release this information to my insurance company or any other authority?"

"Yes," I reply.

"Then I have none," he retracts.

"But you just said you have three!"

"But now I am saying I have none." He gives me a cold stare again.

I don't dare ask him any more questions about his children. I tell myself, he can have three, five, or ten. It is none of my business. He has a strange look. It's not that he does not speak; he just takes his own sweet time. I am at the stage where I have to ask some critical questions, and I am unsure how he will react; however, I begin.

"How old were you when you first had sex?"

He shifts in his seat. "I didn't have sex. Someone had sex with me." He gives me that penetrating look again, then continues angrily. "Now, you want to know about sex?"

"I have no personal interest in it," I tell him calmly. "I am merely asking you questions from this printed form. How old were you when you were sexually abused?"

He scans my face. "From age nine to thirteen, every night."

"Who abused you?"

He falters, "My father." He takes a deep breath, his eyes fill with tears, and he continues choking. "Every night he came home and ordered me to take off my clothes, and he put his thing in my behind. Is that enough or do you want to know more?" He pauses for a few seconds, stares at me, and adds, "I was raped at age eighteen by five prisoners when I was doing time."

I sit, dumbstruck. I can't let his lecherous father out of my mind for a long minute.

After gathering my thoughts I ask, "Did you tell your mother about it?"

"No," he answers, shaking his head.

"Why not?"

"My father used to tell me that if I told my mother, he would kill her." He takes a deep breath again. "I was scared."

"Is your father still alive?"

"No." He shakes his head. "He is dead. I have forgiven him."

"Beaver, that is wonderful. You also have to let go of those other painful memories of yours."

"I'm working on it," he says quietly.

"Why were you in jail?" I continue with the questionnaire.

"Are you going to report me?" He is agitated and angry again.

"No."

"I was convicted for burglary, theft, possession of a controlled substance—" he pauses for a long minute, "and armed robbery."

"What were the consequences?" I probe cautiously.

"The consequences differed from probation to jail," he nswers.

"How many years of jail in all?"

"I don't remember; seven years, I think."

I rise and walk toward the door. "Okay, Beaver, that is enough for today. Thank you for answering the questions. I will see you soon." I take a deep breath as he leaves my office.

* * *

A few days later, I begin group with the statement, "Humility is a human virtue. We witness a lot of hatred and violence around us. We need to be humble in the face of hatred and violence."

"I am learning to practice humility," says Maria. "I need to be humble."

"For example," Beaver jumps in, looking at me, "you are walking on the street with your wife and some passerby messes with her. Wouldn't you be mad at him and try to get even?"

I interject: "First, you are asking a hypothetical question, and I don't feel comfortable answering hypothetical questions. However, every situation is different. As far as I am concerned, I would try to understand the situation and act accordingly. I know in this given hypothetical situation, I have every right and reason to protect my wife and myself, but I wouldn't use unreasonable force or try to get even with a street person. I would take appropriate steps and not rush and cause more trouble. If necessary and if possible, I might call 911, but as I said, it differs from situation to situation. What would I achieve by getting mad?"

"If you kick his ass, your wife will feel proud of you," Adam suggests.

"It is not a question of making my wife feel proud of me,"

I explain. "It is a question of protecting our right to live a peaceful and dignified life. And, by keeping my cool, I will definitely be in a position to handle the situation more effectively and appropriately. In the *Bhagwad Geeta*, the sacred scripture of the Hindus, Lord Krishna, the Charioteer, tells Arjuna, *'Keep your heart at the lotus feet of the lord and plunge into the heat of action.'* That means that if you carry your emotions—love, anger, frustration, rage, depression, and anxiety—with you to the battlefield, you won't be as effective as you would be without them. We need humility in the face of violence, in the face of destruction, in the face of hatred, in the face of misery and pain. It helps the person practicing the humility, and in doing so, it helps others."

"You are talking about practicing humility, but how about a non-believer in humility?" Beaver chips in again.

"This is not something like religious beliefs," I reply. "Why wouldn't anyone believe in humility? There are only advantages in humbling oneself. There are no disadvantages whatsoever if you practice humility."

"You haven't seen the world." He scans my face. "How old are you?"

"It's irrelevant Beaver," I tell him. "It doesn't matter."

"It does," he shouts, "because it looks like you don't know the world. The world outside is full of crooked people, and you keep on saying life is like a banquet and stuff like that. It seems life hasn't kicked you enough; you look to be in your twenties. There is still a long way for you to go, and then you will certainly change our view about life."

"You're not listening," Maria intervenes. "You are too busy preparing to say something before he is done. You are preoccupied."

"I am listening!" He glares at her.

"No," she goes on, "you are not. If you were listening, you would have understood what he said about practicing humility in the face of hatred, pain, and adversity."

"So," Beaver begins, "he's saying even though others cause us pain, we still have to remain humble?"

"Yes, that is called practicing humility. It's easier to go down a hill than up," Maria explains slowly, "but the view is from the top. It's easy to slap someone when you are angry, but difficult to remain calm in aggravating situations."

The next day, Adam expresses his antagonism: "When everyone is practicing violence and hatred, how would my practicing humility change the world?"

Adam is forty-eight with a thirty-two-year history of using cocaine, marijuana, and alcohol. He is homeless and extremely negative in his attitude. He is antagonistic as well as pessimistic.

"Adam," I interject, "if you think you are too small to make a difference, then you are underestimating yourself."

"Even mosquitoes make a difference," adds Maria. "They are capable of making you dance."

"You bitch!" he shouts. "You have no right to call me a mosquito."

"Why would I call you a mosquito?" There is no visible change in Maria's composure. "I was using it as a figure of speech. I'm sorry if I hurt your feelings."

Adam stares at her. "Listen, Maria. I am not going to take shit from anyone. I believe in tit for tat, in giving as good as you get!"

"You don't have to be sorry, Maria," I tell her. "Adam should apologize to you."

"I'm sorry," he says, not looking at Maria, but staring at me instead.

"Let me back up and remind you all of something. Do you remember the other day when Adam said that he is homeless, had othing to eat, and has no one to rely on? Who do you think is responsible for this?" I look over the entire group.

"We are," answers Maria.

"No. Not true," Beaver attacks. "The answer is circumstances."

"Circumstances do play a part, but how about you claiming responsibility for your part in it? Drugs don't just jump inside you. No one gets high until one starts using." I look him straight in the eyes.

"What did we know then? We were kids," he rationalizes.

"But you know it now," I respond.

"Yeah, and now we are already hooked," Beaver continues. "It's mpossible to get rid of it now."

"That kind of attitude won't help anyone in recovery," I explain. "I know it's not easy. It is difficult, but not impossible. You have to learn to walk the extra mile. You have to turn over every stone in your way if you really desire to stay clean."

Adam attacks again: "You haven't slept without food. I've been there, and I have slept in the cold my whole life. You haven't experienced loneliness, depression, rejection, and being treated like shit. Those who go through aches and pains don't remain idealistic. Hopelessness sets in, and you become realistic. No more daydreaming. So don't give us idealistic talks."

I look straight at him. "Adam, you always talk about your plight and try to justify your behavior by talking about how you lived your life. This kind of talk won't do you any good. You haven't seen the plight of poor people in third-world countries. If you were to visit the country I come from, you would see the real plight of poor people. Forget food, they don't even get clean water to drink. The able-bodied are unemployed because of the scarcity of work. Most people are living in slums. They have no sanitation, or drinking water, or no electricity. They use the railway tracks as toilets and are frequently run over by trains. The homeless sleep in the sidewalks and get run over by drunk drivers. They cannot send their children to school. They live below the poverty line. They have next to nothing. Since you have never seen real tragedy, you feel your life is more tragic than others'. At least you play an active part in your addiction, but they have nothing to do with their plight. Their fate is that they are born in poor countries and have no means to overcome it. Therefore, you need to stop saying, "Poor me, poor me," and start working on your recovery! No one else can do it for you; you have to do it yourself."

He looks at me as though I have lost my mind. Bewildered, he utters, "Okay, okay. So you mean, if I eat, I got to shit."

"If you understand that expression better, then take it that way." I smile.

"Fine," he says. "I'll start working for my recovery tomorrow."

"Start today!" I tell him. "You can't wait for tomorrow to come and then start working. You cannot start digging the well when you are already thirsty."

"I never experienced happiness. It's not that I don't want to be happy, I have just never found happiness," he says.

"Happiness is not something to be found," I tell him. "Nothing can bring you happiness. Happiness is uncaused. We make a mistake when we search for happiness in things and people. We postpone happiness for want of something more. If you want to enjoy your life, start enjoying it at this moment."

"How do we do that?" Maria wants to know.

"By living in the present as if you are living for this moment alone, you can leave the worries of the past in the past," I say, "and worries of the future to the future. You have to learn to overcome circumstances."

"But you haven't experienced what we have experienced," Beaver argues.

"No doubt about that," I agree. "We do have different experiences, but we all have feelings, worries, and problems. We all experience pain and joy. We all have desires and dreams. We all experience emotions and possess the courage to live. We all have needs and requirements. We all have an ability to grow. We are connected. The only difference is that we handle things differently."

"But how can I experience happiness when I have gone through so much shit in my life, and I'm still going through it?"

Beaver whines.

"Beaver, if you want to experience happiness, you should be willing to change your attitude. Let me explain it with the help of a story that I came across recently.

"A senior citizen is being cursed at and harassed by teenagers. Whenever they see him working in his garden, they start taunting and scheming against him. He is deeply troubled and disturbed and begins to feel unhappy and depressed. Days go by, and he starts feeling more and more miserable. He starts drinking heavily. On a sober day, he says to himself, 'This is not how I want to be. I don't want to be miserable and gloomy anymore. I have to do something constructive and pull myself out of this situation.'

"After giving deep thought and consideration to the matter, he decides to speak to the teenagers and make them a proposal. He offers them five dollars on the first day for harassing him and tells them to come back again. They are happy with this development. The next day he gives them two dollars, a dollar on the third day, fifty cents on the fourth day, and twenty-five cents on the fifth day. He offers them a penny on the weekend and says, 'From now on, every day you will get a penny for cursing me.' The teenagers are very disappointed with the new offer.

'Forget it,' they say and never bother him again."

"It was a wonderful story." Maria is smiling. "I used to read stories; I stopped reading while in my active addiction.

I need to start reading again."

"Books are our best friends," I say. "You have to cultivate a reading habit. Stories bring joy and happiness and explain things better."

"Bullshit!" Adam snaps. "No one is going to be happy by just listening to stories. You need money, you need other things to be happy."

"Speak for yourself," Maria replies vehemently. "I had everything, but I wasn't happy. Money didn't make me happy. I relied on drugs to make me feel happy. Now I have nothing, but for the first time, I am experiencing happiness because I'm developing a positive attitude and a willingness to move on with my life."

"If you don't get food to eat for two days," he reasons, "you're not going to be happy."

"Food is food. I need it to survive, not to be happy. You're talking crap now," Maria says.

"And you're talking as if you are a philosopher," he retorts. "I'll call you Maria the philosopher."

"Call me whatever you wish," she responds.

"Then I will call you Plato," Adam teases. Everyone laughs, including Maria.

"Whatever," Maria says.

"Adam, you need to grow up," I intervene. "You think and act like a child."

"Isn't that good?" he says with a smirk on his face.

"No," I reply. "It's childish."

"You told us on several occasions that we should be child-like," he reminds me.

"You are taking it out of context," I tell him. "That time I was talking about the striking innocence of children. I was referring to their ability to stay in the present, not live in the past or future and their tendency to forgive and forget. There is no innocence in what you say or do. You scheme day and night."

"Christopher is the eliminator; don't ever try to mess with him. He doesn't say what you want to hear. He says what you need to hear," John chuckles. "Adam only schemes during the day; at night he sleeps. I'm his roommate and hear him snoring. I can't stand his snoring." Everyone laughs.

"I scheme at night," Adam admits. "I love it. I get a kind of pleasure doing it. I think that's the best way to enjoy life. There has to be some spice in life. You guys don't know what you are missing."

Sometimes, I do feel these folks really want to change. They want to grow. But when I come across a person like Adam, and there are many like him, I think they don't. They don't want to be happy. They want to be miserable. I remember a wise old saying: "Don't try to teach a donkey how to sing; it is not his cup of tea." Not everything is for everyone.

* * *

Beaver comes to my office early in the morning puffing and fuming. "She is crazy. I can't stand her."

"Have a seat." I point to a chair.

He sits down.

I look at him carefully and ask, "Who are you talking about?"

"Irene. She came right out and told me that I'm here because I'm homeless." He hesitates. "I am homeless, but it's none of her usiness."

"I know it's none of her business. I don't know why she said that. Do you want me to speak with her?"

"No," he replies. "I can handle it on my own."

"Are you sure you don't want me to talk to her?" I ask him gain.

"Yes, I'm sure," he says. "I don't want you to talk to her."

"Then let it go," I suggest. "Don't sweat the small stuff."

"It's not small stuff," he snaps.

"Everything is small stuff," I insist.

"Not for me," he says. "She pissed me off."

"Beaver, you are angry at her because she is treating you negatively, but you are making the same mistake and acting out the behavior you claim to despise. Two wrongs do not make a right. I know it is none of her business, but still she got into it, you need to let it go or just accept the fact and move on," I tell him. "It's not the incident that made you angry; it's your reaction to what she said."

"Are you trying to tell me that I shouldn't react?"

"Yes." I hold his gaze.

"I'm a human being!" he roars.

"Did I say you weren't?"

"It's human to react," he insists.

"Since your reaction is causing you stress and anxiety and making you angry, wouldn't it be better if you didn't react?"

"Christopher, I don't want to be somebody's psychological slave."

"I don't know what you are talking about." I shake my head.

"You are a psychological slave to drugs; you don't become a psychological slave to a person because you are not reacting to a particular situation. In fact, you become a master of that situation because you are keeping your emotions and the situation under your control."

"I believe that people should respect each other, and when they show disrespect, I hate it."

"Beaver, I understand you want respect. But you can't force others to respect you. You need to command respect, not demand it. Respecting others is an admirable quality. You expect people to be respectful, but it doesn't always happen."

"I have a hard time accepting the realities of life," he admits. "I'm struggling with it. I need to be realistic. I want to learn to live life on life's terms. Most of the time what you say sounds cruel, but the truth is always bitter, and when it hits, it hits hard. I can't shy away from the truth."

"Stay focused," I suggest, "and things will turn out well."

"I'll try." He pauses. "Another thing, I always feel angry. I need help with it. Basically, I am not an angry person by nature, but other people always anger me."

"Beaver, you are not the only person in the world who experiences anger. However, some people handle anger effectively whereas others are ineffective in handling it. Just for your knowledge, understand that anger is not external, it is internal. You have a choice to be angry or not. When you allow others to control your emotions, you get upset and angry."

"But I need to express my anger," he responds.

"Why?"

"It makes me feel better."

"After expressing your anger you may feel better for a while, but it doesn't make your situation any better," I interject. "In fact, you start practicing anger, and then you become an expert at it."

"But, Christopher, I feel strong and powerful when I am angry."

"You might feel effective when you use anger to get what you want, but you make the situation worse. Anger is not strength; it s a weakness, and by not getting angry, you can protect yourself and exercise effective control over the situation."

"I hate it when people tell me what I should and should not do," he says. "I get very angry."

"You possibly experience anger in those situations," I explain, "because they tell you something different than what you are prepared to hear. Try to understand that you cannot hate someone without suffering yourself."

"I always think negative," he continues. "I have always been involved in criminal activities."

"If you feed bad, then bad will win," I tell him. "If you feed good, then good will win. You have to unlearn your old behavior in order to learn new behavior. Let me explain it with the help of an analogy: if a bottle is full of contaminated water, no matter how thirsty you are, you can't drink it, can you?"

"No."

"You have to empty the bottle and refill it. You cannot keep a single drop of the contaminated water because it will contaminate the fresh water. Therefore, the bottle must be thoroughly cleaned.

If you don't empty that bottle, you can't refill it with fresh water."

* * *

While engaged in a one-on-one session a few days later, Beaver pens up: "My life is messed up. My past keeps haunting me. I can't forget my past, and I keep worrying about my future, too."

"Beaver, why ignore the present for the sake of something that happened in the past or something that may not happen in the future? If you live in the present, it automatically becomes a source of power and strength that you need for living a healthy and happy life. You need to remember that yesterday is history, tomorrow is a mystery because it is not promised, and today is a gift—that's why it's called the 'present.' So learn to enjoy it, and let the past go."

"That's easier said than done," he responds. "You say don't dwell in the past, but don't you think recalling the past helps us?"

"You have to learn to observe what's happening within and around you. It will reveal you to yourself. Recalling the past is one thing, but dwelling in it is another," I explain. "Recalling past mistakes in order to learn from them or anticipating the future to plan a further course of action is okay. But you have to make sure that you don't let anything take you out of the present for long periods of time."

"You make it sound so easy, but I know it's not," he grumbles.

"Beaver, I know it is not easy, but you can make it easier if you practice new behaviors sincerely and diligently."

After a week or so, I tell Beaver, "You can't keep bumping into life over and over, again and again. You have to stop that circle somewhere, somehow."

He responds flatly, "I'm not ashamed of my mistakes."

"Beaver, you don't have to be ashamed if you make a mistake; it's human to make mistakes. However, you have to learn from your mistakes. You can't keep making the same mistake again and again."

"I make mistakes to learn from them," he rationalizes.

"Your actions speak otherwise. You have chronic relapse issues, and you need to do something about it."

"Now you are making me feel inferior," he snaps.

"How ?"

"By talking about my relapses."

"Tell me, how many times have you relapsed?"

"Seven or eight times." He looks away from me.

"You are ashamed because you keep making the same mistake over and over."

"So what?" He shrugs.

"Look who is saying 'so what?' You have the nerve to ask 'so what?' You have to learn to be responsible. Instead of feeling shamed and blaming it on others, you have to own responsibility for your actions."

"I don't want to listen to this crap so early in the morning," he retorts.

"If you don't listen, you will never learn. However, it's all up to you; if you don't want to listen, don't listen. No one can force you to listen. Why bother yourself?"

"People are always unfair to me," he complains. "They criticize me for being inconsistent."

"Beaver, it is quite acceptable to change your mind and be inconsistent. We all waver. You're a human being, not a robot. You can always choose a different course of action. We can't expect people to be fair and not to criticize."

"What's wrong with expecting people to be fair and not to criticize?"

"There is nothing wrong with that; but when we expect something and it doesn't happen, we become anxious and stressed. We suffer because of our expectations."

"There is lot of injustice and unfairness in the world," he says. "Sometimes I think life is very cruel."

I nod. "You have a point. Sometimes life itself is unfair, and we can't do anything about it. We have no control over it. We can't explain all the suffering in the world. Children are born with deformities. Innocent people suffer. You see all the killing that is going on around the world. Can you keep blaming the Creator for his unfairness?"

"Do you think, sometimes, you try hard to change and things get worse?" he asks.

"Things don't get worse because you try hard," I answer.

"Things might get worse because you don't plan well, or your approach isn't right."

"People think I am antisocial."

"You are," I chuckle. He laughs for the first time since he arrived. "All kidding aside, if you keep presuming and trying to read ther people's minds, you will never be at peace. Trust me, you are asking for trouble. You worry too much about other people's opinions. What you think and do matters the most."

* * *

While in group, I see John staring at the floor, so I ask, "John, what's the matter?"

"I can't be happy when I have lost practically everything."

"Why not?"

"How is it possible?"

"Can we discuss happiness today?" I ask the group.

They agree that it's a good topic.

I begin, "Happiness is an ongoing journey, not a destination. It's determined by internal circumstances, not by external ones. You have a choice to be happy or not. It does not cost you anything to be happy, but it does cost a lot to be unhappy. You lose peace of mind and become sad, depressed, lonely, frustrated, and irritable, and you lose sleep. It affects you emotionally, physically, and spiritually. You pay a high price for the wrong choice.

"Don't postpone happiness by telling yourself that you will be happy when you are married, after having children, after getting a job, after buying a house, after buying a car, after retiring. If this is our thinking, you will never be happy. You will always be anxious to acquire those things. And if you don't get them, you will be disappointed. If you don't know how to handle disappointment, you may end up miserable.

"You will not achieve happiness by chasing what the world has to offer. It has already been tried and found wanting. Happiness is not in tomorrow; happiness is in the present. Do not refuse to be happy just because you don't have something that you desire. Joy, love, and happiness are all around you. You fail to see it because you are self-absorbed. You have blinders on your eyes. You are seeing and focusing on the external world. You have become materialistic and are ignoring your own internal spring of happiness. Life is full of passion and love. There will be ups and downs in life; we can't escape them, but we can learn to see good in everything around us. However, it calls for a positive outlook toward life. Life is like a banquet; learn to feast on it, and remember don't postpone joy."

"Oh shut up!" Adam shouts "That's all crap. Life may be a banquet for you, but it's not for us. We have no place to live, nothing to eat, and no one to rely on. We don't see happiness. We see darkness everywhere! How can someone who has lost everything be happy?"

"Happiness is a state of mind. One might have billions of dollars and not be happy. On the other hand, someone may have almost nothing and be happy. It has nothing to do with what you have or don't have. Let me explain it with the help of a story I heard long ago.

"Once upon a time, there was a prince who had a beautiful wife and two angelic children. He also had very loving and protective parents. He had everything that one could desire. However, there was a growing discontent and unhappiness in his heart. He decided to speak to one of his trusted friends. 'I have everything I need, but I am very unhappy; where can I find happiness?'

"'I know a mystic,' his friend said, 'who will be able to answer your question. His name is Luke, and he lives seven hundred miles from here. There is no transportation; you will have to walk. And if you really want to see him, you will have to renounce everything you have: wealth, parents, wife, children, and all material possessions.'

"The prince agreed and made an announcement before all the people in the palace. Everyone tried to convince him otherwise, but he had made up his mind, so he paid no attention to the advice. He left the palace carrying a few basic essentials: a towel, some underwear, a toothbrush, toothpaste, and food. After walking seven hundred miles, he started looking for Luke.

"'Do you know Luke?' he asked a bearded man.

"'Why?'

"'I want to meet him,' the prince replied.

"'I am Luke.'

"The prince just couldn't believe him. How could such an unimpressive-looking man be Luke?

"'Are you really Luke?' he asked in awe.

"Luke smiled. His smile was so mysterious the prince couldn't help but believe him.

"'Well! I have come to find out an answer to my question.'

"'What is the question?' Luke asked.

"'I am the prince and heir to the kingdom. I have a beautiful wife and two beautiful children, a boy and a girl.' He continued talking about his wealth, and how he had renounced it all for want of happiness.

"'It's interesting to know that you renounced everything,' Luke commented. 'Why don't we sit on these steps and talk some more?

What are you carrying ?'

"'Oh, nothing important.' The prince shrugged. 'Just a few basic necessities for the trip.'

"'Why don't you place them here?' Luke pointed to a spot between them.

"The prince placed his sack between them and kept talking.

"Suddenly, Luke grabbed the sack and ran. The prince was shocked; he jumped up and ran after Luke, trying to catch him. However, having walked seven hundred miles, he couldn't keep up.

"He went round and round and finally ended up at the same spot and sat back down, gasping for breath. Opening his eyes, he saw, to his surprise, that Luke was sitting next to him with the stolen sack. He immediately snatched his sack back and started berating Luke up one side and down the other. 'I heard such great stories about you; I can't believe what you did. You are a thief. You must have a split personality.'

"'Are you finished? May I say something ?' Luke asked.

"'Go ahead,' the prince said. 'Let me hear what you have to say'

"'You said you renounced everything. Evidently, you haven't renounced anything. You are still possessive. I stole your meager belongings, and you became unhappy. You had this sack with you before, but you were still unhappy. You snatched it back from me, and you became happy again. What does this indicate? This indicates that physical renouncement of material items is not a solution. What you need is understanding. Happiness comes from within. Happiness will not be found in the outside world. Happiness is a journey, not a destination. One can never be happy if one is self-centered and engrossed in oneself. I suggest you go home and stop being self-centered. Go, do your karma, your duty, and start enjoying life on life's terms. Renunciation is not the solution. Understanding, only understanding, is the solution.'"

"I have seen nothing but pain," Beaver states impatiently. "You appear to have been born with a silver spoon in your mouth."

"I haven't seen a silver spoon in my entire life, and you say I was born with one in my mouth?" I joke.

Everyone laughs except Beaver. "Don't try to make fun of me!" He suddenly gets up and walks out of the community room. A few minutes later, he comes back and sits down opposite me. He fixes his gaze on me.

"Christopher," he says slowly, "you are pissing me off, and you are making me very angry."

"It's your decision whether to be angry or not," I tell him calmly.

"You crack those fucking jokes, and all these cronies laugh, and now you are telling me that I can decide whether to be angry or not!"

"You're lucky that you have a choice in this case," I say. "There are many situations where you don't."

"Well, I wasn't angry, but now I choose to be angry." He continues to stare at me.

"Go right ahead." I smile.

"You're lucky that you are not seeing me on the street," he retorts. "I would blow you up."

"Beaver, what is wrong ? Why are you refusing to be happy?"

After a long pause, he opens up: "I told you. My whole life, I have seen pain and nothing else."

"But why do you want to hold onto that pain?"

"I have experienced nothing but pain," he repeats.

"Your outburst has nothing to do with your past pain," I tell him. "Your problem is that you don't want to grow. You keep saying that you have seen nothing but pain. However, the simple truth is that painful events help us to grow. Painful events make a person strong emotionally as well as physically. But there is no growth in you. You are not grateful for the painful events in your ife. Happy events bring joy and pleasure, but happy events do not lead to growth or self-awareness. Happy events do not possess enough power for us to grow. Life brings changes; some we plan, and some just happen, so be prepared."

* * *

A day before John's discharge I ask him, "Are you sure you want to live with your parents?"

He nods. "I'm positive. It's my house."

"What support system do you intend to use to maintain your sobriety?" I continue.

"I plan to make meetings, work the Twelve Steps, get a sponsor, pray to my Higher Power, surround myself with positive eople, and find work because I remember you saying 'happiness lies on busy feet and an idle mind is the devil's workshop.' He pauses, thinks for a few seconds, and adds, "I will keep my anger under control, not put too much on my plate, and I'll stay away from girls, especially those who get high."

"John, if you do everything that you are saying, you will definitely be able to maintain your sobriety."

The next day, he collects his Certificate of Completion of Treatment, and I wish him all the best. A few months later, he informs me that he is doing well, although he has hooked up again with Bill who is back on the street getting high. John stays in contact for a year or so, and then I stop hearing from him. I get a feeling that something is wrong. One day, I hear that he relapsed because he started messing with a girl who was getting high, and he fathered another child and couldn't handle it. It is important to listen to yourself when you speak, and John apparently didn't learn that while in treatment.

During the editing period of this manuscript, it was a pleasant surprise to hear from John. He said that he was doing well and he is in recovery for over two years. He is off his probation and got full custody of his three-year-old son. He is working full time and saving money because he wants to take his children to Disneyland next year. Before getting off the phone he tells me that he is not messing with junkies anymore. I hope he walks the walk.

Two days later, Adam leaves treatment for missing a smoke break. He was upset because there aren't enough smoke breaks and he wanted to be able to smoke when he wanted. He wanted freedom, and he wanted to fight for his freedom. But freedom from what? He was a slave to his addiction. He should have worked to free himself from that slavery. That fight would have been worth his struggle.

Chapter 12

Beaver is Back to His Sliminess

Late at night, Beaver was seen coming out of Mary's bathroom. There was a lengthy and detailed note about the incident in the communication log book. The next day, I call him to my office with Dawn present as a witness. Any time when I feel the need for Dawn to be present in my office, I ask the clients whether they have any objection to it. If they don't, then I request her to be around. She has been a great help on numerous occasions.

"Beaver, what's going on between you and Mary?" I begin.

"What are you talking about?" He stares at me.

"What were you doing in Mary's bathroom?"

"Who told you?" he demands.

"It doesn't matter," I reply.

"I was just standing at her door to get a brush. I didn't come out of her bathroom." He avoids eye contact, which is unusual for him. He usually stares into other people's eyes in an intimidating anner.

"You know you are not supposed to stand in another client's doorway, and especially not in the doorway of a female client," I remind him.

"We are just friends," he insists.

I sigh. "You are not here to make friends or enemies. You are here to work on your issues. No friends, no enemies. Get it?"

"Yes, I hear you," he says halfheartedly.

"Another thing—" I begin, "is there a problem with your medication?" I ask him since Eboni had mentioned to me that Beaver is non-compliant with his medication.

"I don't have any medical problems," he says carelessly.

"What's your sugar level?"

"Three hundred and forty or something."

"Doesn't that worry you?" I scan him. He says nothing, just keeps playing with the carpet with his right toe. "Well, I have decided to put you on Contract. Effective today, you are not to have physical or verbal contact with Mary for the next seven days. After seven days, the Contract will be reviewed, and if you improve your ehavior, you may come off the Contract, or it will be extended if no improvement is shown. This also includes the possibility of termination of your treatment on administrative grounds."

He shrugs. "Okay with me."

"Good." I stand up. "I'll have the Contract prepared; we'll go hrough it together, and then you can sign it."

He leaves my office. "You handled that very well," Dawn comments.

I just smile.

Suddenly, Alana comes down the hall, announcing, "Mary and Beaver are both leaving because they are not allowed to speak to each other."

I fail to understand this. Beaver expressed no problem with the Contract. I find Beaver in his room packing. "Beaver, what's he matter?"

"Nothing." He does not look at me.

"I hear you're leaving ?" I say.

"Mary is leaving because she is not allowed to talk to me," he answers, his back turned to me.

"I am talking about you!"

He still avoids looking at me. "If she can't stay, I have to leave, oo."

"Why do you have to leave because she is leaving ?"

"She is sacrificing her treatment because of me," he answers.

"It's not a sacrifice." I shake my head. "It is suicidal."

"I'll be fine." He avoids eye contact.

"You have no place to live," I remind him. "You have no money; you can't even buy a pack of cigarettes."

"I'll stay with Mary. She will help me in the beginning, and then I'll find work." He looks up for the first time. "You don't need to worry about it."

"Beaver, you are being impulsive and making a wrong decision."

"You can't make me change my mind," he snaps. "Please, leave me alone. Let me pack my stuff."

"Are you sure you really want to leave?"

"One hundred percent," he replies.

"It's not going to be easy for you. You aren't ready to handle your life on your own. You need help." I insist.

"I know what I'm doing," he mumbles.

"Beaver, you are taking advantage of her."

"That is crap," he shouts angrily. "We are in love." He averts is eye. "We'll help each other."

"You're lying. Mary is so messed up, she can't even think straight. She received her SSI check yesterday. She has a place to live. You will use her for a while and then leave her."

"Whatever! I'm leaving." Grabbing his belongings, he storms out of his room and out of treatment with Mary right behind him.

What an irrational decision! They need to grow up. Their focus is momentary pleasure. They conveniently forgot the consequences that will follow their actions. I hope that good sense will prevail upon them and they will not have to start from scratch again.

Chapter 13
Irene's Mental Masturbation

I open the group saying, "It is very necessary to stay focused and committed if you want to build long-term sobriety. If we have clarity of our goals and are willing to work diligently and honestly, we stand a greater chance to achieve our goals. Many of us don't work hard enough; or sometimes we start off well but later we become sluggish, start drifting away from our goals, and then subsequently we give up. We need to remember that consistency plus intensity equals success. Any questions? Any comments?"

Maria begins, "The world wasn't built in a day, so how can we build recovery in a day? We didn't become addicts in a day. Recovery requires time, and time calls for more time. So give time a chance. Give it a shot; things might work. Nobody knows that works or what doesn't work. The thing that didn't work last time might work this time. We just have to keep trying. We have to have patience. No shortcuts. Recovery calls for perseverance. If we sincerely desire recovery, we will definitely make it. But we have to do our part diligently, honestly, and sincerely. We need to be committed to our recovery. God will do his part. He is never wrong. He doesn't make mistakes. He is all powerful, and He is everywhere."

What a sharing! I want her to go on, and I think she could go further. Suddenly, I see a hand raised in the air: it is the irrepressible Irene. I nod my head toward her, indicating that she will be given permission to speak. But it appears that Maria's chain of thought has suddenly cut off. She says, "I'm done. Thanks for allowing me to share."

Irene looks all over the community room and finally fixes her eyes on me. "God is watching over you; he is watching every step. We have to learn to bless our enemies. When someone slaps you on one cheek and you offer the other cheek, it doesn't necessarily mean you are a pushover or that you are letting others walk all over you. It requires courage, a different kind of temperament, and a high-quality mental make-up to be able to do that. It's a rare personality trait, and it's only possible if you are a humble and peace-loving person. No matter what, you are not allowing outside forces to rule you. You are just being yourself; you are in full control, and that means you are the master of your emotions. You simply do not let anything bother you. It's possible. I have seen those kinds of people; they are a rare breed, but they have acquired his quality by practice. We became addicts by practicing addiction. Now we have to practice different behaviors—behaviors that are acceptable to others and, more importantly, acceptable to us! It's easy to see a speck in the eye of another person, but we often fail to see the splinter in our own eye. Pointing fingers at others is easy, and we all do it. We forget that when we point one finger at someone, three fingers are pointing at us."

Irene is forty-five and homeless. She started using alcohol at fifteen and cocaine at twenty-five. Although she is college-edu-cated, she lacks insight into her issues, and she is in denial of her addiction. Her father died when she was barely three, and she grew up with her mother and a stepfather. She was gang-raped twice during her teens and again in her twenties. She is on pro-bation after convictions on two counts of assault. Her mother has a restraining order against her.

The next day, while engaged in a one on one session, I ask,

"Irene, do you think abusing drugs is a problem?"

"Drugs are not a problem for me. I can handle them," she answers. "They keep me alive. I have a choice between death and drugs, and I choose the lesser evil."

"What do you mean by a 'lesser evil'?"

"Well," she begins, "I don't hurt anyone, I don't steal, I don't hurt myself, and I don't do some of the crazy stuff that some people do. I don't want to die. If I don't use drugs, I'll die. Drugs make you or break you. In my case, they made me. It's other people who keep pointing out my perfection and imperfections. I'm tired of it. I believe in 'live and let live,' as long as it does not impede the progress of another person, and God is there to do the rest. Our job is to regulate justice between each other. Don't try to force our opinion on anyone else. If what you are saying is true, then life will back you up."

"Irene, do you know that you are trying to intellectualize and ationalize your addictive behavior?"

She snaps, "No, I'm not. No one can really disagree with my feelings; what I feel is what I feel. Only I know how I feel inside of me. No one else can experience the same pain or feelings that I experience. You can't detach someone's emotions by using apathy or sympathy."

"What do you mean?" I ask.

"My experiences are not yours," she answers. "They're mine. And everything has a domino effect. One chip falls on another, and then on another, and it makes a chain of falling chips."

"What you say sounds nice, but you are contradicting yourself."

"So what?"

"You don't achieve anything by just trying to prove your point of view, do you?" I continue looking into her eyes.

"What you see as wrong may not necessarily be wrong for me," she insists without any hesitation. "I have my own mind. I think my own thoughts, and I try to live them. I am an independent thinker."

"But what good is it when it causes you so much pain and misery?"

"I want to live my own thoughts and my own ideals. I want to follow my own inclinations. I want to live free. I don't want to please others; I have my own taste for life." She speaks like a philosopher.

"What taste are you talking about, Irene?"

"I don't like structure," she replies. "I don't like structured programs. I like to be in a place where I don't have to please others by ollowing their directions, their rules, and their regulations. I love freedom."

"What kind of freedom?"

"Freedom from all rules and regulations."

"Freedom comes from four thoughts and our actions," I tell her. "When you do drugs, you are never free. Your body becomes a slave to drugs. If you want freedom, you have to stop using drugs; otherwise, freedom becomes phony and illusory."

"What you consider phony and illusory may not be true for others." She pauses to gather her thoughts. "Everyone is unique. Every person thinks in his own way and has a right to think his own thoughts. You can't force your thoughts and ideas on others."

"Am I forcing my thoughts and ideas on you?"

"No," she answers. "You're not. But..."

"But what?"

After a long pause, she says, "Never mind."

"Irene, you are simply indulging in mental masturbation."

"Mental masturbation?" Her expression shows her confusion.

"You keep analyzing things," I explain. "You try to intellectualize everything, but you go nowhere. What you keep talking about has no real substance to it. You are just trying to satisfy your cunning ego. It sounds as though you get pleasure from indulging in futile discussions. I think you get a kick out of the rationalizations that you dream up."

"You may be right." She shrugs. "So, what's wrong with it?"

"It's an unnecessary indulgence, and you don't understand the futility of it. Or rather, you refuse to understand the futility."

"I really don't know. Sometimes I feel so confused that I should stop spinning my wheels to find the meaning of life and just go along with the flow." She bursts into tears.

"Irene, we all experience confusion in life. It's normal to be confused. The best thing about all this is that you are acknowledging your confusion."

"But no one else seems to be confused; they have such straight hinking," she sobs.

"I doubt that," I say. "We are all confused sometimes. It differs in degree and the way we handle it. However, you don't have to worry whether other people experience confusion or not. You have to learn to get out of your confusion and clear your mind."

"I don't think I'll ever be able to live a normal life." She continues sobbing.

"Why not? What you need is a desire to live a normal life, some planning, a willingness to follow directions, and clarity in your thinking."

She nods. "I understand what you are saying, but I won't be able to do it. I'm not cut out for a disciplined life."

"What do you mean by 'not cut out'?"

"I mean," she says, "I can't lead a so-called 'normal' life."

"Irene, would it be more accurate to say that you refuse to lead a normal life?"

She nods.

"In that case, it's going to be very difficult for you to stay in he recovery process, Irene."

"I really don't want to stay in recovery. I want to be able to use drugs. I can't live without them!"

"No! You don't need drugs to live."

"Christopher, you say that because you don't know my problems."

"That is your illusion. Irene, you have been here for the past few days feeling perfectly fine without drugs."

"How do you know that I feel perfectly fine?" she demands.

"Are you feeling any physical discomfort now ?" I ask.

"Now ?" She hesitates. "No."

"Isn't that evidence of your well-being ?"

"No! I mean, I don't think right, like so-called 'normal' people think. I am insane."

"You do have some errors in your thinking, but stopping drugs will help you to restore your sanity."

"Sanity by whose standards?" She appears offended.

"You just told me you are insane," I remind her.

"I meant that I am insane because people keep pointing out my perfection and imperfections."

"Irene, why are you so defiant?"

"Because the whole damn world is crazy, and they keep pointing fingers at me," she answers huffily.

"So, you feel that you have no problems?"

"I can't say that," she says, "but using drugs is not my problem."

"If that's the case, why did you come here in the first place?"

"Because of the legal system," she answers.

"What about it?" I ask.

"Mom has a restraining order against me," she explains calmly.

"The police talked her into it."

"Why did she ask for a restraining order?"

"I was doing drugs," she admits, "but I wasn't causing any

problems."

"Again, you are rationalizing your behavior, Irene. You are in denial."

"No, I'm not!" She shakes her head.

"Irene, you were convicted of assault and other drug-related charges. You are unemployed and homeless, you put yourself in vulnerable situations on many occasions, and you are still saying that drugs aren't your problem. Isn't that denial?"

"I'm using drugs because I want to live," she repeats.

"If you stop using drugs, not only will you live, but you will live a better life."

"I don't know," she mumbles.

Chapter 14
Maria Swings at Dee

Over the weekend, Maria and Dee get into an argument about Jerome leaving treatment. Dee is so upset she is close to leaving her-elf. Scott suggests I speak with both of them together, but I decide o speak with them separately before bringing them together in an ffort to settle the issue amicably.

Maria is on the defensive. "I didn't do anything. She put her and in my face. I didn't start it."

"How are you doing now ?" I ask.

"Oh," she says, "I'm doing fine, except for what happened over he weekend."

"Okay," I say, "tell me what happened."

"Jerome was leaving AMA, and we were discussing it and Dee didn't like it. She became verbally and physically aggressive."

"Maria, you know you are here to work on your own issues, and this kind of indulgence can take away your focus from your own recovery. It can also cause you unnecessary problems."

She nods. "I understand what you are saying."

"Don't lose your focus; stay committed to your recovery, Maria. If someone is leaving, it is his decision. You need to stay away from that person or discussing that person's problems."

"I'm sorry Christopher. I'll do whatever you say."

"So are you willing to let it go?"

"Yes," she nods. "I don't want to hold onto it. It's not good for my emotional health, and it can affect my recovery process."

"Good. Now I am going to speak with Dee because I want to hear her side. If she agrees, I am planning to get you both together to resolve the issue. Is that okay with you, Maria?"

"It's fine with me." She smiles and leaves.

Dee is around fifty, heavyset, with light skin and unusual features. She is angry and agitated.

"Dee, how are you doing today?"

"I guess I'm fine," she says, shaking her head in a "no" motion.

"I heard there was a problem between you and Maria. What happened?"

"She was physically aggressive toward me. She swung at me.

I didn't do anything. I'm scared of her. Christopher, I don't trust her and I feel uncomfortable around her."

"What was it about?" I ask.

"Jerome wanted to leave, and he had no money or any means of getting home. I offered him some money and two bus tokens, but Maria said I couldn't do that. I told her to mind her own fucking business and she took a swing at me."

"Dee, I know it's none of her business to tell you what you can or cannot do; however, don't you think she was right in telling you not to help a client who was leaving treatment against medical advice?"

"Well..." She hesitates. "Yes, but I didn't like the way she told me."

"It's not the way she told you that upset you. The fact is, you wanted to help Jerome and you couldn't. And because of Maria's nvolvement, you had to give up the tokens that you had been holding against regulations."

She stares at me without saying anything.

I continue, "Dee, you were enabling him to leave treatment and you call that help?"

"Christopher, I was just trying to help him because he had no money to get a bus or train, and I didn't want him to be on the street."

"But it was his decision, and he has to suffer the consequences. If you want to help others, then help them stay in treatment. Or is there something you aren't telling me?"

"What do you mean?"

"Was there anything going on between you and Jerome?"

Suddenly, she drops her eyes. She stammers, "Are you nuts?"

"Dee, you are here to get yourself together. You are in treatent, and there is some purpose in that. You need to be honest and transparent in your behavior. If you have hidden agendas, neither you nor anyone else will be able to help you here. You have been trying to seduce men since day one. You rub the backs, hands, or thighs of your peers, and when questioned, you rationalize your behavior as being loving and caring. I have told you about that before. If you desire recovery, you need to be committed and sincere. You lack both, don't you?"

"No, I don't," she snaps. "I am very sincere and committed to my recovery."

I shake my head. "I don't think so."

"Believe me, I am very committed, focused, and honest," she insists.

"If that's the case, let me check your honesty. Why did you try to help Jerome and even consider leaving yourself?"

"I liked him." She avoids looking at me and adds, "I'm talking about platonic love. But I wasn't leaving because he was leaving. I was leaving because of Maria."

"All right," I say. "You know you are here to work on your issues; you are not here to make friends or enemies."

She nods. "I know that."

"No, evidently you don't." I sigh. "You were trying to be friends with Jerome and enemies with Maria. You need to focus on yourself. If you do the right things, you will be able to avoid future troubles. You will be stress-free, and you will be effective in anger-producing situations."

"But I am not going to be comfortable with Maria." She shakes her head in her peculiar way. "I don't want anything to do with her."

"Dee, you are both in the same program; it's not possible to avoid one another. Your peers have elected her as a chairperson, and you as a co-chair to facilitate group activities. So considering the current circumstances, it does not seem possible for you two not to meet. It isn't necessary to be friends, but holding resentment against someone is unhealthy. It will cause you unnecessary pain, anxiety, and stress, and you can avoid it if you see the futility of your action. I have spoken with Maria, and she is willing to let it go and move forward."

"No," she says decisively. "I'm not going to shake hands with her. I don't want anything to do with her. I'm absolutely fine with the current situation. It's okay with me, even if you ask me to leave."

"Dee, why do you go from one extreme to the other? No one suggested that you leave. You don't have to leave treatment over such a trivial issue. If you are planning to leave, it will be your decision. However, I suggest you don't even think of leaving. It's not in our best interests. You need to take one day at a time. Get organized, put your priorities in order, work on positive thinking, and focus on your issues and your life. Listen, Dee. You keep saying that you love your child and that you want to see him succeed. How can you help him grow up if you can't get yourself straight? May I call Maria and Dawn now, so we can amicably settle your differences?"

"I'm not going to shake hands with her," she insists.

"With whom, Dawn?" I try to inject humor into the conversation, and she smiles.

Maria and Dawn enter my office, and sit in the chairs opposite

"I have listened to both of you," I start, "and I am not going to get into who is right and who is wrong. You have to let it go and not dwell on it anymore. If you both want to shake hands, you may do so; if not, then don't." Maria extends her hand toward

Dee, but Dee does not even look at Maria.

"Maria," I say, "it's okay if she does not want to shake hands with you. However, she is willing to let it go. I believe as time goes by, everything will be fine."

The next day, Dawn decides to remove both Dee and Maria from their respective chair positions and makes Ishmael a chairperson. I am not pleased with her decision, and I tell her so. I explain that Dee should have gone but not Maria. Maria did play some part in the episode, acting as if she were staff, but she'd been willing to make amends. Dee lost her position as co-chair and she lost Jerome, too, as he is gone forever.

After a few days, Dee is sitting in my office because she was seen kissing Ishmael. There is no sign of guilt or remorse. "Why did you call me here?" she demands.

"Dee, what's going on between you and Ishmael?"

"Nothing."

"Did you kiss him this morning ?"

She hesitates. "Yes, I did. But it was motherly love."

"Motherly love?" I almost choke. "Kissing a grown man on the lips is not motherly love!"

"It was a motherly kiss," she insists.

"You left an imprint of your lipstick on his lips. Dee, you don't kiss someone on the lips so intensely that it leaves an imprint to show motherly love. You need to stop this inappropriate behavior.

Didn't I tell you to refrain from indulging in any relationships?"

"I didn't know you guys would make such a big deal out of it," she huffs. "I'm telling you, it was just a gesture of motherly love."

"Dee, let me tell you that this is not the place to demonstrate our so-called 'motherly love' for a thirty-three-year-old man. You have a son, don't you?"

She nods. "Yes, I have a fifteen-year-old son. He lives with his father in New Jersey."

"How is your relationship with your son?"

"We frequently exchange letters."

"If your heart is so full of motherly love, why don't you shower our love onto your son?"

"Y-yes..." she stammers.

"When did you last see him?"

"Four years ago."

"How is he doing now ?"

"Not well." She looks down at the floor. "He spends too much time out of the house and comes home late at night." She takes out letter written by her son's stepmother and reads it to me.

"Dee, your son needs a mother's love and affection."

"Yes, I hear you," she responds softly.

"He needs direction in his life," I continue.

She nods. "You're right. But I don't know how to help him."

"It's really very simple," I explain. "Stay drug-free, and get your act together so you can be there for him physically and emotionally."

"Well—" she rolls her eyes, "that's easier said than done."

"But there is no other way, Dee."

"I plan to find a room," she volunteers, "and bring my son to live with me."

"Dee, it is too early for that. You need more time for

yourself."

"I think I will be strong enough when I finish this program," she insists.

"I don't think so."

"Why not?" She looks at me quizzically, and visibly upset.

"Because you have many issues you haven't learned to deal with yet," I reply.

"What do those issues have to do with bringing my son to live with me?"

"You are unrealistic," I explain. "I am not trying to discourage you. I am just trying to help you to get in touch with reality."

"I know the reality," she snaps.

"Dee, listen to me carefully. You have severe anger-control issues. You have been experiencing intense loneliness, and you have behavioral problems."

"Behavioral problems?" she echoes.

"You are sexually preoccupied." I choose my words carefully.

"You behave inappropriately, you don't want to deal with your lust ssue, and when someone tries to bring it to your attention, you don't want to hear about it. You start rationalizing and justifying your acts, and you lie."

She pouts. "You are talking me down."

"Your actions make you feel that way."

"My actions?" She stares at me.

"For instance," I begin, "you were found kissing Ishmael right in the lips, and when confronted, you said it was motherly love.

You were lying, weren't you?"

She is in tears now and avoids looking up.

"Dee, you are twenty years older than he is! And it is inappropriate to indulge in sexual behavior while you are here. You need to stop projecting yourself as someone you are not. Get a grip on reality, and start working on your basic issues if you really want to help yourself."

She nods and leaves my office, smiling and visibly relieved because she didn't get any consequences for her behavior.

Dee has been smoking cocaine for many years. She claims that she was recently clean for almost three years. She projects herself as very spiritual person and constantly recites verses from the Bible: sometimes Matthew, sometimes Mark or Luke, but she is dishonest with her feelings and tries to project herself as someone she is not. She is not in touch with her feelings. She is very negative in her thinking but tries to project herself as very positive. It leads to severe inner conflict and causes her agony. She is confused and immensely lonely. Then she withdraws from the world to avoid embarrassment. Sometimes she appears totally cut off, and it frightens me. I want to help her, but I am unable to do so. Helpless! I feel helpless, thinking that helplessness is so pervasive in the world. This reminds me of someone who said water, water everywhere, but not a single drop to drink. How tragic!

A few days later, Dee is caught kissing another client – a female this time. We are discussing it at the treatment team meeting. Scott says, "There is no need to talk with her about this issue now. She is completing her treatment and will be discharged in three days." I, however, do address the issue with her before her discharge, hoping that she might realize it is unhealthy behavior. Who knows? Something might strike a chord, and she might wake up.

She completes her program and is discharged to a shelter and an IOP. I hope she pours all that motherly love onto her son and finds herself a suitable life partner so she can stop the craziness of kissing everyone who crosses her path. I am apprehensive, but hopeful because hope is free. Everything is so expensive nowadays, but "hope" is free, isn't it? Sometimes I hope against hope. Who knows? She might make it.

Chapter 15

Fredrick—Spits Right Back

Within a few days of Fredrick's arrival, I receive many comlaints against him. He is fifty-two years old, single, and homeless. His face is sunburned. He walks and talks with attitude. He seems to be in treatment for the wrong reasons. When he is angry he starts pacing back and forth and his eyes pop out like a frog's.

He enters my office looking anxious and preoccupied. Without my permission, he closes my office door behind us. He pulls a chair and sits down casually. I scan his face, and after a pause, I ask, "Fredrick what's going on?"

"Nothing," he answers without looking at me.

"What happened over the weekend?" I persist.

"It was that agency staffer." He shrugs. "She didn't know how to handle weekends. She messed it up."

"Did you play any part in it?"

"I don't really remember." He avoids eye contact.

"Stop lying," I tell him.

He suddenly gets up from his chair. "Enough is enough. I am done here." His voice is trembling.

"Fredrick, please sit down."

He sits stiffly.

I nod. "Good. Now, can you tell me honestly what happened?"

"The staffer insulted me in front of the community. I am

an adult. She could have talked to me in private and told me not to old hands. But she said nasty things, and I became defensive."

"You say you are an adult. So don't you think you should behave like an adult?"

"Just holding a girl's hand is not a big deal." He leans forward.

"You have been warned on several occasions that holding hands is unacceptable behavior, haven't you?"

"Yes," he answers coldly.

"Why did you call the staff person names?"

"I lost my cool."

"Frederick, anytime you are angry, that is bound to happen. In the heat of the moment, you say things you wouldn't say otherwise."

"But she started first!" he protests.

"Who started first doesn't matter."

"If someone spits at you, what would you do?" he challenges.

"The first thing I would do is clean my face," I reply.

"Well, I would spit right back."

"Then what's the difference between him and you, Frederick?"

"I don't care."

"Look at the irony: you despise his spitting, but you would resort to an act just like his. Do you see anything wrong with it?"

"No," he says rudely. "It looks like all of you are out to find my character defects."

"What would we accomplish by doing that?"

"I don't know."

"You don't know because what you are saying is baseless."

Suddenly, he jumps up and starts pacing heavily around my office; the next minute he is out the door and down the hall.

"Fredrick, wait!" I run to the door. "Listen to me."

He pretends not to hear me.

A few minutes later, he comes back. "I'm sorry. I didn't mean to be disrespectful to you. I want to apologize."

"Apology accepted. Just don't repeat the same behavior; that could give little meaning to the word 'sorry,'" I tell him.

"Okay. I'll keep that in mind." He leaves my office calmly.

* * *

A few days later, Fredrick is back in my office. "I had a nightmare."

"About what?"

"Sean kept me awake all night snoring."

"That can be frustrating."

"I want him removed from my room."

"That's not possible."

"Then can I be shifted to another room?"

"No."

"Why not?" he snaps.

"Fredrick, you are showing no tolerance. Sean just came in last night; he needs some breathing room."

"I'm not asking him to stop breathing. He can go to another room."

"We do not have a single room."

"I know that."

"Then how can you suggest putting him in another room? Wouldn't his snoring disturb his new roommate?"

"It would."

"Well?" I stare at him.

"But I can't stand his snoring."

I shrug. "You have no other option."

"Why should I have to tolerate this nonsense?" he demands.

"Fredrick, it's not his fault. Some people snore. He is not snoring with the intention of disturbing your sleep. The night shift nurse offered you earplugs but you refused to use them."

"Whatever!"

"You need to be more considerate."

"I don't care. I know you guys like him. He told me that. That's why he keeps coming here again and again. I want him out of my room. I need a peaceful place to sleep, don't you get it?"

"Weren't you homeless before coming here?"

"Yes." He looks down.

"Why didn't you demand a peaceful place then?"

He just looks at me stonily.

"Fredrick, how can you forget so fast where you came from?"

"I'm sorry." He looks down, lowers his voice and asks, "Can I sk you something ?"

I nod. "Yes."

"If someone leaves, would you consider shifting Sean to that room?"

"No."

"All right," he sighs.

"Just be happy. Don't focus on his snoring, and you will be fine. When you were homeless, sleeping on the streets, there was no quiet. Didn't you sleep then?"

"Yes I did."

"Wasn't that situation worse than this?"

He nods.

"Fredrick, you should consider yourself lucky to have a roof over your head, three meals a day, and an opportunity to stay clean. Just think about it."

* * *

One day, we are in the middle of serenity prayers when I interject, "Excuse me, Fredrick, stop it!" *While we are busy praying, he is busy massaging Jennie's body.*

"Stop what?" he says, feigning innocence.

"Stop rubbing Jennie's body."

"I'm not rubbing her body. I'm just saying the serenity prayer."

He averts his eyes.

"I don't want an explanation." I give him a stern look. "And stop lying."

"I'm not lying!" he shouts.

"So, am I hallucinating, seeing things?"

He shrugs. "I don't know."

Neither Jennie nor anyone else says a word. Jennie looks shamed and worried. I look at her, expecting her to say something, but she sits mute.

"Listen, what's the use of saying serenity prayers when you cannot even be honest? Here you are praying and still behaving dishonestly. Isn't an honest atheist better than a dishonest theist?"

"An athi-, athi-what?" Ishmael stumbles over the word.

"An atheist," I explain, "is a person who doesn't believe in the existence of God. A theist is a person who does believe in the existence of God. Now, think about it!" I walk toward my office, and Ishmael follows me for a prescheduled one-on-one session.

While settling in a chair he boasts, "I am working on my issues seriously."

"Which issues?"

"I am working on staying clean, overcoming my impatience, gaining assertiveness, and managing my anger issues. I am also realizing that things don't always happen the way I want them to. I m no longer looking for immediate gratification, and more importantly, I am finding a way to get closer to my higher power, Allah." He relates this all in one breath.

"How do you plan to get closer to Allah?" I ask.

"By being honest and having love in my heart for others."

"Do you really think that you are getting closer to your Higher Power ?"

"Of course," he says confidently. "I have no doubt about it.

However, guys like Fredrick and Jennie won't find a higher power because you caught them red-handed. We all saw that he was playing with her breast, and still they went on lying."

"And why didn't you say anything then?"

"Not my business."

"Oh, I see. So you can be selectively honest and still find a higher power?"

"I am close to Allah."

"What about you and Dee kissing the other day?"

"Everybody makes mistakes," he mutters. He quietly walks out of my office without any further comment, and Jennie walks in.

"I'm sorry, Christopher, I was very inappropriate during the serenity prayer."

"Well, at least you realize that you were inappropriate. So you repent?"

"Yes."

"Remember that mistake," I say, "and don't repeat it."

"I won't," and she leaves.

Chapter 16
Lusty Fredrick

While in my office, Fredrick tells me, "My weakness is women." *At least, I say to myself, I don't have to worry about him groping Jennie's breast as long as he is here.*

"I have a serious lust issue," he admits, looking down. "All my relapses are women-related. I left several programs AMA. I walked out with women thinking we would have sex. But we didn't; before sex we always got high, then either I couldn't perform or they lost interest!"

"How do you plan to deal with it this time?"

"I need to keep reminding myself about my past mistakes." He pauses. "And I need to maintain a distance from women."

"Fredrick, do you have any mental health issues?"

"Not really! But I do suffer from depression and loneliness sometimes."

"Do you think there is a relationship between depression, loneliness, and your addiction?"

"I don't know. I think I need a companion. It would help me to get rid of my depression and loneliness and stay clean."

"Do you really think a companion will help you banish loneliness and depression?"

"Yes," he replies, "I know it for sure."

"Have you been in a relationship before?" I ask.

"Of course I've been in relationships before."

"Significant relationships?"

He pauses, then says, "Three."

"What is the longest relationship that you ever had?"

"Four years," he replies.

"What is the shortest relationship?"

"Two and half years."

"What is the longest period that you were chemically free?"

"Six months."

"That means your clean time has nothing to do with you being in a relationship, do you understand?"

"I wasn't in good relationships," he rationalizes.

"You are just giving excuses and trying to prove your point of view."

"I'm not trying to prove anything," he snaps.

"Then what are you doing ?" I ask.

"You have only known me for the last twenty-five days. I know what will help me stay clean."

"What?"

"A female companion."

"You are living in an illusion," I tell him, "and your thinking is distorted because evidently you don't know what is best for you."

"My thinking is not distorted," he counters. "You just say that because I don't agree with you."

"Fredrick, agreeing or disagreeing has nothing to do with it. I m just trying to help you to unlearn and deprogram yourself. You say that a female companion will help you stay clean and get rid of your loneliness and depression. This is illusionary thinking. You were in relationships before, but you didn't stay clean. Were you depressed and lonely in those relationships?"

"Everyone feels depressed and lonely," he answers.

"We are not talking about everyone. We are talking about you."

"Okay," he says reluctantly, "I was depressed and lonely,

but only when I was frustrated in those relationships."

"Well, doesn't it prove that having female companionship doesn't get rid of loneliness and depression? Do you see my point?"

"Yes, but..." He trails off, as if unsure of what to say next.

"But what?"

"Nothing." He shakes his head.

"Fredrick, don't indulge in relationships. You need to stay focused."

"I know. I don't need to be reminded of that."

"Fredrick, you keep saying you know, but you don't act! Women are triggers for you! It's obvious to one and all that you are trying to develop relationships with two female clients at the same time!"

"That's crap," he snaps. "Who says that?"

"Who is not important," I reply. "But I have seen you spending a lot of time with Jennie."

"I'm trying to help her," he insists. "We have a lot in common."

"Why are you here?" I ask.

"I am here to receive help and to help others."

"No, you are not. You are here to help yourself, only yourself. There is professional help available for the other clients. You don't have to worry about them. It is very important for you to stay committed and focused on your own treatment. You can't afford any diversions at this stage."

"I like helping others," he insists.

"Can you give me the names of clients you are helping ?"

"I'm helping Maria, Jennie, and Debbie."

"What is common between these three?"

"They all have issues."

"Fredrick, everyone has issues. The issue here is that they are all women!"

"I help them because they seek help from me."

"You are not in a position to help others. You yourself need help. This is like the blind leading the blind. You need to watch your actions."

"I know what I am doing," he snaps. "I won't risk my recovery."

"Well, remember that actions speak louder than words."

* * *

The weather is nice and we are holding group outside at the picnic table. Fredrick is sitting next to Jennie opposite me, and we are discussing the importance of self-discipline and the need to keep our own behavior under check.

"A woman's body is sacred, and it is only the woman who can preserve the purity and sacredness of her soul and body," says Jennie.

A bit of thoughtful science follows her observation. A few imnutes later, when I look up I see Jennie's hand on Fredrick's high.

"Fredrick, change your seat!" I order.

"Why?" he protests.

"Please do what I am asking without questions," I snap.

"That's not right," he grumbles. "I need to be treated with respect."

"We will discuss respect later," I respond. "But I will say this: respect is a two-way street: you have to earn it, and you have to give it. If respect is the issue, then are you respectful? Now, move!"

"I'm not moving!"

"Then I will have to send you back to the unit."

"I don't want to go back," he whines.

"Fredrick, you cannot dictate what you will or will not do."

"You are really getting on my last nerve," he mumbles, moving to the other side of the table.

No one shows any visible sign of guilt, and Fredrick does not speak for the rest of the session.

Later in my office, I tell him, "Fredrick, you really need to seriously think about your lust issues before it is too late."

"She was cold. We were just holding hands."

"I don't want to discuss it anymore. Scott said that I should put you on a Behavioral Contract. I am not in favor of forced discipline, but it appears your lustful behavior is affecting the other clients, too. I am giving you an oral warning. Any further inappropriate behavior on your part will compel us to take action against you. Therefore, you keep your hands off the female clients! ALL the female clients!"

He leaves and Jennie comes into my office. She appears contrite as usual and promises to behave, also as usual.

Although they are careful around staff, they have been spending a lot of time together. One Friday, Jennie walks into my office crying.

"Jennie, what's wrong ? Why are you crying ?" I hand her a tissue.

"Fredrick called me names," she hiccups.

"Why did he call you names?"

"He demanded to know something," she answers, sobbing, "and when I refused to tell him, he started calling me names. You need to take action against him."

"I will do what is appropriate," I respond. "But you need to know that you are equally responsible for this situation."

She nods. "Yes, I did play a part in it."

"Jennie, you always agree with me, but you act otherwise. I have been telling you for the last fifteen days or so to stay away from him. You agree, but you don't keep your word."

"I'm serious now about changing my behavior," she assures me. "I won't put myself in any more vulnerable situations."

She leaves my office, and I call Fredrick.

"Fredrick, why did you call Jennie names?"

"I didn't call her any names. Why don't you ask her now? Why is she telling you things behind my back?"

"Don't worry about her. You tell me what happened."

"She is nasty. She was yelling at me."

"Why?"

"I don't know." He looks away from me.

"You were involved in the argument, and you don't know?" I roll my eyes. "Tell me what happened!"

"I asked her what was she saying to Dawn, and she got mad."

"Frederick, it's none of your business what she says to other people. Leave her alone."

"Why do you always hold me responsible?"

"Because you behave irresponsibly and you tend to get away with it."

He drops his head into his hands and murmurs wearily, "I don't know, Christopher, something isn't right with me."

I feel bad for him. I know he has made many mistakes. He's made wrong choices in the past and he is still making wrong choices. He has very poor impulse control, lacks coping skills, and he is impatient. He is sexually preoccupied and always wants his way. He suffers because of his thoughtless actions. I hope he will learn to think before acting.

"Well, that's a first. Most of the time you feel victimized."

"I need friends," he sighs, "otherwise I feel closed in."

"Fredrick, you will be free to make as many friends as you want. Right now, you need to concentrate on completing this program successfully. Stop fooling around. You better get your act ogether otherwise you will be in real trouble. No further discussions on this topic; I am tired of it. Have a good weekend."

Monday morning, I see Fredrick and Jennie talking to each other and apparently enjoying being together. This goes on for a few more days. There isn't anything obviously objectionable about it, but there is nothing obviously healthy about it either. They have been constantly reminded that too much closeness is not good, but they don't see what we foresee: relapse. The week was not over before Fredrick was gone.

* * *

"I was about to kick loverboy out early this morning, but I didn't get a chance." Scott shrugs.

"Why? What happened?" I ask.

"They were on their way to breakfast, and a fight broke out between him and Jennie. When I tried to intervene, he became verbally abusive and took off."

I shake my head ruefully. "You know, Scott, some people just don't want to change. He wasn't working on his real issues. He was not focused and was just wasting his time in rationalizing."

"You're right," says Scott. "Speak to Jennie; she is as responsible for this as he was. Put her on a Behavioral Contract."

I draft the Behavioral Contract restricting Jennie from getting nvolved in any kind of relationship that the treatment team finds unnecessary and inappropriate.

She is in my office crying. I let her cry for a while. After she regains control, I read the Contract to her. She is unhappy because the Contract will be in effect for the rest of her stay. However, she eluctantly signs it.

Chapter 17

I Don't Want Your Fucking Counseling

"I am so embarrassed to be here again," Sean declares the moment he settles in a chair in my office. "I am almost fifty, and here I am again." He looks down at the floor.

"Sean, it's all right," I reassure him. "You don't have to be embarrassed. You did the right thing by coming here; at least you are not on the street."

He smiles. "I knew you would say something like that. Believe it or not, I missed you."

"Stop lying," I tease him.

"I'm not lying."

"You didn't call me for months, so how can I believe you?"

"I did call you when I was clean," he says. "I stopped calling you when I relapsed and became homeless."

"How are you now ?"

"Miserable."

"What happened?"

"I've been drinking heavily," he says in a low tone of voice.

"How long did you stay clean after you left here the last time?"

"I was clean for five months, and then I got into a fight with someone."

"Did you get into a fight with that guy on the street you had a grudge against?"

"You remember that shit?"

"What happened?"

"We went at it!" He puffs out his chest and throws his right fist in the air.

"But why?" I ask.

"When I left here last time, I told you that I would get even with him, didn't I?"

"Yes, you did. But I didn't think you were really going to do it

"When I decide to do something, I do it." His green eyes sparkle.

"So, why don't you use the same determination to stay in recovery?"

He just smiles.

I continue, "What did you achieve by getting even with im?"

"Happiness," he replies.

I shake my head.

"I am happy because I beat the shit out of him!" he says with pride.

"But a few minutes earlier, you told me you were miserable."

"Yes." He hesitates. "I am miserable, but I'm still happy about getting even with that bastard."

"How can you be happy about the incident that led you to start drinking again?" I challenge him.

"I proved to him that I'm a man." His eyes sparkle again. "No one can play with me like that."

"That's ridiculous! You don't have to prove your manhood by fighting. If you are man, you are a man, and it ends there."

"You don't understand because you're from a different culture."

"Sean, I don't think it has anything to do with culture."

"Christopher, you haven't lived the life I live. It's different on the street."

"But you don't want to live the street life anymore. You want to live a sober life, don't you?" I look straight into his eyes.

"Yes, but things happen!"

"How many times? You can't keep bumping into life over and over, again and again."

"But you told me it's human to make mistakes."

"That doesn't mean you need to keep repeating the same mistake again and again. You need to learn from your past mistakes. Sean, how many programs have you been in so far?"

"Oh, twenty or so."

"Doesn't that concern you?"

"I don't cause any trouble," he says. "I never steal. I spend my own money."

"That's not the point," I tell him. "The point is that you are not living a happy life."

"I am a caring, loving, and affectionate person. Everyone says that I am very affectionate."

I nod. "Yes, no doubt about it. But what's the point if you don't love yourself ?"

"I'm not crazy, and I don't need your fucking counseling," he snaps.

"Sean, you are abusing your body and ruining your mind. Think about it!"

* * *

Early the next morning, he walks straight into my office, shouting, "Good morning! How are you doing, buddy?"

"Fine, thank you," I reply. "What's up?"

"Did you guys miss me when I left here last time?"

"Sean, everyone remembers you. They all like you."

"What about you?" He looks straight into my eyes. "Did you miss me?"

"No. I didn't."

"You're full of shit," he says.

"I know that. Nothing new there."

"Why can't you simply say that you like me," he prompts, "and that when I leave here, you miss me?"

"Liking you and missing you are two different things." I smile.

"I enjoy your company when you are here. When you leave, someone else takes your place, so there is no question of my missing you. We meet to separate, don't we?"

"Don't give me that shit again!" He leans forward in his seat.

"Sean, it's reality. But you don't want to face it. Because it doesn't make you feel good. You want to glorify yourself."

"Glorify?" He looks at me quizzically.

"You want to hear that I miss you, don't you?"

"Yes. I do want to hear you say that, but not to glorify myself.

It will just make me feel good."

"Sean, I am not going to say something which isn't true."

"But I missed you. I missed everybody," he admits.

"Because you are messed up," I tell him, smiling.

"I'm messed up? You are the craziest person I ever met. Are all Indians crazy?" The sparkle is back in his eyes.

"I hope so," I answer. "Wouldn't that be great?"

"You're a nut." He smiles.

"A nut that you can't crack." I smile back at him.

"I love you!" he says, smiling.

"So what?"

"You are full of..." He pauses, and then says, "Whatever." He leaves my office all smiles.

* * *

A few days later in my office, I tell Sean, "You really need to gain some insight into your issues."

"Insight into what?" he asks innocently.

"Sean, you have to try to understand the seriousness of your issues and their impact on your life."

"What life are you talking about?" he snaps. "I never had a life. I grew up in a dysfunctional family. There was a lot of trouble between my parents. They fought like cats and dogs. It was a real fucked-up family, and you are talking about life. You crazy?"

"How was your relationship with your mother?"

"She was a whore. Instead of being a mother, she was busy pursuing her affair with a political aspirant. She had no time for me. I hated her. I didn't even attend her funeral." His green eyes sparkle, making him look like an alien.

"How old were you when she died?"

"Forty-three."

"She died seven years ago, and you are still harboring this resentment." I look at him incredulously.

"I was ashamed to call her my mother." He takes a deep breath.

"Sean, you have to let it go. She is dead now."

"I don't think it's possible."

"Why not? Just try it."

"My father started drinking heavily because of her extra-marital affair." He looks angry and shifts his sides.

"It's in the past now," I say quietly. "You don't have to suffer because something happened in the past that you had no control over."

"Okay, I'll try." He looks away from me.

"Anything else?" I ask.

"I'm severely depressed. You have to help me with it."

"No problem," I assure him. "We will work together."

"Whenever I remember my childhood, I become more

and more depressed," he continues.

"It's good that you know the possible source of your depression. It makes it easier for us to tackle it."

"I am depressed almost all day."

"That is not true," I respond firmly. "Every time you are here, you are depressed for a few days in the beginning, and then you become more enthusiastic than the rest of us."

"That's true," he concedes. "But that's only when I am here."

"When you are outside, you drink all day," I point out.

"Christopher, I don't drink all day. I drink a few times a day."

"Oh, let me correct myself: you drink a few times a day, but you are high all day."

He smiles sheepishly.

"Sean, do you understand the relationship between depression and drinking ?"

"Sure. When I am drunk, I don't feel depressed."

"That's because you are high."

"But I feel depressed when I am not drunk."

"Sean, that's the point. When you're high, you don't feel anything. You are in an illusion. But when you are sober, you come back to your original self. Your senses are back and you start feeling everything that you are supposed to feel."

"But how do I get rid of my depression?"

"Are you depressed now ?"

"Not really."

"Are you drunk now ?"

"Are you giving me a drink here? You are so full of shit."

"I just wanted to be sure. Now listen: you say you feel deressed only when you are not drunk. But today, you are not drunk and not depressed, either. It proves that you can stay sober and still not feel depressed. Trust me; your depression is an after fefect of your drinking. You have to stop drinking and thinking bout your past, and you will be all right. Time will take care of it. Last time you were here for more than two months, and you weren't depressed your entire stay here. Isn't that true?"

"Yes."

"Sean, I don't have to do anything for you to get rid of your depression. You just need to stop drinking and start doing the right things. Be active, and time will take care of it. Time is a great healer."

"Time!" He sighs. "You always talk about time. Time is almost God for you."

I nod. "Indeed it is. I believe in time as you believe in your Higher Power. Time doesn't wait for anybody. We have to learn to make use of time."

"I do lack a sense of time," he admits.

"One of my friends emailed me some important information about time; let me share it with you." I meet his eyes. "Every morning, our bank account of time is credited with 86,400 seconds. Whether you are rich or poor, black or white, no matter what your theology or religion is, we all get the same amount of time every day. Some use it constructively, but many don't.

"The clock keeps running. If you don't use your allotted time, you lose it. Time can't be saved; there is no overdraft facility. You have to use today's deposit before the night is out. You have to invest it carefully to get the most out of it. In reality, we are careless: we waste our time worrying about silly stuff that happened in the past or about things that may or may not happen in the future."

"I lack patience." He avoids eye contact.

"So you need to keep practicing patience," I say. "And we'll talk about it later."

"Are you kicking me out?" He acts surprised.

"It looks that way," I reply smiling.

He smiles back at me.

* * *

After a few days, Sean enters my office again, looking sad. He sits in the chair across from me. "I don't know how to start," he says. "Let me put it this way: I am very frustrated, but please don't be mad at me, just listen to me. I think I need to drink. I'm really depressed. I have been in these programs so many times, and I am tired of them. I don't think I can ever stay clean. I have tried everything. Nothing works. People here and even my friends outside tell me that I can't make it. That's even more frustrating. The agency tech told me that I am simply wasting a bed here that someone else could make better use of, and I agree with him. I just don't think I can make it."

"Sean, I know you can! You just have to believe in yourself," I tell him firmly. "Don't worry about what others say. People will say what they want to say. You are a nice person, and you know it. You don't cause any problems here. The tech was probably trying to motivate you with a negative statement. However, whether others motivate you or not, it shouldn't matter. You have to be self-motivated. You have to prove them wrong."

"But I don't think it's possible. You wouldn't believe how many people are telling me that I can't make it. I am really frustrated."

"Do you think I would tell you something that is not possible?" I look straight at him. "You know how many people have made it, don't you? Look at Scott, Stanley, and Dawn. They had worse addictions than you did, and they have been clean for decades. You have to be confident. You need to believe in what you are doing. You have to continue doing the right thing. You have to be consistent in your efforts. What matters is perseverance - the results will follow. You have to be patient and don't be discouraged just because others tell you that you can't make it. Let me tell you a beautiful story that I heard somewhere.

"A group of people trapped in a deep well had no way to climb out. Passersby gathered to see what was happening. Someone in the crowd slide a pole down in the hope that they could shimmy up. All of them tried but the pole was too slippery, and no one could get to the top. The onlookers began to discourage them saying, 'Don't try, give it up, why do you want to torture yourself more?'

"All but one man gave up. After many attempts, several hours later, he managed to get to the top. A curious reporter asked,

'How did you succeed when everyone else failed?'

"'I gave 100 percent!'

"'Weren't you discouraged by the onlookers advising you to give up?'

"'I didn't hear any discouragement,' he replied. 'I thought they were rooting me on. I'm partially deaf.'"

"You make up these stories, don't you?" Sean asks with a broad smile.

"No," I reply. "I just modify the stories; they keep floating around."

"Can you take me out to smoke?"

"No."

"I didn't expect it from you anyway," he chuckles. "I just thought I'd try my luck."

I smile. "Your luck is bad."

Sean has been clean for two years. He calls at regular intervals. Recently he left the recovery house where he was living, and when I called, the manager of the recovery house refused to give me his contact information. One morning, however, I received a call from Sean. He told me he was living with his friend and family, he was fine, and he wanted a copy of my book. He wanted to know what was written about him. He also warned me to write good things about him—otherwise he would tell everybody that I am a useless therapist and know nothing about recovery except bullshit stories from the east. Then he said that he has two Indian neigh-bors, and he likes Indians. I replied, "I am not an Indian; I am American as long as I am in America, and when I go to India, I become Indian."

"You are full of shit," he said, and promised to see me soon.

Chapter 18

Frank With a Sparkle and Craig With His Pants Down

Frank has prominent facial features and his beautiful eyes carry a sparkle in them. But he is so frail now that every bone in his body can be seen and counted. He's in a wheelchair, looking depressed and tired. I walk up to him and introduce myself: "Hi!

I am Christopher, and I will be your therapist. We will be working together as long as you are here."

"I don't care!" he shouts. "Get away from me." He wheels his chair in the other direction.

I instantly realize that it is not going to work today. I decide to listen to my heart. I leave him alone and walk away from him.

The next day, I approach him again. "How are you doing, Frank?"

"Miserable." His eyes are wandering all over the place.

"Frank, would you like to speak with me about your issues?" I look at him and add, "You might feel better if you talk it out."

"On one condition." He carefully scans my face. Stressing every word, he says, "Can you promise to make me feel better?"

"I can't promise, Frank, but it usually helps when people get things off their chest. It might work for you, too."

He shakes his head, looking unconvinced. Then he stares

at me indifferently but prefers to stay tight-lipped.

I continue, "Well, take your time. When you are ready, come and see me in my office."

"I might as well come now," he says, resignation in his voice.

I show Frank to my office and help him get his chair through the door. His eyes are wandering all over my office and his muscles are tense.

"Frank, get yourself comfortable, relax, and don't hesitate to ask for help when needed. You might—"

He abruptly cuts me off. "Do you think I'm fucking stupid?"

"No," I reply. "I don't think you are stupid. But why do you say that?"

"No one has ever helped me," he declares. "I had a few problems in the past, and now I have millions of problems. You said you would help me. That's fucking crap. You're bull-shitting me."

Neither of us says anything for several minutes. I think silence will help him calm down, and if I say anything, it may intensify his anger. He might snap. It works; he calms down a bit, looks at me with watery eyes, and appears as though he is ready to talk.

"I have a drug problem." He pauses for a few seconds, takes a deep breath, and adds, "I have been using all kinds of drugs daily. I just can't live without them." Abruptly, he stops and starts sobbing.

After a few seconds, I say, "Tell me about your problems."

"Well," he says, "for starters, I have full-blown AIDS."

He looks at me, as if searching for something. I feel he is trying to read my mind. He is looking at the expression on my face. I am surprised, mainly because he wasn't willing to talk at all a few minutes ago, and now suddenly he tells me he has AIDS. We had rarely begun our preliminary talk. Where did that confidence come from? Or does he just not care anymore? Is he tired of his situation?

"When were you diagnosed?" I ask.

"Way back. I'm dying." His eyes fill with tears.

Suddenly the beauty of his eyes disappears. His face turns pale. Am I seeing the fear of death in his eyes, or is it just my wild imagination? He gathers his strength to continue.

"I was diagnosed HIV positive in 1981 and with AIDS three years ago. I also have hepatitis A, B, and C."

"How did you contract HIV?" I ask.

"Sex." He manages a weak smile. "I slept with every girl who gave me a lift."

"A lift?"

He smiles with difficulty. "I don't mean that kind of lift. I mean, I had sex with every girl who showed an interest in me. I was well-built and handsome then. I was macho. I was a player. I was a male gigolo. But look at me now. Look at my bones: they are about to fall out; look at my skin hanging everywhere. Just look at me. I'm alive due to the mercy of others. I need help with everything I do. I can't move on my own. I'm tired; I'm tired of everything!" He is sobbing again. I let him cry. He cries as though he has never cried before and probably will never cry again. He finally comes to a gulping stop. "I hope you will keep everything confidential. I don't want the others to know that I have AIDS or that I cry like a baby. I don't want anyone to think of me as a weak person."

"I can feel your pain Frank, and I mean it." *I say this with some doubt in my mind, wondering whether I am empathetic enough. Am I reassuring him?*

"Thank you," he says heavily.

I can see that he is a heartbroken soul and that he feels helpless. There is no doubt that he made some bad decisions in his life, but today he needs empathy, love, encouragement and dignity.

"Frank, why are you in a wheelchair?"

"I can't walk. I had hip-replacement surgery. The doctors say it will take an abnormally long time to heal because of my chronic health condition."

"Frank, I have a suggestion. Try your best to be cheerful and happy as much as possible. I know it is difficult but—"

He cuts me short. "That's easier said than done. It's easy to give advice."

"That's true." I nod. "But that's the only way out at this stage.

A cheerful attitude will help you maintain your health, and you will be able to stay in the recovery process."

"I don't care," he snaps. "Everything sucks here. These people are inconsiderate. They don't give a fuck for us."

"Give them some time," I suggest. "You will find that they do care."

"Oh bullshit," he snaps again. "I've been trying to see Stanley for the last two days, and he keeps avoiding me. He says that he will get to me, but he never does."

"He must be busy," I tell him. "Why do you want to see him?"

"Being staff, obviously you'd defend him." He gives me a hard look. "Birds of a feather flock together. He tells me that I can walk, and that I am only pretending to be sick. What the fuck does he know about my condition?"

"Frank, I know you are very sick. And I wouldn't advocate for anyone who is fundamentally wrong. Again, why do you want to see Stanley?"

He lets out his breath. "I want to contact my case manager from another program."

"I will request that he see you as soon as possible." I help him push his chair through my office door. An hour later, when I enter the community room to run group, I see him; he still looks miserable.

Frank does nothing but complain. His bad attitude and poisonous sharing go on for ten to twelve days, and the treatment team assumes he will not last long in treatment. He constantly grumbles about his medication and food and is convinced that the staff are gainst him and that they just don't care. He is paranoid and suffering from emotional and mental breakdown. He is distrusting of people. He is always looking for the ulterior motives and questions others' actions. He is easily offended and unable to relax. He feels very uncomfortable around others. He is stubborn and has difficulty saying he is sorry, even when he is wrong. The sad thing is that he is paranoid.

One day in complete hopelessness, he tells me, "I have tried everything, but nothing seems to work. I don't think I'm ever going to be normal again."

"If you give up hope," I tell him slowly, "nothing will work. I know it's frustrating at times, but you need patience. Patience always pays. Recovery calls for perseverance. Many of us find it difficult to follow through until the end. We like quick solutions, quick responses, and immediate gratification. One thing is certain: you will never see the desired results if you give up, but if you follow through, you will achieve your goals. You will be at peace and start feeling like a normal human being again. Giving up is not an option if you want to do that."

As time goes by, Frank does start to change. His mannerisms and attitude improve, but we are unable to see it. We refuse to acknowledge the changes in him. We have stereotyped him. We see the difference in him but do not recognize what we see.

He begins attending group on a more regular basis and is compliant with his medication. He has stopped complaining, and has started lifting his head to greet others with a smile. He has been ollowing directions without grumbling. He has stopped being sarcastic. He listens carefully and has stopped getting ready to reply. He does not seem anxious to have the last word any more. His case manager from another program is also supportive and provides helpful information from time to time.

* * *

One morning, Craig boasts in group, "I have never been in trouble because of my addictive behavior."

"Craig," I start slowly, "you are very fortunate that you haven't been in trouble. But sooner than you think possible, your addiction will cause you legal complications, bad health, relationship conflicts, unemployment, and homelessness, and it could kill you."

"I was clean for many years," he continues. "I know everything about recovery. I really don't need help."

"Craig you need to stop bragging about your past and take inventory of your current situation. You were using drugs before coming here, your life was unmanageable, and you were powerless over your addiction. That's why you are here, and now you are saying you don't need help. You do need help," I say, looking directly at him.

"I know how to build a recovery," he responds.

"Craig," I look at him carefully, then continue, "I know you were clean for a long time and that was a great achievement. It wasn't by fluke. Without hard work, you wouldn't have remained clean for all those years. However, something was amiss as evidenced by your relapse after so many years of sobriety. You spent many years building your recovery, but you destroyed it in a minute."

"I don't know." He shrugs. "It just happened. I can rebuild it, and for that I don't need to be here."

Frank interjects, "You weren't forced to come here, Craig; you came on your own. You didn't come here for a picnic, did you?"

"This program can't offer me anything new. I want to leave." Craig's eyes are wandering all over the place.

"If you feel that way, then why don't you leave?" Frank stares at him.

"I don't want to mess up my future chances for treatment with the insurance company," Craig says, looking away.

I interrupt, "Wait a minute. You said you are going to stay clean, that you are not going to use again. So why do you care about future chances?"

"Oh, who knows? Anything can happen." He looks at me.

"Craig, it's obvious that you are apprehensive and unsure." I meet his eyes. "That is reason enough for you to stay in treatment.

You just need to take things one day at a time and complete this program."

"Nothing is certain in life," he rationalizes.

"It cuts both ways," I tell him. "So you might as well stay."

"I can stay through this weekend at the most," he says.

"Man, you are talking as if you are doing Christopher a favor," Frank says in exasperation. "If you want to stay, stay; otherwise, just leave."

"Did I ask for your advice?" Craig snaps.

"No," Frank replies calmly.

"I don't want your free advice," he retorts.

"Okay, then you can pay me for the advice," Frank teases. "After all, we are all in the same boat."

Everyone laughs except Craig.

"No, we're not! You are all junkies; I was clean for many years. We are not the same. I just had a momentary slip. I have three-hundred thousand dollars in my bank account." He holds up papers for everyone to see.

"Frank," I intervene, "don't worry about him. He will be okay."

"I'm not worried about him," Frank says politely. "I don't like the way he talks to you."

"You have seen clients talking worse to me than this," I respond, "but it doesn't bother me."

"I'm sorry for being a pain in the butt." Craig suddenly

changes his stance. "But the thing is that I'm a paralegal. I have responsibilities, and that's the reason I need to leave."

"Craig," I say slowly, "the issue is not about your leaving; you can leave when you feel mentally and physically stabilized. The issue is your closed-mindedness and bragging about your past sobriety. You have to understand that is in your past. Whether the past is good or bad, you have to let it go, and start fresh."

I wish them all a good weekend and ask Craig to come to my office before I leave.

"Craig, did you speak with your wife about the family session as I advised?" I ask.

"No," he answers. "I don't want my family involved. I had a great upbringing. They didn't ask me to do drugs. I did it on my own. So I have to do recovery on my own."

"Craig, a family session might help you and your wife to rebuild a good relationship."

"Please don't get me wrong," he tells me. "I love my wife. I share an honest and transparent relationship with her. But I just don't want her to know my whereabouts."

"Why not?"

"We have a lot of money in a trust," he answers. "If she finds out where I am, she will line up all the attorneys after me."

"But didn't you just say your relationship with your wife is honest and transparent?"

"She is after my money. I'll let her know where I am at the right time. I love her. She has been in recovery for the past three years, and she wants me to stay clean. I'll be going home to live with her once I am done here. I am just playing it safe for the time being. If I end up staying the entire length of the program, then we might end up having a family session."

"All right. I'll see you on Monday; have a good weekend," I say

* * *

Early Monday morning, Dawn asks me, "What are you going to do about Craig ?"

"Why? What happened?" I ask.

"You don't know ?" She appears surprised. "He was caught with his pants down in his room, and Virginia was hiding under his bed! It happened over the weekend."

"Really? But he's married and says he loves his wife very much."

"He is full of shit. Don't believe what he says." She shakes her head.

"Can you bring him to my office?" I ask. "We'll speak with him together."

Dawn returns followed by Craig.

"Hi, Craig! What's up?" I ask.

"I'm doing fine," he says, smiling.

"What happened over the weekend?" I ask.

"Oh, nothing major," he answers. "They are blowing it out of proportion."

"No one is blowing it out of proportion," Dawn snaps. "You haven't even received any consequences for your actions yet."

"I didn't have sex with her!" he says. "I was wearing a towel around my waist because I was getting ready to get into the shower when staff entered my room."

"Then what was Virginia doing in your room?" Dawn asks.

"She came to ask for a pencil," he answers, looking away from her.

"Then why was she hiding under your bed?" Dawn presses.

"She got confused when the tech knocked on the door. He avoids looking at her. She didn't know what to do."

"You do know that other clients are not allowed in your room," she says impatiently, "don't you?"

"Yes, I do," he replies, looking down at the floor. "I didn't invite her in, but you can't expect me to throw her out; that would be ill-mannered!"

I step in: "Craig, keep your manners to yourself. Where was our roommate at the time of this incident?"

"He was out somewhere."

"Was it planned?" I ask.

"C'mon," he says. "It was a coincidence."

"Why was your door locked from the inside?" Dawn is relentless.

He fumbles, thinks for a moment, and says unconvincingly, "She was confused, so she locked it."

"So, you are saying that you two didn't have sex?" I stare at him.

"No." He shakes his head vehemently. "I am not here to have sex!"

"You know this kind of behavior is detrimental to your recovery process," I remind him.

"Aw c'mon, don't blow it out of proportion," he repeats, looking down.

"Craig," I say softly, "you need to learn to take responsibility or your behavior. You need to muster the courage to own responsibility for your part in this incident."

He appears desperate and lost for words. After a brief pause he says, "I want to be transferred to another facility."

"Transferred for what?" I ask.

"Because you guys are trying to kick me out of here."

"No." I shake my head. "We don't want you to leave. We just want you to follow the rules of the program."

"You haven't said you are sorry yet," Dawn reminds him.

He falters. "I didn't make a mistake so why should I apologize?

I'm a human being, and I maintain contact with other human beings. I know Virginia from the streets, so obviously I will befriend her."

"Craig," I sigh, "didn't I tell you last week to stay away from Virginia?"

"Yes, you did." He looks away from me.

"So, why didn't you do what I said?"

"I can't do everything you tell me to," he snaps.

"Why are you so rude?" Dawn intervenes.

"I don't take shit from others," he retorts.

"That's enough," I state. "I am putting you on a Behavioral Contract stating that you are forbidden from maintaining any verbal or physical contact with Virginia. Breach of the terms and conditions will lead to appropriate action against you, including the possibility of an administrative discharge."

"That's okay with me," he responds hastily.

I draft the Contract, and he reads it thoroughly before signing.

"Can I nod when she says hello?" he inquires.

"Craig," I tell him decisively, "you are not to have ANY contact with Virginia."

The next day, there are a slew of complaints about Craig's behavior. He exchanges things with Virginia, he shares the same lunch table with her, and he talks to her through other clients. When pulled over by staff for being defiant, he says, "That's not written in my Contract."

He is in my office complaining about a staffer who objected to his behavior. "These people are trying to throw me out of this program."

"It's your behavior that is causing you problems," I say.

"My Contract says I am not allowed to have any physical or verbal contact with Virginia," he rationalizes, "but it doesn't say anything about non-verbal communication."

"Craig, why are you here?"

"To get my shit together," he answers resignedly.

"If that is true," I counter, "then why don't you surrender yourself fully to this program and follow directions?"

"I am talking about the terms and conditions of my Contract!" he cries.

"Craig, stop harping on an invalid point." I tap my pen on my desk. "I know you have worked as a paralegal, but now your life is at stake. You are already over fifty. It is high time that you get your act together. You have to give up your manipulative ways. The laws you have learned and practiced are good for winning cases, but the laws for a happy life are different. Laws for life require honesty, open-mindedness, sincerity, enthusiasm, and courage. Stop dwelling in negativity and start developing a positive attitude. If you persist in using drugs, you will always be in trouble."

"My mental health issues make things difficult for me," he sighs.

"But you have been maintaining for so long that you have no mental health issues and now suddenly, you are saying that your mental health issues are making things difficult for you." I frown at him. "However, you do have behavioral issues, and you lack the desire to do the right things that are required to live a happy life."

"I want to be happy." He scowls.

"You can't be happy when you rationalize, intellectualize, lie, and justify your wrong behavior," I explain. "Why do you want to screw up your own life? You are intelligent. Use your intelligence to better your life, to get back on track and move forward."

"You hit me hard," he responds. "No one has ever told me in so many words exactly what I have to do. I will do what I need to do."

"I hope you really mean what you are saying."

"I am sincere," he says, avoiding eye contact.

"Remember, actions speak louder than words," I tell him. He nods.

* * *

There is no apparent change in Craig's behavior. He behaves during the day, but once the day staff leaves, he resorts to his manipulative ways, his controlling behavior, and his lustiness. I receive multiple complaints about his behavior and unwillingness to honor the terms and conditions of the Behavioral Contract. Whenever he's confronted about his behavior, he rationalizes it.

One day I begin group by stating, "The winner is not the one who wins, but the one who never quits. So in recovery, you are a winner as long as you don't quit; otherwise you are a loser."

"I don't like that word," Craig challenges.

"Whether you like it or not, it won't change the reality of life."

I shrug.

"Don't ever use that word again." He gives me a warning look.

"It's not in my dictionary."

"You can find it in *Webster's Dictionary*." I look straight at him. "It is a common word."

"I'm not a loser!" he shouts. "I'm a winner!"

"If you believe you are a winner, then why are you so upset by hearing the word?" I ask.

"Because it affects my self-esteem."

"If you truly believe you are a winner, then what I say shouldn't matter at all," I tell him firmly. "And just for your information, winners don't blame the world when they fail. They take responsibility for their behaviors and actions, and work to move forward. They don't quit. However, losers blame the whole world for their failures, and they refuse to take responsibility."

"People like you piss me off," he snaps.

"Well, I guess you are choosing to be pissed off," I shoot

back.

"That's fucking crap!" he yells.

"Craig, you are refusing to accept the truth. You empower me to piss you off. You are giving me a space in your head."

"Fuck it, I can't stand you any longer," he says impatiently.

"Craig," I sigh, "just learn to be a man."

"I am a man. I have fathered children, and they are older than you are. You don't need any other proof, do you?" He suddenly stands up, touching his zipper.

"Just fathering children is not enough," I tell him gently. "You have to learn to look at the bigger picture. If you are a man, you will learn to take responsibility for your behaviors and actions and inactions and muster the courage to live life on life's terms. You will not run away from problems. You will handle depression, loneliness, petty frustrations, and setbacks with courage. Fathering children is one thing ; being a responsible father is another. You have to learn to be responsible, loving, and caring to yourself and others."

A female client interjects, "I blamed the whole world in the past; instead of taking responsibility for my behavior and doing anything to better the situation, I kept complaining and being resentful about everyone and everything. I went to a conference once with recovering addicts, and I trusted them. I had a very expensive leather jacket and hung it in the coatroom, but when I came back, it was gone. I blamed everyone there and stopped going to meetings and conferences, which resulted in my relapse. I didn't realize that my judgment was lousy. I failed to understand that just because someone is in recovery doesn't mean they have changed their entire behavioral pattern. I wasn't smart enough. I was a loser in that sense."

"I have every right to hold onto my beliefs and ideas. I don't vave to listen to anyone," Craig snaps.

"Of course you have a right to your beliefs, thoughts, and

ideas, but you have to check their legitimacy," I say.

"I don't know why the fuck people expect me to live up to their expectations!" he retorts.

"Craig, do you expect other people to behave appropriately?" I ask.

After a pause, he says, "Yes, I do!"

"Well, Craig, if you expect an appropriate response from people, then what's wrong if they have the same expectation of you? Think about it."

He sits spellbound until the end of the session.

Over a period of time there are several complaints about Craig's behavior, and when he tries to seduce Serena, Virginia's new roommate. Virginia does not take it well. They almost come to blows.

"Craig, what is wrong ? Why are you so defiant?" I question him.

"I'm not doing anything objectionable," he answers. "She keeps asking for help, and I've been through the process, so I'm just trying to guide her, trying to make her life easier."

"No," I almost shout, "you aren't making life easy for anyone; in fact, you are making life difficult for both of you. You are working hard to get kicked out of this facility."

"Kicked out for what?" he snorts. "For being outspoken?"

"It has nothing to do with you being outspoken." I resist the urge to roll my eyes. "You are in constant violation of the terms and conditions of your Behavioral Contract and the rules and regulations of this facility."

"No." he shakes his head. "That's not true. I didn't violate the terms of the Contract. Have you personally seen me doing anything wrong ?"

"Of course," I say. "The other day, I saw you cutting your nails and Virginia sitting beside you."

"After that, you didn't see me doing anything else," he asks, "did you?"

"Craig, the staff has a list of complaints about you, including how you are trying to seduce Serena."

"Don't believe them," he tells me quietly. "They have something against me. Maybe because I'm more intelligent than they are."

"Craig, that is what YOU think. What I think is that you are too smart for your own good. You need to accept the truth about yourself and start working on your issues. And you need to keep away from Virginia and all the other female clients. Time is running out. Time will not wait for you. So make use of the time available to you."

"All right." He nods. "I'll do it."

"Good. Now, what are your aftercare plans?" I ask.

"I'm going home to my wife and I'll attend IOP."

"In that case, I still suggest that a family session will be of great help in your recovery process."

He shakes his head. "No, I don't want my wife to know where I am."

"Who are you fooling ?" I counter. "You received two greeting cards and a letter from her last week. So how is it possible she has your address, and yet doesn't know your whereabouts?"

"No," he says. "You don't understand. I have a situation with her."

"Situation?"

"I told her that the director of this place allowed me to use his address for communication purposes and that I'm in another program."

"Why are you lying to your wife?"

"They say when in Rome, be like a Roman," he says carelessly.

"You do know that you can't build recovery on lies," I ask, "don't you?"

"They are going for a smoke. I need to go." He is up and by he door.

"Okay." I shrug as he runs out of my office.

* * *

I relate my conversation with Craig to the treatment team. "That is to be expected when you deal with this population. We don't kick out clients for behavioral issues such as having sex on the unit," Scott states.

"But he is dishonoring the Behavioral Contract," I stress.

"No," Scott insists. "I'm not going to kick him out; the purpose of the program is to help clients who have behavioral issues."

"All right," I groan, leaving his office.

Later, Craig begins instigating clients to sue he facility for negl-igence, and it becomes a matter of concern for Scott. "If I were a betting man, I would bet one thousand dollars that Craig is setting the stage for clients to fall, and that he has a lawyer ready to pay him for clients," Scott tells me one day in the treatment team meeting. Now Scott is trying to get rid of him, but he doesn't want to discharge him administratively. He advises Stanley not to request any more days from his provider. The plan is executed as stated.

I explain the situation to Dawn. She is back in my office accompanied by Craig. "What's the matter?" Craig demands.

"Have a seat." Both of them settle in chairs across from my desk. "Craig, you have to leave today," I tell him.

"What?" He appears shocked.

"We are completing your treatment here," Dawn explains.

"How can you complete my treatment so abruptly?" he demands.

"The treatment team feels that you aren't making any progress here. Whatever you had to learn, you learned, and we feel that you have reached the saturation point," Dawn patiently tells him.

"But I'm not ready yet," he whines. "I need more time."

"You have been here for more than thirty-five days," I interject, "but your focus was on having sex with Virginia, challenging and disrespecting the outlined program, and deliberately annoying the staff to gain control."

"I can't change my behavior in thirty-five days!" he protests.

"I'm sorry I can't help you now," I reply.

"I knew I would be thrown out for being outspoken," he says angrily.

"You should be happy that you are getting your Certificate," Dawn cuts in.

"I'm okay with it." Suddenly, he stops resisting. "I'll go pack my things."

Dawn comes back later, complaining, "Craig is talking with the clients and saying all sorts of stuff and poisoning the entire community. He should be moved as quickly as possible."

"We can't do anything," I tell her, "until Stanley has completed his paperwork."

"I'm not going to have him in my group," she states. "I am aking the clients out at 10:00. I'll tell him to stay with you."

"That's fine."

* * *

Craig is in my office, sitting in the chair across from mine, panting and breathing heavily.

"Craig," I begin, "what's the matter?"

"I'm mad!" he spits. "You are completing my treatment when I am not ready. I am going to use."

"I don't think you should think about using just because you are unable to stay here any longer."

"I don't want your fucking advice," he snaps. "If I am going to use, I am going to use. You are the one who made this decision. Stanley told me that you didn't ask for more time."

"The decision was made by the treatment team," I explain. "I told you before that you weren't willing to give up your old behavior, and you weren't learning anything new. You were wasting your time as well as everyone else's. You didn't want to be here in the first place, but now you want to be here because of Virginia, don't you?"

"I want to call my insurance company," he states.

"You are free to make that call, but not from my office," I tell him. "I am not allowed to let clients call their insurance company; those calls are to be made through Stanley."

"All right, all right, I'll do what I need to do." He glares at me and stomps out of my office.

Dawn walks in again. "Now he is talking to Virginia."

"We can't stop him from talking," I tell her with a touch of annoyance. "The only thing we can do is speed up his discharge."

We step into the hall and notice that Virginia is also leaving.

"You're not putting both of them into the same cab, are you?"

Scott asks Stanley.

"Of course not," he replies.

Stanley is out with Craig, and he stays there until the cab comes for him. Meanwhile, Virginia completes her paperwork and walks out of the facility. I wonder where they will meet; the cab was taking Craig to his wife's house. I didn't have to wonder for long, because Sam, our van driver, and a client coming back to the unit report seeing Craig and Virginia walking down the road with all heir belongings.

Craig calls the next day and tells me that he is trying to get into another residential program and that he is doing fine, but he needs to speak with Dawn, because Virginia got upset with him and left without leaving her phone number behind. "Absolutely not," Dawn tells him, "I can't give you her phone number because of the confidentiality law." And that was that.

Chapter 19

Cherry and Frank— What a Contrast

I start group stating, "It is your recovery. You have to seek help. Don't expect others to work for your recovery; it doesn't happen that way. It is very important to stay awake and ask questions. You can't sit back, do nothing, and expect recovery to happen. My job is simple: I just have to provide you with knowledge and information. Your job is difficult, because you have to grasp it and apply it to real-life situations. But the first step is to recognize that you need help."

"I expect you to help me when I'm in trouble. Aren't you here to help us?" Cherry cuts in abruptly. She is a heavy-set woman whose eyes seem ready to pop out of their sockets, making her look fierce.

"Of course it's my responsibility to help you, but you can't expect me to anticipate all your needs and wishes," I respond.

"You, being a counselor," she says, "should be sensitive to my needs and wishes."

"I have no way to be sensitive to your needs and wishes the way you expect," I explain. "I am not a mind reader. You have to tell me your needs."

"No, I am not going to tell you anything," she retorts.

"Christopher, ignore her. She is just trying to give you a hard time," Frank says, rolling his eyes.

"She needs to clear her thinking," I respond. "I need to

help her set her thoughts straight."

"God can't help people who refuse to accept help, or who don't recognize the help that they are receiving!" Frank states emphatically. "Christopher, please repeat the story about the man who refused the help God sent him."

"Anything for you Frank."

He beams.

Frank may have AIDS and many other opportunistic infections, but he still has his charm. When he smiles, it lights up the room. And he is a fighter.

"Once upon a time, it rained heavily. The rising water threatened the village. The villagers were told to move to higher ground where they would be safe. Almost everyone complied except for one man. His beautiful, two-story house sat on the riverbank. The river kept rising. He was on the first floor watching the water lapping at his front porch when a boat came by. The people in the boat advised him to get in the boat, but he flatly refused, stating, 'don't worry about me. I firmly believe in God, and he will take care of me. You don't have to worry about me. There are others who need your help; go and help them.' The boat left and the water kept rising.

"Slowly but surely, the first floor of his house flooded, and the man moved up to the second floor. Another boat came by, and the people onboard offered him help. Again he refused, repeating that he had told the people in the first boat. The second boat went on without him, and the water rose above the second floor of the house. His only option was to climb out onto the roof.

"While on the roof, a helicopter pilot helping in the rescue effort spotted him and offered to lower him a line. He refused, stating, 'My God will help me. You don't have to worry about me.' The helicopter left without him, and shortly afterward the flood-waters washed him away. After his death, he went to heaven, for he had been a good man. However, he refused to enter the gates of heaven because he was very angry with God. God asked him the reason for his anger. 'I was so spiritual. I went to church every day. You helped everyone but me. I am the only person who died in that flood. Isn't that unfair?'

"'No,' God replied. 'I sent you help three times, but you refused it every time. You know that I work in mysterious ways.'

"That is why it is very important that when you need help, ask or it and be receptive. You have to learn to help yourself. You have to be help-seeking. You must understand that your life is at stake, and you need to take charge of your life and not let drugs ruin it."

The group responded positively to the story, saying, "Thank you," and "that was a good one." Cherry just shrugged indifferently.

At the end of his first thirty days in the program, Frank is the only one who is always cheerful and enthusiastic. He is ready for group early and exhorts the others to attend. It is a wonderful sight to see him pushing his wheelchair with one hand while calling the others. He shares his feelings and thoughts freely. What a reversal! He doesn't project negativity anymore. He shares positive thoughts and feelings. His enthusiasm and love for life are obvious.

One day in group, he states, "I have full blown AIDS and hepatitis A, B and C." *How's that for absolute honesty? I think. What faith! Now he is being unselfish. He has purity and clarity in his thinking. He has repentance. At the same time, he doesn't want to look back. He wants to keep moving. Bygones are bygones. He seems to have learned from his past mistakes.*

On another occasion, I ask, "Frank, how are you feeling now ?"

"Excellent! I want to live," he responds. "I want to live my life to the fullest extent. It's never too late. I made mistakes, but I don't want to dwell in the past. I want to live in the present and just take one day at a time. I want to enjoy every moment of my life on this planet. I want to experience real joy, real peace, and real happiness. I don't want to be miserable anymore. I have had enough misery. I m ready to say goodbye to it. Better late than never."

Another time, he asks me, "What is the difference between loneliness and aloneness?"

I lean back in my chair. "Well, Frank, loneliness is a state of mind where you miss people, things, and places. In aloneness, you like to be alone. In a state of aloneness, you are with yourself. Alone, you are serene, joyful, and happy. You see things more clearly. You are in contact with reality. You see everything with its real value, nothing more and nothing less. When you are lonely, you are self-centered. You refuse to see what is good in and around you. You don't see the beauty of nature. You are self-engrossed but you are cut off from yourself. You miss people, things, and places that do not belong to you. You forget that people belong to life and not to you or me."

"How do I learn to be alone and not lonely?" he asks.

"You have to learn to take time to be alone to observe what's appening within you and around you," I reply. "The prophets, he mystics, and healthy children miss nothing. They are happy to be themselves. They enjoy things without clinging to them. They are like birds. The birds of the air neither sow nor reap nor gather in barns."

Frank is progressing well in his recovery process. He is goal-directed, focused, and enthusiastic. He is gaining control over his emotions, and he is listening from his heart. He is asking questions with openness and a willingness to learn something new. He wants to be transformed. He wants to deprogram himself. He wants to unlearn his old ways and learn new ways of behaving. He wants to re born again. There is a risk involved in change, and he is willing to take that risk. He is no longer self-absorbed; he is far less self-centered. He is in a state of self-observation. He has decided not to feel lonely anymore. He understands the

*meaning of aloneness, and he has learned to enjoy it. What a
wonderful change!*

"Frank, you are close to completing your treatment here.
How do you plan to maintain your recovery?" I ask in a one-
on-one ession.

"I am committed to give it a sincere and honest try," he
answers. "I have acquired some knowledge and information,
but I will not make that an end in itself. I will try to apply
that knowledge and information in my day-to-day life. I will
also attempt to continue to learn and remain teachable. I will
take life one day at a time."

*He completes the program and is referred to a residential pro-
gram. A year goes by without hearing from him, so one day I
call him.*

"Hey, Frank, how are you doing ?" I ask.

"Fine," he responds cheerfully.

"Is everything well with you?"

"Yes," he answers, "everything is good."

"Frank do you know who this is?" I ask, chuckling.

"Yes. You are the therapist from The Orthodox Institute for
Drugs and Alcohol."

"You have a very good memory. What is going on with
you?"

"I had an operation a few days back for liver cancer," he
says with no self-pity. "I also had a kidney operation last
December. I have only one kidney now."

"Oh... things sound tough."

"Yeah well, that's life," he responds.

"How is your hip?"

"The same."

"So, what are your new plans?" I ask.

"I don't have any plans as such," he replies. "I just want to
stay in recovery. I want to die without using drugs."

"Frank, I am deeply impressed with your attitude and

determination. Your strong spirit is an inspiration. I will keep you in my thoughts."

"Thank you," he says, his voice almost musical.

Chapter 20

Cherry Blames the Program for Her Pregnancy

Within a few days of her stay in program, Cherry walks into my office and declares, "I don't want to be here."

"Why not?"

"This program sucks." She settles down into a chair.

"For that matter, every program sucks," I tell her.

"Not every program," she snaps. "This one specifically sucks. This program made me pregnant the last time I was here."

"How can a program make you pregnant?"

"Well, it did. I'm not lying," she says defensively.

"What I meant to say is that normally, unless and until you have sex, you can't get pregnant," I explain.

"Well, yeah," she admits. "I had sex with a guy who was very handsome."

"So, don't you think it's unfair to blame the program?"

"If I wasn't in the program, I wouldn't have got pregnant."

"If you had not had sex, you wouldn't have gotten pregnant!" She shifts uncomfortably.

I ask, "So, why do you really want to leave this program?"

"I don't know," she responds wearily.

"Cherry, you need to find out the real reason. Now, go and relax for a while and come see me after lunch."

She comes back to see me, and I'm glad she is still here.

"Cherry, how old are you?"

"Thirty-nine," she says hesitantly.

"Are you married?"

"No," she answers. "I don't intend to get married. I hate marriage."

"Why?"

"Men are fucking—" she pauses, "assholes."

"How is your relationship with your parents?"

"Good," she answers.

I think of asking if she hates her father, but instead, I ask, "How is your relationship with your father?"

"Excellent," she replies. "I have a good relationship with both my parents."

"When did you see them last?"

"Eight years ago," she answers. "I moved here from California; they are still there, and they send me money. Oh, and I'm a paranoid schizophrenic, and I am also diagnosed with bipolar disorder.

I suffer from depression and loneliness, and I have serious anger-control issues."

"I see," I respond. "It looks like you have several mental health issues. Does anyone else have mental health issues in your family?"

"No," she says. "I am the only black sheep."

"Well, Cherry, I'm glad you are in treatment. Just hang around and things will get better. See you soon."

* * *

A few days later, Cherry stomps into my office again. "Fuck him!" she spits out. "He stole my money." She is pacing. "That fucking bastard ran away with my money."

"Cherry, sit down and tell me what happened."

She sits but is still furious. She is breathing heavily and

has fire in her eyes.

"Who stole your money?"

"The black guy who worked here last night," she answers.

"How much?"

"A hundred dollars."

"Why did you have a hundred dollars on you when you know you are only allowed to have twenty dollars?"

"My mom sent me a money order, and the staff person who received it said he would give it to me, but he ran away with it."

"Do you know his name?"

"No," she answers angrily.

"Don't worry. I will find out. For the time being, just relax. We will take care of it. I will have to speak with my supervisor, but I can assure you that you will get your money back."

"I want it now!" She slaps my desk.

"That's not possible," I tell her firmly.

"Why not?" she demands.

"I need to find out the whole story."

"I told you everything that happened," she insists.

"I cannot come to any conclusion right now."

"Why not? Do you think I'm lying ?" She looks hurt and leans forward.

"No," I answer calmly.

"I want your decision now," she presses.

"I can't make a decision now. I have to talk to Scott. Please, have patience. I need some time."

She stands and starts pacing my office.

"Cherry, did you take your medication this morning ?"

"Yes," she answers, fuming.

"Did you have breakfast?" I ask.

"Yeah, I ate that nasty breakfast," she snaps.

"What do you like for breakfast?"

"An egg with a glass of juice and some fruit," she answers.

"That sounds like a healthy breakfast."

"I always like healthy breakfasts," she boasts.

"Well, that's smart," I say. "A nutritious breakfast is necessary for your health."

"Yeah, but here you get nasty things to eat," she grumbles.

"But they have a lot of fruit and juices," I say.

"I like cherries, pineapples, and blueberries." She settles in a chair across from me.

"When did you last have cherries and blueberries?"

She gives me a rueful smile. "Not in years."

"Do you watch movies?" I change the subject.

"I love movies!" she answers enthusiastically.

"What kind of movies?"

"Action movies," she replies without a blink.

"Do you go to the theater?"

She shakes her head. "No. I watch them on TV. Theaters cost too much."

I nod. "Theaters are expensive."

"Do you watch movies, Christopher?"

"Yes, I do."

"Do you watch Indian movies?"

"Sometimes."

"What kind of movies do they make?" she asks, leaning forward.

"Action, comedies, and romance," I reply.

"Romantic movies," she responds with twinkling eyes. "Wow!

I would like to watch them."

"You can find them on cable usually on Saturdays," I tell her.

"What kind of movies do you watch?"

"Comedies."

"That's so boring." She shakes her head.

"Possibly," I respond.

"I can't stand comedy," she says, moving backward.

The change of topic has had a magical effect. She is now calmer and less anxious.

"Cherry, please go back to your room. I will get back to you after I talk with Scott."

She leaves, and I go to find Scott.

"I know, I know," Scott says. "I heard all about it. The temp from the agency ran away with a hundred-dollar money order."

"What do we do?"

He just shrugs.

"Scott, what should I tell her?" I insist.

"She will have to wait," he answers tentatively.

"How long ?"

"Till we get the money order back. I have already called the agency manager."

"But it isn't her fault." I look at him quizzically.

"I know that," he responds sternly, "but the truth is that she has to wait. There is no alternative."

"Well," I say, "in the meantime, I will see if I can pacify her."

* * *

Cherry is standing in the door of her room, agitated again.

Before I can open my mouth, she shouts, "Did you get my money?"

"Please come to my office."

She yells, "Where is my money?"

"Cherry, come to my office, please!"

"Oh, all right." She rolls her eyes and then follows me. After entering my office, she stands breathing rapidly, and I wave her to a chair.

"Cherry, we will get your money back, but we need some time. Please have some patience, and everything will be okay."

She jumps out of her chair, snapping, "What the fuck are you talking about? Have some patience? I want my fucking money right now! It's my money, and I need it. I called my mother and told her to put a stop on the money order so that guy can't cash it."

"Oh! That's very smart thinking," I compliment her.

"I want my money, or I am going to call my lawyer," she threatens, still standing. I again request her to sit. She pulls another chair and sits down looking away from me.

"You just told me your mother is going to put a stop on it," I remind her.

"Yeah," she utters without looking at me, "but I don't know when Mom will send me another one."

"Okay, how much money were you planning to spend out of the hundred dollars?" I inquire.

"Forty."

"How about if I give you forty dollars today," I say, "and you pay me back when you get your next money order?"

"Wow, great!" She beams, turning her head toward me.

"Okay, let me run this past Scott. If he approves, I'll give it to you."

Scott gives me permission, and I give her the money.

Later that day, during group, she complains about what had happened and how she lost a hundred dollars.

"Cherry," I interject, "you need to stop talking about how you lost your money. You didn't lose anything. Yes, you were put to some inconvenience, but the matter is already taken care of, so just let it go and move forward."

"But staff stole my money," she repeats.

"Your money isn't stolen—"

She cuts me off: "That fucking bastard did steal my money."

"You don't know that for sure," I tell her. "He might have forgotten to give it to you when he left. It's over and done with. We are in the process of resolving the issue, so don't dwell on it. You can't be happy obsessing over the past."

She looks offended. "You know," she sobs, "I have been put down by men my whole life. In my opinion, men do nothing more than inflict pain on others."

A rather broad generalization, but in her case, I could understand.

Cherry is homeless. It was getting too cold, and she couldn't take it any longer, so she got herself admitted to treatment. She doesn't know what she wants out of this program. While in my office, she says, "The main reason I am here is because I am homeless."

"If you were homeless and you wanted a place to live, you should have gone to a shelter," I tell her.

"But I was sick, too. My stomach was flipping, and I felt like I was dying. I was stressed out, depressed, and very lonely. The nurse here doesn't care. She won't give me any medication. She shouldn't be working in this kind of place," she complains.

"Do you plan to work on any goals while you are here?" I deliberately ignore her complaining.

"Drugs are not my problem." She looks at me and adds, "I want to get some kind of place to live where I don't have to get up early and do what staff want me to do. I am tired of being told what time to get up and what time to go to sleep. Programs like this get on my nerves.

Cherry is a chronic complainer. Having a one-on-one session with her is always a hell of a job. She keeps complaining that her back hurts and that she is not getting any medication. The doctor was trying to clean out her system and bring her back to a baseline before starting any new medications. Cherry seems to be unsatisfied with the explanation; it doesn't make any sense to her at all.

One day instead of having group, we go for a walk. The temperature is above fifty degrees even though it's February. We are enjoying ourselves on the diversion road behind our facility. We had snow two days earlier, and now it is melting.

The ice melting from the trees makes them appear as though they are bathing in the open. The ice crystals fall on our heads, as if mischievous kids were hiding in the trees and showering us. Birds are chirping. There are no cars, no trucks. The entire road belongs to us, as if we own it. How wonderful!

Everyone is having a good time except Cherry. She is complaining about the pain in her back, and she blames it on the weight that she has gained by eating too much since she has been in our facility. No one is paying any attention to what she is saying. Some clients try to sneak off and scan the garbage on the roadside, but I remind them that that is addictive behavior, and they don't want to practice addictive behavior anymore, so they stop.

After a while, Cherry picks up a small stone and starts kicking it. I cannot resist from joining in, and suddenly the whole group is involved. Now we are playing football. Only instead of a ball, we are using a stray stone. We try to kick the stone on top of the pot-holes. When anyone gets close, we happily shout, "goal!" Once or twice, we kick the stone into the snow, and we hunt for it. There is nothing special about this particular stone; it's just an ordinary stone, but it is the one we want. We are happy when we find it and start the game all over again.

Cherry has been playing with the stone for over forty-five minutes and has not complained about her back. How interesting!

Back on the unit, we share our experiences. Everyone says, "That was wonderful." We can take a lot of pleasure in small things. We discuss the ordinary stone, and the seemingly childish game that gave us such sheer pleasure.

"I was free. I never felt freedom like this before. I was out of this prison, and I was having a drug-free walk," offers Cherry. "My mother always told me that we have to stay in touch with nature. The pleasure that you receive by being in contact with nature is real; you experience real happiness. However, I need to stay clean to experience real joy, real heaven. When I started using drugs, I slowly lost everything. I lost my spirituality, I lost my children, I lost my apartment, I broke up with my boyfriend, and my family refuses to have anything to do with me. Worse still, I lost me, my soul. I remember the pain and my losses, and I repent. I'm sure I don't make the same mistake again. I'm going to make it this time.

As Christopher says, I'm taking it moment by moment, like baby steps. I'm not in a hurry; my goal is to complete this treatment by aking things one day at a time. Step by step. I'll do whatever it takes to stay clean. I need freedom from these institutions, freedom from drugs. I was born free, and I want to live free."

What repentance! What soul searching! What determination!

I am impressed, as are the others by her thoughtful sharing and her mother's advice. I think to myself: "It seems the pain and loss have hit her hard. It does look like she has hit rock-bottom. Who can stop her from staying clean? She will definitely learn to watch out for weak moments. It's just a matter of time. Time heals everything. The only requirement is patience."

How little I knew that what I heard was nothing more than just idle chatter.

The next day, Cherry comes to see me at 7:45 a.m., saying, "I want to leave." To my astonished why, she responds, "I have more important things that need to be taken care of." When I remind her about her determination toward completing this program, she retorts, "I know what I'm doing."

I had forgotten for the moment that actions speak louder than words. This reminds me again of the fact that yesterday is history. Cherry conveniently forgot the determination that she had expressed while sharing her thoughts in group. The moment she left was the moment of weakness, and she, in her desperation, failed to guard against it. One more tragic relapse!

Chapter 21

Ruby and Roger

Ruby is six feet tall, forty year old, hefty woman. She is homeless and has been using mood-altering chemicals for twenty-five years. She gave her four children up for adoption. She was gang-raped by six men and has been arrested for prostitution many imes. A bench warrant was issued against her for a violation of a court order. She is still on probation. She tells me, "Wigs trigger me to get high."

"Wigs?" I repeat, confused.

"Whenever I wear wigs, I prostitute," she explains.

"Ruby, I don't understand the connection between wigs and prostitution."

"Whenever I wear a wig, I feel beautiful, and that leads me to prostitution, and then prostitution leads to addictive behavior."

"Ruby, are you in contact with your probation officer?"

She nods. "Yes. My probation officer told me that I might have to go to jail because only the judge has the power to lift the arrest warrant, but I know they won't lock me up when I'm in treatment.

I'm not worrying about it. If I have to go to jail, I will, but I don't think I will end up in jail considering the current situation."

It turns out she was correct. She presented herself before the court and stated that she was going through a drug and alcohol rehabilitation program. She produced supporting documents and was ble to get her arrest warrant lifted and stay in treatment.

Ruby is highly intelligent. She understands human behavior and analogies so well that I wonder why she doesn't use her exoraordinary intelligence for her own welfare, including staying clean. She is close to completing her program, and she has never lost her temper. She also avoided getting into any relationship issues. I never had to reprimand her for any behavioral problems, either.

In group one morning, I mention that one of my colleagues confessed to me that he had relapsed even though he was teaching Twelve Steps and believed himself to be very spiritual. I ask for omments.

Ruby starts: "A changed life is more graceful than his so-called spirituality." On another occasion, when I had asked the group to share their understanding of love and spirituality, she spoke so movingly about love, spirituality, and awareness that it became a living and life-giving experience for me.

"For I was hungry, and you gave me food. That is love. For I was thirsty, and you gave me drink. That is love. For I was a stranger, and you gave me shelter. That is love."

She explained love in general with the help of verses from the Bible. It was very moving.

* * *

Over the weekend, Roger, a chairperson elected to lead unit meetings by his peers, was involved in a power struggle. He has a habit of making other people's business his own. He told a peer, "You are not allowed to have two cups of coffee."

"You mind your own fucking business, you fag," was the instant retort.

This incident turned into an intense argument, and the staff on duty had to involve security guards to separate these two so-called grownups.

While in my office, I ask, "Roger, what happened over the weekend?"

"We were at the cafeteria, lined up for coffee, and Albert was behind me. He muttered some comments. I demanded to know what he said, and he didn't take it well. Then he picked up two cups of coffee, and I told him that he couldn't have two. He got mad and started calling me names. He called me a fag and said that everyone knows it. I was about to kill him. I'm not going to take crap from people! I'm still thinking of killing him; he better keep away from me. I gave him cigarettes and stuff when he had nothing. He has seen only the good side of me. I can be a real bad man. I'm ready to kill him."

"If you kill him, you will end up behind bars."

"I don't care," he scoffs.

"Incidentally," I casually mention, "I was told that you started the trouble."

"Who said that?" he demands.

"Two separate incident reports speak volumes against you."

"She's a fucking liar," he says, referring to the female technician on duty at the time of the incident.

"Roger, you are being disrespectful." I frown at him.

"The staff here is full of crap."

"I am also one of the staff here."

"I'm not talking about you," he responds quickly.

"You need to stop being disrespectful to others," I warn him.

"I am not here to respect anybody," he snaps.

"Do you need to be respected?" I ask.

"Yes."

"Well, Roger, if you want to be respected then you need to learn to respect others."

"I'm going to file a law suit against this place." He threatens.

"For what?"

"Because my information has been leaked, and Kathy told me that the staff talk about clients behind their backs." He smacks his fist into his palm. "And I am going to file a suit under the confidentiality law, and I will see to it that this place has its license revoked."

"Why are you listening to Kathy?"

"She is my friend."

"I don't think so."

"But I know for sure," he insists.

"Kathy is causing you stress and anxiety, which you do not need," I explain to him.

"It's okay with me. I can handle it." He shrugs.

"Really? You don't seem to be handling it all that well."

"I'm handling it just fine," he snaps.

"If what you are saying is true, then why are you so stressed, anxious, and agitated?"

"I told you, I am not here to take crap from others!" he shouts.

"Roger, you have serious anger issues; you need to learn to handle your anger or one of these days, you will get into serious trouble." I lean back in my chair.

"I don't need to learn anything," he says. "You need to tell the others who are full of shit to get rid of their shit."

"Roger, you simply must clean up your language and be more respectful."

"Yeah, well you wouldn't be so polite if someone called you a fag," he sneers.

"You are making it personal," I tell him.

"Oh, the hell with it, I'm signing out." He jumps up from his seat.

"Why?"

"I'm tired of being a scapegoat."

"Roger, no one is making you a scapegoat. You have to get that out of your head. And you have to stop getting into other people's business and start minding your own."

"I don't want to hear that crap again," he snaps. "I don't take crap from others. I've had enough of it."

"Roger, you need to listen and think before you say anything or act."

"I'm packing my stuff and leaving right now. If I stay here any longer, I will kill him."

"What would you achieve by killing him besides ending up in jail?"

"I don't care." He shrugs.

"It's your life; you better care."

"I don't need any more advice. I'm leaving right now." My door slams behind him.

Although Roger did not attend group that day, he did stay in the program. The following morning he is sitting in group.

I begin, "It's very important to learn to enjoy every moment of life. Heaven and hell are states of mind. We choose where to live. Things are simple in nature, but we complicate them. We make mountains out of molehills."

"I can relate to that," Roger admits spontaneously. "I made a mountain out of nothing yesterday and complicated everything. I was angry with you for no reason. I guess I was angry because I wasn't ready to hear what you were saying."

"Basically," Ruby joins in, smiling, "you did not hear what you wanted to hear. Instead, you heard what you were ought to hear."

"Right!" Roger exclaims. "But I always look for emotional support!"

"Depending on other people for emotional support is not healthy or desirable. You have to be independent emotionally. You don't want me to make you feel good or bad, do you?" I ask.

"Yes, I do. I want you to make me feel good," Roger says emphatically.

"If you depend on me to make you feel good, you automatically give me the power to make you feel bad. It cuts both ways," I explain.

"How ?" Cat questions.

"Okay, let's say that one day I get up on the right side of the bed. I say all good things about you because I'm in a good mood, I appreciate everything you do. You are glorified, you feel good, and now your mood is elated. The next day, I get up on the wrong side of the bed. I say bad things about you because I'm in a bad mood. I insult you by finding fault with everything you do. I say things you don't want to hear. You felt good when I appreciated you, so obviously you will feel bad when I say bad things about you. That's why I said it cuts both ways. I acquired the power to make you feel good as well as bad. But who gave me the power?" I ask.

"I did," Cat replies.

"Correct," I say.

"Can I say something ?" Ruby looks at me.

I nod. "Go ahead."

"Roger," she begins, "you have been here for more than fifty days, and you are well aware of the rules and regulations, but you chose to address Albert's behavioral problem as if you were staff, and it almost cost you your treatment. It's like a power struggle, whatever it is. We have to consider the worth of everything we indulge in. You want everyone to follow the rules and regulations, which is good, but at what cost? You almost ended up leaving treatment. You don't want people to follow rules and regulations at your expense, do you? Do you understand?"

"I sure do," Roger agrees. "I know I was wrong. I wasn't ready to hear what I heard. I didn't want to hear what I was supposed to hear, and I didn't get to hear what I wanted to hear. Christopher tells us the truth, but we don't want to hear it because it is bitter. I have been there. I was angry and walked out of his office slamming the door just because I didn't get to hear what I wanted to hear. We have been conditioned to want to hear something that sounds good to our ears, even if it is untrue and harmful. Christopher, I am sorry for being disrespectful and nasty. You know I respect you. I love attending your groups. I have never met any person as wonderful as you. I sleep in all the other groups, but I have never slept even once in your group. I am indebted to you for teaching me the meaning of life."

"I do not know the meaning of life myself, so how can I teach you?" I chuckle.

"You are being modest, Christopher. You know the meaning of life; if you don't know, who does?" Roger asks.

"Roger, I don't know who knows, but as far as I'm concerned, I don't feel any need to find out the meaning of life as long as I live happy, serene, and truthful life," I say.

"Do you have a higher power?" Brenda, my new client, wants to know.

"How does that matter?" I reply.

Everyone starts laughing hysterically.

"That's typical of Christopher." Roger is holding his sides, laughing.

"He won't answer questions if you ask him out of curiosity." Ruby is smiling. "According to him, that is not learning. He says curiosity kills."

"You may reframe your question," Kathy advises Brenda

"No. I'm okay," Brenda says without looking at her.

"Brenda, I wasn't trying to be smart, but it's my philosophy that I shouldn't reveal my beliefs," I clarify. "It could prejudice someone's mind. And I'm sure that in the due course of time, you will form your own opinion about my beliefs and prejudices."

Roger nods. "He's right. He never told us whether he is theist, theist, or agnostic, but I believe he is agnostic. Now, he is like, ho cares? That's just him."

"You've got to wait," Kathy explains. "Have patience and everything will be revealed to you as an unfolding truth. I was just like you in the beginning, but now I am changing. I am willing to wait and see. I am ready to give chance a chance. I am giving time, time."

Chapter 22
Kathy's Brother is Quacko

Kathy, a large woman walks into my office and takes her time settling into a chair. After being sure that she is comfortable in a tiny chair for her large size, I ask her, "Do you have a criminal history?"

"Yes," she replies, looking into my eyes.

"What were the charges?" I ask.

"Three counts of aggravated assault," she responds, "and involuntary manslaughter."

I am stunned. Kathy is obese and needs a cane to walk. However, she looks upbeat and talks non-stop. She is funny. She makes me laugh. I enjoy and love the company of people who make me laugh. Murder was the last thing I expected to hear.

"Who did you kill?" I sputter.

"My husband," she answers with no visible sign of remorse.

"Why?" I am still struggling to come to terms with her original response.

"He was a very controlling and physically abusive man," she answers placidly. "I was always walking on eggshells with him. Behind closed doors, it was a living hell."

"How did it happen?"

"It all started when he hit me over the head with an iron bar." She shrugs. "I stabbed him once in self defense, and he just collapsed and died. I didn't intend to kill him, but he had to die to release me, to free me."

"How old were you when this happened?"

"Thirty-four."

"How many years were you in jail?" I ask.

"Do you mean for the murder?"

"Yes."

"I served a year and a half in jail." She pauses. "And I did thirteen years of probation."

"What? That's all!" I exclaim.

"Well," she says, "it was in self-defense, and I have explosive disorder."

"Do you have any children?"

"I have a son and a daughter, eighteen and sixteen," she says. "I love my children."

"Are they by your late husband?"

"No. They are by two different men. My son doesn't know anything about his father."

"Why not?"

"Well, I was raped and got pregnant, and I kept the baby."

"Are there any other traumatic experiences in your background?"

"My aunt used to rape my brother every day in front of my yes when we were growing up."

"Did you tell anyone?"

"We tried to tell our mother," she sighs, "but she didn't do anything about it. That's why I ran away, and then I got raped!"

"How is your brother doing now ?"

"Oh, he's a quacko!" she declares, laughing.

"Do you mean wacko?" I smile.

"Oh no, he's more than wacko." She is still laughing. "He is quacko!"

"Does he do drugs?"

"No, he is gay. He hates women. He went for sex change surgery and married a man from Africa. He believes he is

Buddha and doesn't believe in Jesus Christ. One day he wore a woman's dress when we went to visit our father in the hospital, and when my father saw him, he suffered a heart attack and died. Now he wants to do the same thing to my mother because she holds her responsible for what happened to him. He is also trying to evict my sister from our house and take over the property. He keeps sending his money to his man in Africa. He says that's what all Buddha's do. I tell him that Buddha's don't do that. But he disagrees. He is nuts! I can't understand why he would become like a woman when his whole life he was raped by a woman. That's why I say he is quacko. I didn't want to be a man after I was raped. And that African man, African men don't do things like that, they don't marry homosexuals. I think he just wants citizenship. My brother is so quacko." She laughs non-stop. Her laughter is so infectious that I start laughing myself.

She regains control and continues, "I lost one-hundred-and-forty pounds in the last two years."

"How much do you weigh now?"

"Two-hundred-and-seventy pounds."

"So you were really heavy," I state.

She nods. "Yeah, I had trouble walking. I was frequently in a wheelchair."

I am impressed. "How did you manage to lose so much weight?"

She sits up straighter in her chair. "You know, I was addicted to junk food, and I kept on eating it until it started affecting my health. I had to do something or I was going to die. I said to myself, if I cannot manage my food, how can I manage my life? So I decided to change the way I was living. The first thing I did was go on a diet. Then I started walking a minimum of two hours a day. I signed up for night school and completed my senior year of high school two years ago."

"That's fantastic. Congratulations!" I beam at her. "You

should be proud of yourself. You showed perseverance and real strength of character!"

"I have to tell you, man," she goes on, "before coming to this program, my life was unmanageable. My psychotic anger was over-powering. It was tearing my life apart. I was accustomed to using drugs every day. I had to have it at any cost. I was depressed, lonely, stressed, angry, guilty, hungry, sleepless, filthy, broke and homeless. While in my active addiction, I didn't keep appointments with my dentist or my doctor, and I would skip work whenever I wanted to. No show, no call was my pattern, and as a result I was fired from every job I had. I'm learning new ways of behaving after coming here. I am learning to stop, think, and listen before acting. I am gaining a better insight into my problems. I am learning impulse control techniques. I think one hundred times before I say or do anything. This is now possible because I sincerely desire recovery. I am committed! I am open-minded; I am devoted. I don't want to make the same mistake again. I want to build a home for myself. I want to start doing the things I stopped doing. I want to be a good mother to my children. I want to give them the love and affection they deserve. I never want to use again. I know the baffling and cunning nature of my disease."

It turned out that Kathy was full of smoke. The next day Sam, our driver, escorted her to her doctor's office. After waiting two hours in the van, he went to check on the delay and discovered that she had run away. When she shared her thoughts and feelings associated with her recovery process, she gave the impression that she was committed, sincere, and willing to work hard to get her act together, but it wasn't true. What a shame!

Once Scott and I were attending a recovery conference organized by the city; suddenly, I heard someone calling my name. When I looked around I saw a fat man running toward me. I did not recognize him until he introduced himself. "I am Roger,

*your ex-client." He looked heavy; in the neighborhood of 230
pounds, but while in treatment he was slim, around 140 pounds.
Later, he called all his friends accompanying him and happily
introduced hem to me. At the end, I was pleasantly surprised to
hear from him that he was in recovery for almost four years and
was in con-tact with Kathy, who has been in recovery for almost
two years. Isn't that great? Think about it!*

Chapter 23

Sex Ruined Albert

The day Albert is admitted, he is transferred to a hospital because
of his high blood sugar level. An argument with Roger caused
him more suffering than he expected. He remains hospitalized
for four days. When he returns to the program, he is weak and
tired and placed on bed rest.

He attends my group the next day. He seems depressed.
He begins, "Everything is messed up. I need to get myself
together, and I haven't met my therapist yet, so I don't know
what's going on with me. These people are so fucked up, they
just don't care. I'm in the dark. I don't know whether they
even know what's going on with me."

I interject, "I will be working with you. Since you were
immediately hospitalized, I didn't have a chance to meet with
you. We can get together after this group; I need to collect
some information from you anyway."

"I'm depressed and tired. I don't think it's a good idea to
ask me for any information today." His eyes wander all around
the community room.

"Okay," I reply, "don't worry about it. If you still feel
depressed and tired after group, we can meet tomorrow."

His mood improves as group progresses. He actively par-
ticipates and shares information about his addiction. "My
so-called friends introduced me to drugs. Actually, I just
wanted to be part of the 'in' crowd. For years, I have been

using drugs day and night. I was killing myself. I want to stop using. I know how to use drugs but I don't know how to stop. I did try to stop on my own but it did not work. I guess I need help. I do crazy things when I am high. I do things you won't even imagine. I will talk to you about those things when the time comes for me to share in depth." He glances at me.

I smile. After serenity prayers, I ask him, "Do you feel comfortable enough to complete some paperwork now ?"

"Yes, I'm fine." He smiles and follows me to my office.

After sitting down, I ask, "Why did you decide to seek help, Albert?"

"I was at the end of the road," he answers. "Everything I did was wrong. I was killing myself. I lost everything. Everything came down on my head."

"Any substance abuse history in your family?"

"I'm not sure."

"With whom did you grow up?"

"My parents and siblings. But I didn't have a good relationship with either of my parents." He pauses, then continues. "My relationship with my mother was insane."

"What do you mean by 'insane'?"

"Let me make it simple," he says. "When we were growing up, Mom would wake us early in the morning, say around 1:00 a.m., and make us sit on the couch. Then she would tell us, 'I'm going to kill all of you because I don't want anybody else to look after you when I die.' She would do this frequently, and we knew she could do it. I saw her stab another woman once. My mom was razy, absolutely nuts."

"Does anyone else in your family have mental health issues?"

"One of my sisters was in a mental health institution for while."

"Albert, how is your relationship with your siblings?"

"It was never good from the start."

"Are you married?"

"My wife and I are getting a divorce," he says, his eyes downcast.

"How many times have you been married?"

"Twice."

"Do you have any children?"

"I have four: two by my ex-girlfriend—" he ticks them off his fingers, "and two by my first wife. But they are all grown up. My relationship with them is strained."

"Do you have any mental health issues?" I ask.

"Nope. I'm fine. I do have medical issues: hepatitis C, high blood pressure, diabetes, and a bad leg."

"How old were you when you first had sex?"

"Oh, you won't believe it; I was barely five." He looks right at

I think, since I have been in this field, I believe and disbelieve anything and everything that clients tell me.

He continues, "There was a girl from our neighborhood who used to baby-sit us. She asked me one time if I knew how to do pussy, and I said no. She told me to lie down, and I did. She got on me and fucked me good. We did it many times after that, but I never climaxed. My first climax was when I was twelve, with the most beautiful girl in the neighborhood. She gave me a blowjob."

"Do you have any sexual problems?" I ask.

"I have erectile dysfunction. I have been sexually inactive for the last two years." He lowers his voice. "It bothers me a lot. I'm only fifty-nine. I should be able to have sex at least three to four times a week. My diabetes has made it worse. It depresses me. I attempted suicide three times by overdose. I didn't die because I didn't have enough cocaine, and I wasn't in a position to buy more, and that saved my life."

"Albert, I need to conduct a prescheduled family session

with another client, so we have to stop here. We can finish the rest of his paperwork tomorrow. Do you mind?"

"No problem. Oh, I forgot to tell you that I have neuropathy. I will talk to you when I see you next." He leaves my office. The next morning right after breakfast, he walks into my office puffing and fuming. "I'm depressed, and I don't know why. I guess I'm not feeling too good today." He pauses. "My dad was here last Monday while I was in the hospital, and he left some of my medications for me, but no one knows where they are. I'm losing my cool. I'm so fucking angry right now."

"I'll talk to Eboni and find out whether she knows anything about it."

"I already talked to her, and she says she doesn't know anything," he says with annoyance. "These people are messing with the wrong person. I'm basically a good guy, but if somebody rubs me the wrong way, I can get very ugly!"

"Do you want me to convey this message?"

"No. Just let it go." He is suddenly contrite. "They just shouldn't take me for granted."

"You have the right to get your medications. But that doesn't mean you have to be angry. It will just mess up your sugar levels again," I caution.

"Who cares?" He shrugs.

"It's your health. You better start caring."

"Let me tell you something." He takes a breath. "I was barely seven years old, and my baby brother was four. A boy from the eighborhood hit my brother very hard. My sister, who was there, told me that I had better protect my baby brother because if Mom found out that I didn't help him, she would skin me alive. And you know what I did next?"

"No, I wasn't there," I joke.

He smiles and struggles to look angry.

"I went and got a screwdriver and stabbed the boy in the

back. Of course, the police took me away. But I was released when the police received confirmation that the boy was out of danger. I missed his lung by a few inches." He puffs out his chest.

"What's the purpose of recalling this incident today?"

"Just to let you know I can be nasty, if I choose to."

"You also know the consequences, don't you?" I stare at him.

"Jail, but I don't much care."

"Albert, it would be better if you try to let go of the past and move forward with your life."

"I'm very upset today." He appears mellower. "I know I need to calm down."

I nod. "It happens. Just do me a favor: go to your room and relax for a while, and if you feel better, then come to morning group."

"I'll try. Oh, and please let me know if you find out anything about my medication. See you later." He smiles as he steps out.

Later in group, he is angry again. When his turn comes to share, he spits out, "That fucking nurse lost my medication. This place sucks. They are supposed to be professionals. But there is no professionalism in what they do. They don't care. How can they misplace a client's medication? I can sue them for negligence. They are really pissing me off."

"Albert, you need to have some patience," I say, hoping to calm him down. "I have spoken with the nurse, and she is investigating the matter."

"She told me the same thing, but she is doing nothing about it," he snaps.

"Albert, just relax and wait and see what happens next."

"This time, I don't want to fail. I want to succeed in my recovery. But I am afraid of the negativity around here; this place doesn't seem to be conducive to my recovery."

"Albert, your negative attitude will take you nowhere. If

you really want to succeed, then you need to develop a positive attitude. You will depend upon it in everything you do! And if you put your mind to work with a positive attitude and believe that you are going to succeed, you definitely will."

"I have a friend who is absolutely negative in attitude but still doing very well; how do you explain that?" he asks sarcastically.

"There are exceptions to every rule, and everyone has a different definition of success. Have you heard people say that once you achieve success, you become more and more successful?"

"Yes," he responds, "I have heard it before. But my mind is always wandering. I have no control over it. My mind never stops. I have rushing thoughts."

"Albert, it is very important to have control over your mind, and if you lack that control, you will never achieve any worthwhile goals. You have to learn to use your mind. If you don't use it, it will become worthless. It will be rusty. It requires practice. Meditation helps. It's not that disturbing thoughts won't be there; they will, and they will keep rushing. However, they will not have the power to bother you. Their existence will be equal to nothing. You will have clarity about your goals, and you will not be confused anymore. Once that confusion is gone, you will be able to achieve some worthwhile goals."

"I get frustrated very fast. I lack patience and tolerance," he admits.

"Well, that is the result of your negative attitude. You practice nothing but negativity. A negative mental attitude leads to fear, anxiety, restlessness, frustration, resentment, and anger."

"But I didn't expect my life to become a mess like this," he says, averting his eyes.

"It doesn't matter whether you expected it or not. The

results are the same. By the way, what did you expect?"

"I don't know," he sighs.

"If you want to enjoy your life, you need to develop a positive attitude. A positive mental attitude will help you succeed, have peace of mind, maintain relationships, love and be loved, and have sound mental as well as physical health. The result will be sound sleep. Last, but not least, you will have clarity in your thinking ; and it will help you to understand yourself as well as others better. Do you understand?"

"I guess so."

* * *

Now things are changing drastically. Albert has been a different person for the last ten days or so. "When can I see you?" he keeps asking every time he sees me in the hallway. I see him here and there, but due to pre-scheduled session with my other clients, I am unable to give him the time he demands. Meanwhile, his lost medications turn up; his father did drop them off but had neglected to put Albert's name on them. He was delighted that we found them.

I knock on Albert's open door. "Let's meet for a one-on-one now."

"Great." He jumps up. "I do need intense therapy. I desperately want to talk to you; I have so much to share."

"No problem. I can spare some reasonable time for you today."

"You are the man." He smiles.

Back in my office, I ask, "So, what's up?"

"I don't know where to start." He takes a deep breath. "It will take hours if I start telling you about my crazy childhood and the other stuff I did in my adulthood."

"Just start," I suggest.

"I know I have to get this off my chest. This is the time I

have to do it." He pauses to collect his thoughts. "Well, I am here this time not out of fear but despair. If I don't succeed this time, I will die for sure. I've been in many rehabs before but I guess I wasn't ready. I was thinking of using drugs before I even stepped out of those programs. This time, I'm serious and I don't want to die. You know, I have medical problems. I have hepatitis C, my liver is messed up, I have neuropathy in my leg, and I have high blood pressure and diabetes. I can't afford to do drugs on top of all that. I know I'm late in realizing this, but it's never too late. This is a new beginning for me. I want to start over! You won't believe what I am going to tell you next. I have done a lot of crazy stuff." He pauses, then continues, "When I was a kid, my mom had a boy-friend who liked to mess with underage girls, and she would help him. She would get my sisters to invite their girlfriends over, and then he would have sex with them. Mom and her boyfriend tried to convince me to get my girlfriend to sleep with him. I refused because I really liked that girl. Instead, I got him my girlfriend's best friend. One day, Mom asked me to walk my baby sister, who was ten, over to her boyfriend's apartment. I knew what was waiting for my sister. I was afraid to say no for fear she would kill me. On the way to his apartment, I thought of running to Dad's office to tell him what was happening, but then I was afraid that he might kill Mom, so I didn't go to his office. I acted as a pimp for my little sister."

"Your parents have been married for sixty-one years, right?"
He nods.

"How did she have a boyfriend while she was married to your father?"

"She was married to my dad, but she was still messing with her oyfriend."

"Did your father know about her affair?"

"I don't think so." He shrugs. "He's a Baptist pastor. He

was lways busy with his church work. I tried to tell him once after he promised that he wouldn't tell her, but the minute I began telling him about Mom, his expression changed and he went right upstairs. Later, when I asked him why did he leave, he just said, 'she is my wife and I don't want to hear anything about her.'"

"How did she get away with all this?" I wonder aloud.

"Mom is capable of doing anything. She sabotaged both my marriages. She got my first wife shot in the chest, but she survived that attack. My mom was cruel and nasty; she abused me emotionally. My childhood was violent. Once, a boy from the neighborhood tried to mess with me. I told my dad, and he slapped the ever-loving bejesus out of him.

"I never learned to respect women. I always thought they were mean and nasty. I did a lot more crazy things. I had sex with several married women. I had sex with women while they were on the phone with their husbands. I had threesomes.

"I was living in an apartment. One day the landlady told me that I had all the women talking about me; she wanted to see how big I was. We started having sex every day, but I was scared because her husband carried a gun. One day he came home early and found us together. When he reached into his pocket I thought he was going for his gun, but instead, he removed a big diamond ring and told me to look at it. I looked at it and said, 'you must love our wife very much to buy such a big diamond ring.'

"'I love her,' he replied. He could have killed me, but he spared y life. I left that apartment forever. Everything about women excites me. But when women pee, that excites me more than any other thing. I've always been attracted to abnormal women. I even married a woman who was many years older than me. One woman told me when I walked her home, 'you got the meanest eyes I have ever seen. I bet you beat your women.' When we were in the middle of sex, she suddenly got up out of bed and started saying, 'please don't hit me, please don't hit me.' I realized her fantasy was helplessness. I would handcuff her or do something where she would be absolutely helpless, and then we would have sex and it was always very intense.

"Now I want to leave all this behind. I've been in multiple programs, but I never verbalized my issues to anyone before. Now I feel the need to tell someone. I have to start the process somewhere. I think this was the time chosen for me by my Higher Power, and now I feel relieved. I want you to teach me how to learn to deal with my issues more effectively." He takes a deep breath.

"Albert, I like your spirit, but you cannot rush. Time is a great healer. Learn to listen to yourself and others. If you develop listening skills, you will understand things better, and you will definitely be more effective in handling whatever comes up. You need to wait and see what happens in the process. I suggest that you write an essay on the importance of listening skills, and we can discuss it when we meet again."

"I'll do it!" He leaves my office with a determined look.

A few days later, he comes to see me immediately after a group session on anger management.

"I really needed to hear what you said in group today," he says, sitting down. "I have always been careless, and you said that we can't afford to be careless anymore, that enough is enough. If I hadn't been so careless, I wouldn't be in the mess I'm in now. Another thing you emphasized was not to procrastinate. Trust me, I have been procrastinating my entire life. Then suddenly, everything becomes urgent, and I get stressed and it turns into anger, and I end up using drugs."

"It appears you were paying attention and listening carefully." I smile. "I am glad."

"Since the day you told me to start listening, I've been

doing that because I'm here to get my life together. I didn't listen in the past, and the result was a dog's life. I've got to change my lifestyle, and I know I need to follow the right path. I'm confident that I'll do it this time." He hands me his essay. "Here, Christopher, I completed the written assignment on listening as you suggested."

I glance at it and see the line, 'I really like the analogy that anger is like a matchstick; it has a head but no brain.'

"Good job!" I look up. "Now you have to start doing what you have written."

"I will prove it by my actions," he states confidently.

"Well, time will prove it," I challenge him.

"I have a severe anger-control issue," he continues. "I become defensive and react using strong words, and it leads to serious complications. I have to learn, as you say, to stop, listen, think, then act, and not react impulsively. You know, you speak in generalities, but it applies so much to me that I feel as if you are focused on telling me what to do. I felt angry initially, but then I realized that it is just coincidental. I have those characteristics present in me, and they are being addressed in a general way. I told myself I had no reason to be angry. I just started listening, and it became easier for me to understand. I just wanted to confess that I was angry at you."

"If you continue listening from your heart, the end result will be peace of mind," I say.

"I have kind of started to understand what you mean and am trying to follow it." He pauses. "In the past, I never knew what I as doing."

"Try to remember those days and the helplessness you experienced because of unplanned journeys. It will help you stay focused and plan better."

"I don't like a planned life," he says slowly.

"Planning for life means living a disciplined life."

"A disciplined life restricts my freedom."

"Well, a life plan always has to be flexible. A disciplined life never interferes with anyone's freedom. In fact, it helps us to free ourselves and enjoy our freedom. It prevents us from going haywire. It also protects us from the negative consequences of misunderstood freedom. Remember that freedom brings certain responsibilities with it. It's just like rights; you can't have rights without responsibilities, can you?"

"No."

"So try it. See if you can live a disciplined life," I suggest.

"I'll try," he says thoughtfully. "It's never too late."

"But it's late for me," I say.

He laughs wholeheartedly as he leaves.

* * *

The next time when we meet, he says, "I want to tell you more about my life. Where would you like me to start?"

"Start anywhere you wish."

"Okay." He clears his throat. "I told you that my mom sabotaged both my marriages. In fact, I allowed it to happen. When my wife and I were together, my mom would knock at the door late in the evening with the intention of causing a rift between us. My mother didn't like the fact that my wife looked more beautiful than her. My wife looked like Cat in our group. When we were living with my mom, my mom would say, 'Al, there is a nice movie on TV, would you like to watch it with me?' Eventually, my wife started getting pissed off. And if my wife was fixing dinner, Mom would immediately jump in and say; 'I have already fixed your favorite dinner tonight.' Just to screw things up.

"I told Mom a few years ago that because of the way she raised me, I could never have a successful relationship with a woman. She had me helping her cheat on my dad. I could never fully give myself to a woman because I could never trust them. Oh, and you won't believe this: my mom had a lesbian affair!"

"Really? How did you find out?"

"It was right in my face. One day I saw five or six lesbians sitting on the porch. I knew some of them because they were from our neighborhood. My mom was in the arms of one manly-looking woman. I sucker punched her." He throws a punch in the air.

"You punched your mother?" I am startled.

"No, oh no." He shakes his head. "I sucker punched that manly-looking woman. All the women except my mom immediately got off the porch and left. My mom was very annoyed with me.

But she couldn't do anything because she was afraid I might do omething to her, too."

"Did your father know about your mother's lesbian affair?"

"Yes." He looks straight at me. "He knew about it. I guess she told him what happened, and he called me into his office and said, 'This is my house; don't ever come to my house and offend your other's guests like that again. You keep out of our affairs.'

"One day he came home early, and some guy was in my parents' bedroom pretending to do some work. He knew what was happening. I was thirteen, and I couldn't make out what was going on. They had me totally confused. I have asked myself many times why Dad was so passive. I still don't have an answer to that yet.

"This kind of atmosphere at home made me very suggetive in sexual way. I learned to read body language. I even started having threesomes. I started having women do each other, and I got some sadistic pleasure out of it. Sex ruined me. My boss at my first job got me an apartment. She moved in with me after a few months, and she would hold my dick in her mouth and sleep all night. This went on for seven years.

It got to the point where that was the only way I could fall asleep. She treated me like a king. She would run my bath; she would fix me food with a glass of wine and so on.

"Around that time, this country was going through the Black Power movement. I'm talking about the late 1960s. My friends were saying I had to get away from her, so I decided to leave her.

However I didn't leave, we pulled it together for two more years."

"Albert, where do you see yourself now ?"

"I'm in No Man's Land." He struggles to smile. "I want to change. I want to make amends." His voice chokes. "I want to own responsibility for my behavior. I want to stay clean. I want to capture a fort."

"How do you plan to do it?" I scan his face.

"By being honest and letting the past go," he answers.

"Do you think the fort will be yours?"

"I am confident." He touches his chest with his right hand.

"Albert, recovery calls for more than confidence. It calls for hard work. It calls for sincerity. It calls for action, and last but not least, it calls for honesty."

"I am willing," he promises.

"Great! If that is so, then the fort will be yours without a doubt." The session's time is almost up, and I say, "Bye now. I'll see you soon."

"How soon will you see me?"

"Why?" I look at him quizzically.

"I need to talk to you often," he answers. "I need intensive therapy."

"I told you that I can see you twice a week for individual therapy and five times a week in group," I remind him.

"Can I see you in emergencies?" he pleads.

"Yes, of course." I smile.

"Great, thank you." He leaves my office all smiles.

* * *

A week later, Albert introduces me to his parents.

"I am Albert, Senior, and this is my wife." His father shakes hands with me.

Albert had told me that both his parents were in their eighties, but they really look good for their age. His mother is well-dressed and looks healthy. If he hadn't told me about her behavior, I possibly would not have noticed the uneasiness on her face and her strange, cold eyes. She definitely appeared capable of causing harm. When Albert starts talking about his childhood and confronts his parents, his mother appears uncomfortable and suddenly becomes restless.

"I just wanted to let you guys know what's going on with me." Albert looks at his parents. "If you don't hear from me that often, don't worry, because I will be focusing on me. It's high time I take care of me. My whole body and mind are messed up. I have a lot of physical problems and some emotional issues."

"I knew it," his mother interjects.

"Dad!" Albert suddenly shouts.

"What?" Albert Senior appears startled.

"Dad, you are here to participate in a family session, and you're buried in that crappy newspaper."

"No, I'm not." His dad guiltily folds the newspaper.

"I saw you reading the newspaper," Albert insists.

"No, I wasn't! I can tell you exactly what you were all talking about."

"Dad, you gave the impression that you were reading the newspaper." Albert is adamant.

Albert's mom slowly turns her neck in the direction of her husband, and her long, cold stare does the trick.

"Okay, okay," Albert Senior stammers, putting the paper down.

"Listen, Dad," Albert starts afresh. "I just want to let you know that you don't have to worry anymore. I will not come and wake you up in the middle of the night asking for money. It is over. It's done."

"You have said that many times in the past," his dad reminds him.

"Those times were different," Albert states coolly.

"I believe you. You sound sincere this time." Albert's father looks at him affectionately.

"I never had the confidence that I could do it," Albert says, "but this time, I am confident."

"If you really mean what you are saying, I will be very happy."

His dad puts his arm around Albert's shoulders.

"I'm doing it for me, for my liver, my heart, and my legs—and for that matter, my whole body. If I continue using drugs, I will be dead, and I don't want to die."

"What did you say? You have a bad heart? Your liver is messed up?" His mother appears shocked.

"Yes, Mom," he replies. "I am on medication for it."

"I suspected it from the very beginning." She looks at her husband. "I just didn't say anything."

"We both love you!" his father says emphatically. "We can't give you everything you want, but we will be with you emotionally as and when you want us." His father glances at me and continues, "He is the most intelligent of our four children, but the drugs took away everything from him."

"He was a charming child," his mother adds, looking at him lovingly.

"We provided him with the best clothes, the best toys, and every other thing he needed," his father says with pride.

"Then what do you think went wrong ?" I ask. "Why did he pick up drugs?"

"He started hanging with the wrong crowd," his dad

answers.

"No, Dad, that's not right. The problem started much earlier.

Mom, you—for some reason—taught me to use my aunt's address, and every time I gave my aunt's address, the teacher would say 'that s not where you live,' and the other students would tease me. I became defensive and reacted violently. I literally started stabbing other children. Mom, do you remember how I stabbed that older kid with the screwdriver?" Albert looks at his mom.

She nods. "Yes."

"I don't remember anything of the kind." His father appears confused.

"You wouldn't remember, Dad, because you were always busy doing your church work, or going to clubs, or playing ball. I would come to you for help, but you never had time for me, and now you are saying you gave me everything I needed. You provided me with material things, but not love." He stares at his dad.

"There are many parents who don't buy anything for their children!" his dad says defensively.

"So what?" Albert snaps. "You were buying expensive stuff because you wanted to show off your good taste!"

"I was trying to provide my family with basic needs," his father insists.

"Just a few minutes ago you said that you bought me the most expensive things, and now you are saying you were trying to provide your family with basic needs. You are contradicting yourself. There is a lot of ambiguity in what you're saying," Albert retorts.

"Son, we are living in a hotel, but every time you call, not only do I come, but I also bring you cigarettes and anything else you want, don't I?" his dad asks.

"You sure do," he responds, "because you are basically

retired and don't have that much to do. I really don't need anything from you guys now. I want to be a man and take responsibility for my wn behavior."

"Well, if that's what you want, we'll be leaving now." Albert Senior stands and starts walking toward the door.

"Okay, Dad, fine." Albert stares at his dad.

His mother's cold stare does the job again. His father retreats the way a child comes back after seeing a threat in his parent's eyes. He resumes his seat.

I look at Albert quizzically.

He shrugs. "Dad always behaves like that."

"We need to—," his mother begins.

His father interrupts, "We are here to listen, I know."

"Don't you ever cut me short," she snaps, giving him a stern look. "As I was saying, we are here to support Albert." She continues staring at Albert Senior.

"I'm sorry, dear, I didn't mean to interrupt you," he says meekly.

Wow, what a look! She received an instant apology from her husband.

"Mom, don't worry about me anymore. I am done. I have hit rock bottom. I can't afford to do drugs any longer. I don't want to cause pain to you guys any more. That's my promise." He reaches for his mother's hand.

"I know you mean it, Albert. You are our child; call on us anytime, and we will be there," his mother assures him softly.

"No, Mom, no more calling. When I needed a real mom, you weren't there. You were busy doing your own thing. I don't need you guys any longer."

"You're saying that because you are angry with us," his father says.

"No, Dad, I'm not angry. But I do know what's right and wrong. I don't want to say anything more that will hurt you. Mom did a lot of crazy—"

His mother interrupts, "We love you, Albert, but we need to go now. By the way, your brother is outside. He wants to see you."

"I need permission from my therapist to go out." He looks at me

"I'll escort you." And we all go out.

The brothers hug each other but don't make eye contact. On our way back to the unit, I ask Albert, "How is your relationship with your brother?"

"We never had a relationship from the beginning. Did you see how Dad's face changed when I confronted him?"

"Yes. I did notice your father's uneasiness when you said that he never had time for his children."

"Did you notice how uncomfortable my mother looked?"

"Are you getting some sort of pleasure by indulging in this stuff?"

"Kind of," he admits, avoiding eye contact.

"Albert, do you want to change or not?"

"Of course I want to change." He looks straight into my eyes.

"If you really want to change, then you have to let the past go," I insist. "And stop looking for sadistic pleasure."

"You're right," he concedes. "I do take pleasure in hurting people. I need to stop hurting people, especially my parents. I guess they did what they thought was best or right from their perspective. Their turn is over. I'm sorry, you're right; I should not be of such a petty mind. I have to develop a broader outlook toward ife. I need to grow."

"Albert, you speak really well, but you need to learn to walk the talk."

"Christopher, you will see a changed Albert," he states with confidence, "and you will be impressed."

"I will be glad to see a changed Albert. Do you have anything else to talk to me about?"

"No."

"Then see you soon."

"How soon?" he presses.

"As soon as you feel you are changed," I reply.

When Albert comes in for his next one-on-one, he asks, "Do you notice any change in me?"

He has missed two sessions; he was in the hospital for one and I was on vacation for the second. But he appears more composed, more enthusiastic, and happier. He shows more maturity and unserstanding when dealing with his peers as well as the staff. He is handling his anger very well. He is assertive and shows no aggression. He is patient, does not act impulsively, shares his feelings without any reservations, and appears unconcerned about the consequences. He also appears more aware of his strengths and weaknesses. Yes, I am noticing many changes. I am tempted to tell him the changes I've noticed, but I resist because I think it's too early to say anything, and I want him to recognize the change in himself on his own. Instead, I decide to tell him the story about a master and his student.

"A young man desires to attain enlightenment. He is told that he needs a guru to guide him. He finds a guru known for his wisdom. The student works with him for a few days and notices some changes in himself. He is not sure about the changes that are happening and wants his master to validate them.

"'Master, do you notice any change in me?' the student asks.

"'Why are you asking ?' the master responds.

"'I am curious; I just want to know.' The student shrugs

"'How does it matter?' the master insists.

"'It doesn't really matter,' the student replies. 'I am just asking out of curiosity.'

"'I don't answer questions which arise out of idle curiosity,' the master states.

"The young student keeps asking the question repeatedly

and receives the same answer every time.

"One morning, the young man declares, 'I am going to the mountains. I want to meditate and gain wisdom.'

"'Goodbye,' the master says.

"The young man keeps writing about the progress he is making. He always wants to know whether he is enlightened or not.

"The master throws the letters in the trash; he never reads them. Years pass and the letters become thinner and thinner. Then the master does not receive a letter for a long time. Now he wants to know what is happening with his student. He asks a traveler who is going that way to check on the student. When the man returns, the master asks, 'What did my student say?'

"'He said how does it matter?' the man replies.

"'Enlightened! He is finally enlightened.' The master was delighted."

* * *

While leaving the community room after a group on honesty,

Albert asks, "Christopher, do you have a few minutes?"

"Why?" I ask. "What do you want?"

"I need to talk to you."

"Okay, come with me." I lead him to my office.

I rest my laptop on my desk. While plugging it in, I ask, "Albert what do you want to talk about?"

"I want you to know that I fucked my sister twice."

I am caught off guard. The words came so sudden and fast that I had no time to reflect. I don't know how to react. I look at him, hoping to get some clue about his emotions. There is no emotion on his face. For a moment, I think I have every reason and right to hate this guy. Then I say to myself, I should not think that way;

my job is to help him change his addictive behavior and guide him in his recovery process and not to hate him.

I pick the conversation up again. "How old were you when it happened?"

"Fourteen." He pauses. "I was fourteen, and she was twelve. I was watching TV in my parent's bedroom. They were gone, and my sister came in, and I fucked her. I thought it was okay for me to do it because the other guy was doing it anyway."

"But she was your baby sister!"

"She was all right with it," he replies.

"Did she talk to your parents about it?"

"She did." He nods. "But only a few years ago."

"What did your parents say?"

"My mother told me she knew everything that had happened, and my father did not say anything."

"Did your sister speak to you about it?" I look at him intently.

"No." He meets my eyes. "I told her once that I wanted to talk to her about it, but she told me she had a lot of stuff going on in her life, and she couldn't handle anything else right then."

"How is your relationship with your sister now?"

"It's fair. She sent me here and told me to talk about my issues openly. She wants me to get help."

"Does she do drugs?"

"Yes, she does."

"Is she married?"

He shakes his head. "No, but she has a boyfriend. She hangs with bums. Lowlifes. She has low self-esteem and feels depressed all the time."

"Lunch is up!" Dawn shouts from down the hall. "Let's go."

Clients go to the cafeteria every day at about 12:15 in the afternoon to have their lunch and Dawn accompanies them.

"I need to go." He looks at me with no visible guilt on

his face.

I nod. "Yes, you do."

I am left with a million questions in my head. I wonder why he said he "fucked" his sister. Why didn't he say he molested her or something like that? He almost appeared proud of what he had done. I understand the circumstances he has been through in his childhood. I understand the contribution of his family to his addictive behavior. But today he is not under the influence of any mood-altering chemicals. He has good communication skills, he as no mental health problems, and he believes that he has a steady head on his shoulders.

I speak with Alana, and she cannot understand it, either. She says, "Well, at least he spoke about it." I agree with her; I get many patients who talk about how they were sexually abused in their childhood, but very few ever admit that they abused anyone. This is one of the few clients who has discussed his heinous act. I'm not going to hold it against him. However, I have asked him to see me the next morning. I am going to try to find out how he feels about the issue.

The next morning, Albert comes to my office, at 8:00 sharp.

After initial greetings, I ask, "Albert, do you think that you abused your sister?"

"No," he states flatly. "I thought it was all right. We both cosigned it. She walked in the room got in the bed, and I rolled over her. So much was going on in that house; I didn't feel anything wrong about it."

"Why did you say yesterday that you 'fucked' your sister? Why didn't you use a different expression?" I ask.

"Because that's what it was," he replies. "There was no foreplay or any feelings involved."

"But you appeared proud when you were talking about it!"

"I don't know about that. But you just have no idea the relief I felt after talking with you about it. I had to share it with someone, and I shared it with you for the first time."

"Have you ever been sexually abused?" I ask.

"No," he answers. "But I felt emotionally abused when I took my sister to my mother's boyfriend's apartment on her tenth birthday. I also felt funny when I accidentally saw my dad's hard penis hanging down to his knees when he was ready to make love to my mom. I felt inferior. I did everything possible to enlarge my penis."

"You do know that the size of the penis doesn't matter, don't you?" I shake my head at him.

"No, I don't know." He looks confused. "I feel it does matter."

"It doesn't," I tell him. "That's a myth."

"Then why are there so many advertisements about penis enlargement all over the place?"

"Because everyone wants to make money," I reply. "There are people like you who are suckers. What matters is the emotional relationship and how affectionately you make love to your partner."

"I think you might be right." He nods shyly. "I don't have a large penis, but my wife was happy."

"Did you ever have a monogamous relationship?"

"No," he chuckles. "Even when I was married, I cheated. Now I want to stop it. I want to live a spiritual life."

"When do you plan to start?"

"I already have. I am committed." He meets my eyes.

"Well, stay the course!"

"I will! By the way, what are we going to discuss in group today?"

"We will discuss your issues." I tell him just to see his reaction.

"No problem." He leaves with no visible sign of concern.

* * *

Albert thinks Cat is a beautiful creature. In fact, he thinks she looks like his second wife, but he doesn't know that she is really messed up and a nymphomaniac. He thinks that she is seductive as she subtly shows the inner part of her thigh through her miniskirt. While in group, she spreads her legs in such a way that others will not miss noticing what is underneath. I have asked her on several occasions to sit properly. She gathers herself together for a moment but resorts to her seductive ways the moment I turn my back to her. I am surprised that Albert doesn't try to hit on her. Once he did say, "Cat is a beautiful creature, she reminds me of my second wife. She turns me on."

Chapter 24
Cat is a Fuck Baby

She is sexually preoccupied and has difficulty controlling her sexual urges. She claims that her hormones keep jumping, and she needs to satisfy her sexual desires by any means possible. She just can't resist temptation. She doesn't know that most people have difficulty resisting temptation and that it is best resisted at the thought level. I explain that she must learn to control herself because her behavior could cause serious complications, and she needs to stop threatening to leave. She has been prostituting most of her life to support her drug habit. She says, "I became a prostitute, but I didn't contract any sexually transmitted disease. So I don't care what others say." She does not take the risks involved seriously.

I tell her, "You were lucky; time was on your side. But before it takes an ugly turn, let some sense prevail. Let the past be past. Move on with determination to live life more enthusiastically than ever. You have to learn to live a spiritual life. Stop focusing on immediate gratification."

"I know, that's been the problem my whole life," she says regretfully. "I always want what I want when I want it. I don't care about the consequences. I have a 'my way or the highway attitude.'" She takes a deep breath, then continues, "I grew up in a highly dysfunctional family. My mother was an addict, and I don't even know who my father is. My mother was tricking when she conceived me. They call me a 'fuck baby.' My mother had several boyfriends. She was physically abusive, and she had a boyfriend who was physically abusive to her as well as to me. I never had one day without physical pain. I had several boyfriends. I just didn't now how to stay in a relationship. That's not me. Sex is very intoxicating for me. Lack of sex triggers me; if I don't get enough sex, I use drugs. When I'm desperate for sex, I do anything to satisfy my sexual urges. My three children have three different fathers.

I was tricking. I don't even know who their fathers are." After a brief pause she says, "They are in DHS (Department of Human Services) custody for the last three years."

"So you really repeated your mother's history."

"Yeah, I sure did," she admits. "Whatever she was, she was my role model."

"Cat, you will have to continue with sex therapy after completing this program along with drug and alcohol IOP."

"Do you think I will be absolved from my sins?" she asks nexpectedly.

"I really don't believe in sin," I tell her.

"So you mean you aren't born out of sin?"

"I am born out of love and the sexual relationship between my parents," I reply.

"I'm Catholic," she says. "I was taught throughout my life that e are all sinners, born out of sin."

"Cat, that's your belief. I don't have to refute your belief. However, I don't have to believe what you believe."

"So you mean I didn't sin?"

"No, you didn't," I answer. "You either do wrong things or right things. For example, being an irresponsible mother, tricking, using drugs, stealing, and so on are simply wrong things to do. Being a responsible parent and loving yourself and others are right hings to do."

"How about heaven and hell?"

"It really doesn't matter to me whether there is heaven and hell or not. However, I believe that we live either in heaven or hell in the here and now, and not after death."

"But I believe," she says, "there is a hell and a heaven after death."

"No problem, Cat. You are entitled to your beliefs, but don't worry about heaven and hell right now. Just focus on your recovery; that is more important than anything else."

"I am learning to do one thing at a time," she says.

"That attitude will help you to achieve your goals without sweating too much," I tell her.

"But how about my lust? I have difficulty dealing with it," she dmits.

"If you are serious about your recovery and willing to exercise control over your sexual desires, you will be able to manage your lust effectively."

"But it's very difficult," she repeats.

"No two ways about it," I agree with her.

Suddenly she bursts into tears. I think to myself that she is sincere and needs guidance. If guided well in her recovery process, she has a good chance for success. I think she is willing to change, she is willing to move forward. She has shown an inclination to seek help. I always remember a very vital principle of helping. 'You should not help anyone more than they are willing to help themselves'. If you help someone more than that, you are helping parasites grow. But in this case the situation is different; she repents her past but as a difficult time letting it go. She doesn't know how to seek help, but she is willing to try. So in this case, walking an extra mile to help is worth trying.

A few days later, Cat blows into my office. She is furious. "I was oppressed as a child, and I won't tolerate it anymore."

"What happened?" I ask.

"Here I am working hard for my recovery, and people are draging me into more difficulties," she answers.

"What difficulties?"

"The tech says I'm not working on my issues!"

"Cat, do you think you are working on your issues?"

"Of course I am."

"Then what others think shouldn't matter."

"But the opinion of the staff does matter."

"Cat, I am telling you that only your opinion should matter, no one else's."

"But they are here to encourage us, aren't they?"

"They are here to do their jobs," I reply. "If they encourage and help you to stay in treatment it's a bonus, and if not, it shouldn't matter."

"I wish they were more professional. Sometimes I think they are more screwed up than us."

"Cat, you're overreacting. You expect them to behave the way you think is best, and it is causing you anxiety and stress. Is it worth it?"

"No," she replies.

"Then stop expecting people to behave the way you want them to behave. It's not always going to happen, and you will be anxious and stressed most of the time. Why do you need validation from others anyway?"

"I guess it makes me feel good."

"Cat, what's the earthly use of a good that depends on outside forces? Good feelings should come from within. They should be independent. No outside force should have control over your feelings."

"I wasn't appreciated when I was growing up," she continues, "and I guess that's the reason I seek appreciation from others."

"That's possible," I say. "However, you need to understand that if you are satisfied with whatever you do, you don't have to worry about other people's opinion. You have to value your own pinion."

"I have low self-esteem," she continues. "I have never valued my opinion in my entire life."

"I hope that you will grow and become wise," I state.

"Well," she admits, "I definitely need to grow."

"Cat, if you really want to grow, just be open-minded and willing to learn, and you will be surprised at the end results."

"I also need wisdom," she says.

"Wisdom comes with knowledge. So increase your knowledge, and the result will be greater wisdom." I smile at her.

"I owe you so much," she says.

"You owe me nothing," I tell her. "You are open and willing to change, so the credit goes to you."

She smiles. I hope she continues smiling all her life

Chapter 25

Brenda, Rhonda and Wanda—The Innocent Victims of Incest

Brenda is thirty-five, a sad-looking woman and a chronic re-lapser who is addicted to cocaine and heroin. Her parents are still in their active addiction and have no contact with her. Brenda's six-year-old daughter lives with her daughter's father. The sad thing is that Brenda doesn't even remember when she saw her last.

Brenda's grandfather started Brenda on drugs when she was nine with the intent to start a sexual relationship with her. He started molesting her the same year, and it went on until she turned fifteen. He used to pick her up on weekends and have sex with her. She didn't tell her parents about it because her father was never a major player in her life, and her mother was busy getting high. Her parents were living in their own world. One day, somehow she mustered the courage and told her teacher about it. That led to her grandfather's arrest and subsequent conviction for child molestation.

Brenda now finds it difficult to trust men. She started messing with girls and now claims that she is bisexual. She suffers from severe anxiety and manic depression. She's immensely lonely and feels stressed. She is medication-seeking and likes to be sedated. She is very impulsive and lacks patience. She doesn't like herself. She has a history of more than fifty suicide attempts. Her suicide attempts include cutting herself. She has many superficial marks on her forearms and other parts of her body. She doesn't feel there is any way out of her current mess. She doesn't think she is ever going to stop using drugs. To my question, "Why not?" she responds, "I can't answer your question."

She has anger issues. She is holding lots of resentment against her grandfather. She has difficulty letting the past go. Her childhood sexual abuse memories keep haunting her.

* * *

While in group I begin, "Most of us find it difficult to forgive and forget. There are some memories that bring nothing but pain and misery. Clinging to the past prevents us from growing and enjoying life on life's terms. The best way to get rid of resentment is to learn to forgive and let go. I know it's easier said than done, but we have to learn to live in the present."

Brenda interjects haltingly, "I was raped by my grandfather when I was nine. My sexual abuse memories keep haunting me. Would you still ask me to forgive and forget the incident?"

"Brenda, you have experienced hurt in your life." I continue. "Although the pain that resulted is old, you keep recalling those details and feeling the emotional pain of those memories as if it is happening today. You do it because it has now turned into resentment. The only solution you have, is to understand the futility of holding onto it and let it go. Do you see any other solution?"

"Yes, I do."

"What is it?"

"If I can find out where he is. I'll kill him."

"You will end up in jail."

"No." She shakes her head. "I won't. I'll kill myself, too. I have tried killing myself more than fifty times."

"Christopher, she is not going to listen. Ignore her," Michael suggests, staring at Brenda.

"The only thing she does in group is sleep," Rhonda joins the discussion. "She never does anything else."

"I agree with Rhonda," Wanda says, looking at Brenda.

"Wanda," I say, "don't worry about her; just stay focused on your own recovery."

"I am focused on my own recovery," Wanda says. "I come first, and I know recovery is a selfish discipline."

One thing I have noticed about Wanda is that she is changing. She stays calm and doesn't lose her cool. She listens, and tries to prove her point assertively and does not give others the power to take her out of her square; I feel it is a great achievement in itself. Think about it.

In the initial phase of her recovery, she would immediately start crying and resort to rationalizing her behavior. I know sometimes crying can be the best outlet for stuffed up emotions. But in her case, it's different. She still does cry a great deal. She cries instantly as if there is a spigot behind her eyes. Nevertheless, now she is open to feedback and welcomes suggestions. I remember asking her one time if she used glycerin to make the tears flow, and she had given me a confused look and said, "Why do you ask, Christopher?"

"Well, because," I had said, smiling, "you cry instantly, just like actresses do." She had beamed with pride.

"Let us get back to our discussion," I say. "Any one wants to share anything."

"I was abandoned by my mother when I was a child," Wanda volunteers. "How can I forget that and also forgive her for such a shameful act?"

"Wanda," I reply, "I understand your anger, how you feel, and how it makes you vulnerable. The pain that resulted from that incident was real. But if you don't let those memories go, how can you help yourself ? You can't enjoy the present if you are dwelling on the painful memories of the past."

"It's not easy." She is in tears now. "I was thirteen when my mother abandoned me. My aunt was there for me, but she couldn't take my mother's place. I understand the importance of 'letting go,' but it's hard."

"I'm not saying it's easy," I reassure her, "but it is necessary because it will help you to eliminate your emotional suffering. If you don't mind, may I ask your age?"

She hesitates. "I'm forty-one. Why?"

"You were abandoned by your mother when you were barely thirteen," I say, "and now you are forty-one, so that incident took place twenty-eight years ago, and you are still suffering. You have a choice to suffer or not to suffer. Now do you see the futility in clinging to those memories?"

Michael speaks up. "But it wasn't her fault."

"Of course it wasn't her fault, Michael, but that is immaterial today. What counts today is whether she is going to bury those painful memories forever and move on with her life or not. She has a choice to be bitter or better."

"Christopher, you're saying I have a choice, but I didn't have a choice then," she says.

"Wanda, let me try to make it easier for you to understand. I gree, you didn't have a choice then, but today you do. Either you let those memories go by understanding their futility, or you cling to them and choose to suffer. It is entirely your decision now. Do you understand?" I ask.

She nods.

"I was raped," Brenda continues sobbing, "for five long years when I was child. It isn't like I was just beaten or something like that, it was rape. I can't forgive and forget that!"

"I was raped by my older brother," Wanda volunteers, "when I was growing up. I held a grudge against him until I came here. I wasn't willing to speak about my sexual abuse issue; I just held it in. I was angry; I was frustrated, it wasn't doing me any good. Now, since I don't dwell on it, I'm not in pain anymore. In fact, Christopher told me it was not my fault. Whatever happened happened in the past, and I had no control over it. I realized he was telling me the right thing, and I came awake and decided to let it go, and move on with my life. I have no words to express the relief that I feel today. I forgave my brother, and now I have no burden of resentment."

"Well, you all know that I was also raped when I was a child," Rhonda says. "It happened on several occasions. I wasn't willing to forgive him, and it resulted in resentment and anger. It was very difficult for me to let go of my past painful memories. I was a victim of my own resentment. I was irrational and hurting myself unnecessarily. The day I decided to forget the past and remove those painful memories from the computer chip above my shoulders, it started healing the wound that I had aggravated by dwelling in the past. Forgiving him was essential for my own well-being. It had become an obstacle to my recovery process. Since I was holding onto the past, I wasn't making any progress. I was unable to think positively. I was always preoccupied with the thought of getting even. I was worn out spiritually and psychologically."

"Don't I have the right to be angry at the person who sexually molested me?" Brenda retorts.

"Brenda," I say, "it is normal to feel angry and resentful. I remember how you were shocked and offended when you heard the words 'forgive and forget.' There are times when I have felt justified being angry and resentful. But maintaining that anger and resentment causes more harm and pain, and I realized it was a waste of energy."

"It's easy for you to suggest forgive and forget," she says, defensively, "but you don't understand how difficult it is for me to do."

"Brenda," I say looking straight into her eyes, "you are harping on the same thing over and over. I know it's difficult, and it might seem impossible. Nevertheless, there is no other way! Can anyone here suggest a better way?"

"There is no better way," Wanda declares, "than forgiving and forgetting. I had very painful experiences and found it difficult to forgive my brother. I couldn't let go of my sexual abuse memories for a long time, but once I did, I gained a lot. I feel free, and I'm not depressed or resentful anymore. Holding onto those painful memories wasn't doing me any good. It seems impossible in the beginning, but eventually, we always gain from letting go."

"Wanda, how is your relationship with your brother who molested you?" Brenda asks cautiously. "Do you like him? Do you feel uncomfortable in his presence?"

"I don't like him, nor do I hate him," Wanda replies. "I have not forgotten the incident, but I have forgiven him. He will have to give an account of what he did to God. I believe in the law of deeds. You reap what you sow. But I don't have to worry about it now. Worrying about it is a waste of time and energy and is not in my best interest. I don't feel anything in his presence. When he visited me last Sunday, my father was very angry with him, but I was okay with him being here. He apologized for what he did to me. I remember Christopher telling us not to let others rule us emotionally. I no longer give anyone the power to make me feel good or bad. He says that people want monkeys so they can twist their tails and make them jump the way they wish."

"Wow, you have come a long way," Rhonda says admiringly.

"I sure have," Wanda agrees. "I wasn't willing to work on my issues. Now I have decided to grow. For instance, I have difficulty reading. But I have started reading material that Christopher gave us on sexual abuse, forgiving, and resentment. I don't want to be vengeful anymore. I don't see any sense in holding onto the past. I have never felt so good in my entire life. Before, I would say, 'what the fuck is so good about this morning ?' when greeted with good morning. I don't want to be that person anymore. Now I find every morning pleasant. I look forward to morning. I look forward to these groups." She pauses and tears fill her eyes. "I'm not crying because I am unhappy, I'm crying because I am happy. I was a real mess when I came here. Rhonda can tell you that."

"That's why I said that you have come a long way." Rhonda nods. "I didn't want to be friends with you in the beginning because you were so frighteningly aloof and lonely. I was afraid to talk to you. You didn't give a fuck about what anyone was saying. You were so self-centered."

"I know I wasn't willing to share," Wanda admits. "I thought I had reached the end of the road. But since I started talking about y sexual abuse, I don't feel shame or guilt anymore, and I don't feel the need for revenge."

"Holding a grudge against someone mentally handcuffs you to that person," I say. "You become a prisoner. You feel emotional pain. You struggle not to think about them, but you still do. Have any idea why?"

"Because we don't let it go," Michael responds.

"You are absolutely right," I affirm. "The person you resent occupies your mind and thoughts, and you think about them every time you get a chance."

"I don't want to forgive a person who caused me so much pain," Brenda insists.

"You are not doing him any favors by forgiving him," I state. "You forgive him because it is best for you!"

"Of course I'm doing him a favor if I forgive him."

"No, Brenda," I repeat, "you are doing yourself a favor, not him."

"How can you say that?"

"Because," I sigh, "if you forgive him and let go, you are no longer holding onto resentment, which is self-destructive. You stop torturing yourself emotionally. You experience serenity and peace of mind. You need to practice the vital principle of forgive and forget."

The next day, Brenda walks in my office and admits, "I have real difficulty letting go."

"You are not alone, Brenda," I say slowly. "Many people have difficulty letting go. It is strange that people find it so much easier to hold a grudge, to want revenge, to be resentful, than to forgive. We always want to seek justice. We need to understand that revenge is inferior to forgiveness. Forgiveness requires courage and application of mind. We achieve nothing by being vengeful. The moment we become aware, we will stop being vengeful.

"Let me illustrate with the help of this example: imagine that an old classmate of yours insulted you while you were in college. Twenty years later, you still experience the same hurt by vividly recalling the entire incident as if it happened yesterday. You see him accidentally at a party, and you feel very uncomfortable in his presence. You consider talking to him about it, but you don't now how to start. He hasn't noticed you yet. He is enjoying the party, and you are suffering. He is eating chicken wings, socializing, and dancing, and you are busy counting bones. How sad! He has no time to notice you, and you have no time to enjoy the party because you cannot let him out of your sight. At the end of he evening, he suddenly sees you, walks up, and tells you he is delighted to see you. You confront him about the incident twenty ears ago, and he doesn't remember it at all. In fact, he has not thought of you in years. So, you made yourself a prisoner of that memory. You were obsessed with him and that incident. You suddenly realize that you are a fool, a fool of the highest order, for holding onto that incident for twenty years. You immediately let it go and experience peace of mind and real freedom. Now do you understand the futility of clinging to past painful memories?"

"I'm still not sure."

I sigh. "Okay, listen. He lives thousands of miles away. He is focused on making his business successful and enjoying his life. He is unaware of your worries and resentment. You have allowed him to live in your mind and given him the power to control your emotions. You let him have a space in your head. Bluntly speaking, you became a victim of your own imagination."

"I get mad whenever I remember his face," she admits.

"Brenda, you don't realize how badly you are affected by your resentments. You are allowing someone else's behavior to affect your life even though you are powerless to change that person's behavior. Since just thinking of that person increases your stress level and makes you anxious, angry, and depressed, why not stop thinking about him? You must try to let it go. For some reason you are not fully ready; you still want to suffer."

"I need more time," she murmurs.

"Of course you do." I nod. "I am not expecting you to forgive him right now, but eventually, you will have to."

"That seems like a plan." She smiles.

Brenda comes to see me again after a few days.

"I've been thinking a lot recently," she begins.

"Wow! I didn't know you could think, too," I tease.

She laughs.

"What were you thinking about?" I ask.

"My sexual abuse. I was trying to find a better way than to forgive and forget, and I finally realized that you are right. The only way to deal with my resentment and my past painful memories is to do as you say."

"I can't believe you are saying this! Are you sure?" I stare at

"Yes, but now I need to know how to go about it."

"Brenda, the first step is willingness. However, just saying, 'I forgive you,' is not enough. You have to look deep down inside of you and decide whether you really want to forgive that person or not. You need to admit your powerlessness. You have to take an inventory of all the experiences in the past that still disturb you and you want to make peace with. In addition, you need to check the shortcomings that keep you from forgiving others and then make direct amends to them. In the end, you will have peace of mind."

She starts crying. "I want to wipe the slate clean and start over. I don't want to be miserable anymore. I don't want to hold resentments or grudges against anyone."

We sit silently for a while.

She takes a deep breath. "Since I made the decision to forgive and forget, I'm feeling much better. I feel more at peace, and my thoughts are not rushing like before. Thanks!" She leaves my ffice with a big smile.

Chapter 26
Michael's Dilemma

I am with Michael in my office. I say, "Michael, you express a strong desire to stay clean. So why do you continue using drugs?"

"My wife is an active addict," he says.

"Do you guys use drugs together?"

"Sometimes we do heroin together."

"Is she willing to seek help?"

"I'm not sure." He shrugs. "She is living with her father now."

"Have you spoken with her about it?"

"Yeah, she said, 'you go to rehab, and I will go to Dad's house.' My parents are unwilling to let her live with them; they don't do drugs so they don't understand us."

"How about her father?"

He takes a long time to answer. "He does heroin occasionally."

"Michael, do you think there is a possibility that they use drugs together?"

He replies wearily, "I suspect they do, but I am not sure."

"So, what do you think is the best solution for you?"

"I don't know what to do." He slumps down in his chair.

"Do you think your life has become unmanageable?"

"No doubt about it."

"Do you need help with your problem?"

"Yes."

"Do you think you are unable to help yourself ?"

"Yes."

"So, you admit that you are unable to help yourself and that you need help from others. How, then, can you deal with another person who has her own issues?"

"I don't have to deal with her issues." He shrugs carelessly. "She as to deal with them."

I shake my head. "You are not being realistic. You have a wife at home who is an active addict, and she doesn't even want help. You get high together, yet you claim you don't have to deal with her issues. That is like living in water and not tasting it. You need to check your thinking."

"Are you suggesting I should not live with her?" He stares at

"You told me that you relapsed because of your wife," I remind im.

"Yes, I did."

"Michael, you and your wife are getting high together. You are seeking help, but she isn't. If you live together while she is in her active addiction, your chances of staying clean are greatly diminished. Since you already have a chronic relapse problem, you certainly don't need a partner who is an active addict."

"But she is my wife," he protests. "What can I do?"

"Simply stop being with her."

"Are you suggesting I break up my marriage?" he asks.

"No, you don't need to break up your marriage. But you do need some separation from your wife. You need time for yourself.

After you've had a couple of months' recovery, if she is willing to seek help and you feel confident enough to handle the situation, then you can take it from there."

He looks at me. "You make it sound so simple, but it isn't."

"Michael, some people need to be put in the back seat of your life. You cannot have a healthy relationship with a person who is an active addict; it will lead you to destruction. For the time being, you need to cut your ties with your wife."

"I know what you are saying is right." He nods. "But it is not an easy decision to make."

"It will be difficult in the beginning," I agree, "but once you are used to living without her, the fear of separation that is bothering you now will go away."

"How ?" he asks, disbelief in his voice.

"Remember the power of time?" I ask.

"Yes, time is a great healer, and it heals everything." He smiles.

"So, just wait and be patient, and most of your worries will disappear," I assure him.

"All right." He sits up straighter. "Since it's you telling me this,

I will follow your advice."

"Michael, don't do something just because I or someone else says so. Learn to do things only when you understand them and want to do them. You have to live your life based on your own convictions."

"How do I do that?"

"Listen," I suggest. "Listen carefully to what others are saying.

Then listen to your own heart, and if your heart permits you to do t, then go ahead and do it. You will never regret it."

A few days later, Michael comes to see me again. "Christopher, I have decided to leave my wife alone for a few months and just stay focused on me. You are right; I need to learn to handle my issues first. If I don't have the ability to handle my problems, how can I handle someone else's?"

"Your relationship with your wife isn't healthy," I agree. "The two of you would have remained drug buddies. Some people need to be loved from a distance."

"Please don't get me wrong," he stammers. "This doesn't mean I'm not going to do what you are suggesting… but it seems ruthless."

"No," I reply. "You are just trying to help yourself first, and if you succeed, you will be in a better position to lend her a helping hand."

"Sometimes it's so confusing," he says. "Things that should be simple become so difficult."

"Michael, you have to search for and embrace the truth around you; then things will no longer be complicated."

"But, Christopher, the basic question is, do I really want to seek the truth?"

"You are asking yourself a very good question. However, if you want to grow, if you want peace of mind, and if you want to be happy, then you need to seek the truth. Only the truth leads to wisdom."

"What about the people around me?" He gestures broadly.

"You cannot change the people around you," I reply, "but you can change the people you are around."

"I'm referring to my parents," he clarifies. "I can't change them."

"Why do you want to change them?"

"My parents don't trust me anymore," he admits.

"Why not?"

"I have lied to them more than once."

"If you have lied to them in the past, how can you expect them to trust you?"

"They keep digging into my past."

"They were hurt and are not feeling confident about you. Just as you need time to get yourself together, they also need time to heal their emotional wounds."

"That makes sense. Want to know what my other problem is?"

"Sure."

"When ten people say ten different things, I get confused. I don't understand whose advice I should follow."

"If you listen without prejudice, everything will start to make sense to you," I tell him. "You will no longer be confused."

"I do need better listening skills."

"Michael, during our next session, I will tell you a beautiful story which explains what happens when you follow everybody's advice."

Several days later, he confides, "I am looking forward to this session. I want to hear the story you are going to tell me."

"An old man and his son lived together," I begin. "Their sole source of income was a donkey that they used to carry baggage for people. Time passed, and the man grew older and could no longer walk very well. On the way to the weekly market, he and his son decided to sell the donkey. Since it was a long journey, the son suggested that his father ride the donkey. The son led the donkey with his father riding. As they journeyed, curious onlookers started making nasty comments: 'What a selfish father, riding on the donkey and making his son walk, what a shame!'

"The father, deeply troubled after hearing these comments, decided to let his son ride. Now the boy was riding and the father as leading. They went a few miles further, and other curious passersby started commenting : 'What a shame! The boy is so selfish. He is riding, and that old man has to walk. Why don't both of them ride the donkey?'

"That sounded like a good idea, so they decided to ride together. They went a few miles more and then they heard, 'That s the height of selfishness, two guys together riding on the back of that poor old donkey! He is so tired, and he needs rest. These idiots should be whipped for cruelty to animals.'

"Father and son didn't know what to do. They were

252 INSANITY—BEYOND UNDERSTANDING

confused. They decided to tie the legs of the donkey, insert a pole between his legs, and carry him between them. They proceeded onward. Now people were laughing, 'Look at this stupidity; instead of riding the donkey, these idiots are carry-ing the donkey on their shoulders. They seem to be the fools of the highest order.' Father and son were going crazy at this point. They kept walking, hearing all these comments and becoming more and more frustrated. They lost their focus, tripped, and dropped the donkey in the river. Now they had no donkey, no money, and no assistance from anyone. They both died of starvation.

"Did that make any sense to you?" I ask.

"Yes, it did," he replies happily. "I have to follow my own convictions and my own heart, am I right?"

"Yes, you are absolutely right."

"What goals do you want me to work on for the next couple of days?" he asks on his way out the door.

"Practice your listening skills," I suggest.

Michael is doing very well in treatment. He is listening from his heart. He is trying his best to learn new coping skills, and his utlook towards life appears to be changing. Meanwhile, his mother and sister, along with her four-year-old son, attend a family session. The child appears very comfortable playing with Michael.

"He seems to be very good with children," I mention.

"My grandson loves playing with his uncle," his mother declares, "but Michael doesn't care. No one does drugs in our family. We work hard to make ends meet. He doesn't understand our hardship. We begged him not to be friends with a girl who was hooked on drugs. He didn't listen. His father stopped talking to him, and still he married that girl. We allowed them to stay with us, thinking that they would not use drugs around my grandson, but they started getting high in our house too. All her family members are druggies. She gets high with her own father. You see my daughter."

She looks at her abnormally large daughter lovingly and continues, "She has her own difficulties, but now she is living with us and helping us as much as she can. If Mike doesn't separate from his wife, he will never stay clean."

"Mom, please keep my wife out of this family session," he commands. "I am here for me and not for her. My therapist knows everything about it."

His sister speaks up: "Mike, Mom is right. If you want to stay clean, you really need to stay away from your wife."

"Why don't you guys leave her alone?" he says irritably. "She is with her father now. You didn't even let her stay for one day after I came here."

"She was getting high in my home. I have my grandchild at home, and you expect me to keep her there? No way," his mother snaps.

"Last time when you guys weren't together, you stayed clean for four months," his sister reminds him.

"Are you going to allow me to come back home?" Michael asks his mom.

"No. We want you to go to a recovery house and start staying clean. I will speak with your father, and then we might allow you to come home," his mother answers.

"Why can't I come now ?" he demands.

"Because we have lost trust in you," his mother tells him bluntly. "You behaved badly, and your father is very angry. You are his only son. He loves you to death, but he has had enough of you. Now you need to prove yourself by your actions."

"All right, I will go to a recovery house," he says with a resigned look. "Can you give me some money?"

"Yes." His mother hands him a few bills. "Your father gave me this money for you. Mike, please don't cause him any more heartache; he is getting old. He just wants you to stop using drugs."

"I am trying," he says, and we close the session.

Michael completes his treatment and goes to a recovery house. I hope he remembers to love his wife from a distance and maintains his recovery.

Chapter 27

Kevin Turns into a Beast

"This is Christopher, your therapist; Christopher, this is Kevin," Stanley introduces my new client.

"Hi, Kevin." I look at the disheveled man. His clothes are filthy and, apparently, he has not showered in months. He smells to high heaven!

On the way to Kevin's room, Stanley exclaims, "Man, you need to take a shower!"

"Yeah, I am kind of messed up." He smiles faintly.

"Kind of messed up? You are real messed up!" Stanley tells him.

We all share a good laugh.

"You know what we should do?" Stanley looks at me quizzically.

"What?"

"We should take his picture," he replies.

"Sounds good to me," I joke, looking at Kevin.

Kevin laughs in spite of himself and goes to his room for a shower.

Kevin starts attending group on a regular basis immediately. His ICM brings him some clothes, and Kevin gets a few more out of our own storage.

"Why did you decide to seek help this time?" I ask.

"I was using drugs day and night. My body couldn't take it anymore. I tried to stay clean on my own, but it didn't work. I want to fix my problem. I need a long-term program to fix it. I'm homeless. I have no place to live. I'm a paranoid schizophrenic, and that's why I have an ICM. I've been in many long-term programs, but nothing has worked. This time I'm committed and focused, and I know I need to complete this program successfully so my ICM can help me get housing."

"Well!" I say. "It seems like you have a solid agenda."

"Recovery comes first," he responds.

"Do you have any support systems?" I ask.

"I have support from my case manager," he replies. "Can I call him?"

"Sure, but only after we are done," I respond. "Do you have any family support?"

"No," he answers.

"What about your parents?"

"My parents are old," he replies.

"How was your relationship with them when you were growing up?"

"I basically grew up with my mother. My parents separated when I was six. My father used to pick me up for weekends. We did have good times together, but my father drank. I used to catch him drinking. He was a cop, and I was afraid of him. I have no relationship with him now. He is married to a white woman whose husband and son died in a crash. They weren't in love, but till they got married. Now he loves her. She has issues. She does not get along with my sister and her son. She hates them. She is a racist."

"If she was racist, I don't think that she would have married our father in the first place."

He nods. "You have a point."

"What is your drug of choice?"

"It used to be alcohol, but now it's cocaine."

"How long have you been using drugs?"

"I was thirteen when I first started," he says, "and now I

am forty, so you count."

"Twenty-seven years," I answer.

"Wow!" he exclaims. "I can't believe I have been using for that long."

"But you have."

"Yeah! Isn't that crazy?" He shakes his head.

"Kevin, what are you going to do while you are here?"

"I want to learn new tools that I can use when I get out; basically, I want to get my shit—sorry for my French—together."

"So you are committed and focused?"

"On the scale of one to ten, I'm at the top," he replies.

"Excellent! Now you can go ahead and make that call."

I hear him talking with his ICM, telling him how much he needs this program and how committed and focused he is. He remembers to tell his ICM that he has no cigarettes and that his SSI check is due. He requests that his money be brought to him as fast as possible. "My ICM wants to speak with you," he says thrusting the receiver into my hand.

"I'm Robert, Kevin's ICM. I would like to bring him some money and cigarettes tomorrow if it's all right with you."

"What time tomorrow ?" I ask.

"Around 10:00 in the morning," he answers.

"That's fine," I say. "I'll tell him you are coming tomorrow at 10:00."

"Man, I am so glad he's coming tomorrow with cigarettes," Kevin says excitedly.

"Kevin's ICM is here," the administrative assistant announces the following morning.

"Please ask him to have a seat, and inform Kevin of his arrival," I request.

"Aren't you going to be in the meeting ?" she asks.

"No," I reply. "I am on the phone with the insurance company. They can meet without me."

I finished my call sooner than expected and went to meet

Kevin's ICM, Robert.

We shake hands. "I'm glad you came. Kevin was desperate to see you."

"Not me, his cigarettes," Robert corrects me.

We chuckle.

"Come on down to my office," I say.

While we are on our way to my office, Dawn announces a smoke break.

"Can I go smoke?" Kevin is rushing.

"Sure, go ahead," I tell him.

"Kevin is showing some interest in his treatment," I inform Robert. "He attends group on a regular basis. He shares his thoughts and feelings as well."

"Kevin has a pattern of doing well for the first fifteen days or so, and then things start going downhill. He lacks patience, and he is very impulsive," Robert tells me. "He loses interest and leaves treatment."

Kevin appears to be in a very good mood for the next two days. His ICM is in touch with me by phone. I find these conversations helpful, as they provide some insight into Kevin's situation.

"I was never happy when I was using drugs; what I experienced as excitement," Kevin explains in group one morning.

Interestingly, most clients say the exact opposite: that they are only happy when using.

On another occasion, he shared, "I was loyal to nothing but drugs. I didn't do anything on time. I was a master of procrastination, but I was very punctual at smoking crack. It made me greedy and full of hatred for others. I could see the change in me. I wasn't happy seeing myself turn into a beast. I was arrested for corrupting a minor and felony charges. I was becoming a wicked person. I spent a few years in jail. The situation was getting worse. But I still wanted that excitement. I wasn't willing to stop using drugs, even hough I could see my downfall. I focused on immediate gratification. I knew the consequences of my action, and still, at any cost, I wanted those highs, that kick. I would trade anything for that one high. I was preoccupied. I wanted revenge. I had no clue what revenge I wanted, but I was furious all the time. I couldn't handle petty frustrations. I became vulnerable. I wanted sex all the time. Then I reached a stage where I wanted sex but couldn't perform. I would visit whores, pay them, and try to have sex with them. Sometimes I was successful, but there were times I couldn't perform, and in frustration, I would beat the shit out of them. I'm not like that. I'm basically a good person. I have a good heart."

"If you are a good person and have a good heart, why do you keep doing crazy things?" Faith jumps in.

"When I'm not doing drugs," he says, "I don't do things like that. It's my past. I don't want to be like that again. I'm tired of this shit, and I'm sick of being sick. I know there is no life out there when you are on drugs."

"I know things are pretty awful out on the street, especially when you are on drugs," I agree.

"Christopher, I have put myself in situations you can't even imagine," he says remorsefully. "Chasing drugs is not a joke; it is very dangerous. If I didn't pay the dealers their money, they would hunt for me like I was a wild animal. I was hiding from them. I was running from crack house to crack house. Have you ever been in a crack house?" I shake my head "no," so he continues, "Good. Don't ever go there. They are pretty awful places to live. You don't now who is sleeping next to you. Sometimes they put you in dangerous situations. Cops come at odd hours, wake you from a sound sleep, kick you in tender places, and demand money; and if you don't pay, they put you behind bars, and if you do pay, they let you go, but they never leave you alone. You become their permanent customer. They know how and where to get you. Man, you don't know how they scare the shit out of you.

I don't want to subject myself to that kind of torture again. I know what I have to do; I just have to say 'no' to that 'first' drug. I know I can't make up for lost time. But now I can start living my life right."

"You seem to be repenting your past," I observe.

"I don't like my past," he says. "I wish I could change my past."

"I don't think you can do that," I tell him. "However, getting a grip on your present situation is possible, and once you get a grip, you will be in a position to plan for the future."

"That's what I want to do. I want to take life one step at a time. I don't want to rush my recovery. Everything else can wait. Once I have myself together, everything will fall into place. I don't want to lie to myself and the world anymore. I'm tired of lying. I'm tired of living life dishonestly. I'm willing to work hard, and I'm ready to practice rigorous honesty to achieve my goals. I want y recovery no matter what." He sets his jaw in determination.

"Well," I say, "you sound very committed, and it appears you are willing to do whatever it takes to stay in a recovery process."

"I'm doing it for myself," he says. "It's a do or die situation for me. I want to practice tough love on myself."

"Let's take it one day at a time and see what happens," I suggest.

* * *

The next day when I greet Faith good morning, she retorts, "Who are you?"

"I am Christopher. I will be working with you as your therapist. We spoke yesterday."

"I have a short memory," she explains. "I forget things."

"No problem. Faith, I need to get some information from

you."

"Why?" She appears indifferent. "I don't feel like giving any information."

"Can we talk about something else, then?"

"I don't think I want to talk about anything," she says irritably.

"Faith, it is necessary for me to get some information about you today, because without it we cannot complete your review with your insurance company."

"Are you threatening me?" She gives me a harsh look.

"No, I am not," I reply.

"You better not," she huffs.

"What happened with Eboni?" I ask.

"I just refused to take my medication," she answers. "And I don't want them to draw my blood, either."

"How about the therapist you had earlier?" I ask.

"She's a bitch," she replies. "She didn't know what she was talking about. She was getting on my nerves. I was ready to roll out. Good, I have you now. Has anybody told you that you have beauiful eyes?"

"Well," I say, "now you don't have to think about rolling out because she is not working with you anymore. I am. I bet you want to be happy, don't you?"

She shakes her head. "No, I don't."

"What?"

Seeing my confusion, she laughs. "Oh, I was just kidding. Of course I want to be happy. I want to stop using drugs. I was using every drug. I started using when I was fifteen. I use crack cocaine, alcohol, and marijuana, but my drug of choice is crack cocaine. I use drugs three or four times a day."

"How many bags a day?" I ask.

"I don't count like that," she says.

"Approximately?"

"Eight to ten bags a day."

"How about alcohol and marijuana?"

"Every day. Now don't ask me how much," she warns.

"What is your living situation?"

"I'm homeless," she answers. "I will need some place to live after I'm discharged from here."

"Are you married?" I ask.

"Why? Are you going to marry me?" She smiles.

"Are you married?" I repeat.

"Nope. I didn't find anybody cute like you before."

"Do you have children?" I continue.

"I have four boys and four girls."

"Where are they living ?"

She shrugs. "Six of them have been adopted, and two of them live on their own."

"How old are they?"

"I'm tired!" she shouts. "You have lot of questions. I can't answer all of them. My youngest child is almost two. They don't allow me to see him."

"But you said earlier that he's been adopted," I remind her.

"No, he's in the custody of DHS," she says.

"How can you expect them to allow you to see your child when you are still in your active addiction?"

"He's my baby. He needs his mommy," she says.

I think of saying, "what do you care?" However, I don't say it.

"How about their father?" I ask.

"I don't know," she replies. "They all have different fathers. Every man I screwed was getting high."

"Are your parents still living ?"

"They are upstairs." She looks at the ceiling.

"In the psyche unit?" I ask.

"NO! They are dead!"

"With whom did you grow up?"

"I grew up with my mother."

"Did your parents do drugs?"

"I don't know," she says wearily.

"How was your relationship with your parents?"

"Fair with my mother. My father wasn't in my life," she says.

"Did your mother's death affect you?"

"I was on the street getting high," she answers. "I didn't even now she had died."

"Do you have any sexual abuse issues?"

"I was abused by my uncle," she admits.

"Do you have any mental health issues?"

"I'm told that I'm bipolar," she says, appearing unsure.

"Do you have a criminal history?"

"I don't want to talk about it." She crosses her arms.

"That's fine; anything else you want to share?"

"How long am I going to be here?"

"I don't know," I reply. "However, patients are typically here thirty to sixty days."

"My problems aren't going to resolve in sixty days. I need more time. Try to get me at least three months."

"Faith, just take things one day at a time."

* * *

A few days later, while in group, Kevin declares, "I don't want to be here."

"What's the matter?" I look at him.

"I'm ready," he answers. "I've been here fifteen days. I learned that I need to learn."

"He wants to leave because he's getting his check tomorrow," Peter says sarcastically.

"That's not true," Kevin says defensively. "I'm leaving because I am ready. I don't need to be here anymore."

"I've been there," Peter says, shaking his head. "I left treatment every time I received my check. I can tell you, that money does not last even a day. You need this program. I think you forgot that you were like when you first came here."

"I remember how he looked when he came in here," Mel chuckles.

"My check has nothing to do with my decision to leave," Kevin says calmly.

"Where will you go?" Peter asks.

Kevin shrugs. "I don't know."

"You have no place to live, and you are still leaving, just because you want to use. This disease is very slimy. It's the devil that's calling you. Don't leave, Kevin," Faith pleads.

"But I'm ready," he repeats.

"Kevin, who says you are ready?" I interject quietly.

"I do!" He thrusts his chin in the air.

"Yesterday you said that your recovery comes first and that you are not thinking of leaving this time because every time you leave treatment, you relapse. I can't force you to stay; no one can. I know you are going to do what you want to do. Whether you leave or stay doesn't matter to me. However, I will be glad if you stay in treatment. How can you forget how messed up you were when you got here?" I ask.

"You're right," Faith agrees. "He's going to do what he wants o do."

"Ah, he's leaving because he is getting his check," Mel adds. "Please don't waste your time on him."

"Kevin, think straight. Don't make a wrong decision," I entreat.

He gives in. "Okay, I will stay."

Everyone claps, including Kevin.

He comes to see me after group is over. "Can I call my ICM?"

I dial the number for him, because Robert has specifically requested that I not give Kevin his cell phone number.

After initial greetings, I say, "Robert, Kevin wants to talk to you. He was talking about leaving today."

"That's his pattern," he responds. "He's getting his check today."

"Please talk to him about it," I request.

"Sure," he says.

I put Kevin on the speakerphone.

"Are you coming today? I need my money," Kevin tells him.

"No. I can't come today. Are you planning to leave?"

"No," Kevin replies, "I won't leave. I know I need to be here, but I do need my money. Okay, thank you." He hangs up.

"Kevin, take it easy, hang in there, and you will be fine," I ssure him.

"Of course. I'm not leaving," he repeats.

"Just remember your last run," I remind him, "the pain and agony that you have gone through in the past, and all the other consequences that come after using drugs."

"Of course." He nods. "I can't subject myself to that same torture again. Where would I go? I have no place to live. I promise you I won't leave."

He stays one more night and leaves the following day while I am busy doing reviews with the insurance company. By the time I am available, he is gone. I call Robert.

"I saw him on the road trying to hitch a ride," Robert tells me.

"Do you have any idea where he is, where he might go?" I ask.

"No," he responds. "He must be on the street, probably getting high. That's his pattern."

I hang up, hoping that he will come awake one day and change is pattern.

Chapter 28
My Way or the Highway

During a staff meeting, I inform Scott, "My new client Sabina is refusing to attend group."

"Why?"

"She appears to be lazy and non-motivated," I reply.

"Try to motivate her to attend group."

"How ?"

"What do you mean, 'how'?" he asks impatiently.

"She doesn't come out of her room at all, and when Dawn tries to get her out of bed, she snaps at her."

"Just take it easy," he says. "At least try to complete her psycho-social assessment."

"All right."

Sabina eventually starts attending group on a regular basis and sharing her thoughts and feelings about the recovery process. Unfortunately, most of the time there is no consistency in what she ays.

"How long am I going to be here?" she asks during group one morning.

"I can't say for sure," I reply. "It can be anywhere from thirty to sixty days."

"I don't want to be here for more than thirty days," she asserts.

"If I remember correctly, didn't you request sixty days when you spoke with me last time?"

"I changed my mind," she says.

"Why?"

"Every question doesn't need an answer," she snaps.

"Oh! I see."

"I want my Certificate and medication when I leave," she states.

"She is not going anywhere," Mel predicts.

"Of course I am not leaving now," she responds. "I will leave when I complete the thirty days."

"Leave her alone," Peter says scornfully. "She is just seeking attention."

"I am not the person you guys think I am," she insists. "I don't have that 'my way or the highway' attitude."

"But no one is saying that; why are you feeling guilty?" Peter asks.

"Why would I feel guilty? Are you out of your mind?" she yells. "In fact, it's you who should be feeling guilty because you are putting on a false front."

"I'm not putting on a false front," Peter protests, holding his hands out.

"You're lying." She stares at him. "Didn't you say the other day that you are an expert at putting on a false front?"

"I did say that, but I was talking about my past behavior," he replies.

"Well," she says, "I think you are using that expertise now to get your way."

"You are full of shit!" he accuses.

"You are the one who is so full of shit," she retorts. "Don't you know you are not allowed to use that word?" She looks at me for intervention.

"I'm sorry," Peter mutters.

"Let's talk about something more important than leaving," I suggest. "We will handle Sabina's discharge when that day comes."

* * *

One early morning, Faith declares, "I need to be shifted to another room."

"Why?" I ask.

"Sabina is nasty," she replies. "She bitches all day and all night."

"What does she say?"

"She says I'm dirty," she replies, "and I don't keep the bathroom clean."

"Is that true?"

"I don't know," she answers sullenly. "Sometimes I might forget to flush."

"Sometimes?" I ask.

"I'm messed up," she says. "You can't expect me to be clean."

"Faith, you have been here over a week. You are not on the street any longer. You need to learn to be hygienic."

"I need a single room. I can't share a room with nasty people. Are you going to shift my room or not?"

"I don't make that decision. However, we don't have single rooms; whatever room you end up in, you'll still have to keep it neat and clean. Being hygienic is also a part of your recovery process," I tell her. "Have you ever tried to find out why you have difficulty getting along with others?"

"Because all of them are nasty," she responds.

"How can all of them be nasty? Faith, you need to check your attitude."

"There is nothing wrong with my attitude. It's them. They are screwed up."

"Do you know the story of the two travelers with different attitudes?" I ask.

"No," she replies.

"Do you want to hear it?"

"Okay," she says reluctantly.

"There were two travelers traveling around the world. They were looking to relocate. Both had different attitudes; one had a positive attitude and one a negative attitude. Mr. Positive short-listed many places where he could possibly settle down. Mr. Negative could not find one place to settle down because everyone he met was nasty in those villages.

"They both passed through a village near the bottom of a hill. Mr. Positive liked the location and the villagers very much, but Mr. Negative disliked the location as well as the villagers. They decided to check a village located at the top of the hill. They saw a man grazing his cattle. Mr. Negative approached him and said, 'I am a traveler looking for a place to relocate myself. I am looking for a beautiful location and people with the right attitude. I have traveled long distances but have found neither a beautiful location nor people with the right attitude. I found some people who are very loud, others who just don't speak, some who walk with attitude, some who are unhygienic, and others who are too much into others' business. I just passed the village at the bottom of this hill, and I had the same experience as earlier. Since you belong here, can you tell me what kind of people live in the village at the top of that hill?'

"'Nasty people,' the man replied without a blink.

"Now it was Mr. Positive's turn. 'Sir,' he said, 'I am on the look-out for a place to relocate myself. I have traveled a long distance. I just passed a village at the bottom of this hill, and I liked the location; the people there have big hearts. However, the village at the top of the hill looks very attractive, and I think the view from the top will be beautiful. Do you have any idea what kind of people live there?'

"'People with big hearts live there,' the man replied.

"Mr. Positive went to live in the village at the top of the hill. He found a beautiful location and wonderful people as he expected. Mr. Negative never found a place or people that he could settle in with. He remained homeless his entire life and took to heavy drinking and drugging."

After listening to the story, Faith says, "I don't think you are helping me with my situation. I don't want to put up with that bitch."

"Faith, you are unnecessarily cursing Sabina. You need to stop blaming her."

"I am not blaming anyone," she snaps, "but that's the way it is. I don't want to relapse because of her nagging at me day and night. She has issues."

"Faith, stop taking her inventory and look at your own actions," I suggest. "It looks like you are turning a blind eye to your behavior."

"She is obsessed with cleanliness," she complains.

"Look at yourself," I tell her. "Look how dirty your clothes are. Your room smells; everyone is complaining."

"If it bothers them that much, then they can come and clean my room," she says.

"Faith, you are responsible for keeping your room clean. You need to change your thinking."

"What do you mean?" she demands.

"You sound very negative in attitude. Recovery calls for a positive attitude. If you continue practicing the same attitude, you are bound to relapse," I caution.

"Bullshit," she snaps. "I was clean for close to two years."

"Faith, the past clean time doesn't make any difference now. The truth is that you relapsed, and you are here to receive help. A person can be clean for years and still have a negative attitude. You need to be open-minded if you desire help."

"I want to go to my room and lie down," she says.

"No problem," I tell her, "but before you lie down, please clean your room and put the food that is in your room in the refrigerator."

"I'm tired," she yawns.

"You'll be allowed to rest, but you need to clean your room first."

"I'm not going to do it now," she says defiantly.

"You have to do it now, or else the cleaning lady will throw everything you have in the trash, and you will not like it."

"Whatever." She shrugs and leaves my office.

She goes back to her room and jumps in bed without cleaning her room. The next day, Dawn and the housekeeper put the food she had in the trash.

There is no apparent change in Faith's behavior. She is non-compliant with medication and disrespectful to staff. She finds it difficult to get along with other clients. Her room is a mess, and she is not allowed any food in it, which adds to her agitation. She holds everyone else responsible for her discomfort, and she is unwilling to admit the part she plays.

"I'm sick as a dog, and they won't leave me alone. I can't attend fucking group when I am so sick," she whines.

"Faith," I begin, "why are you noncompliant with your medication?"

"I have every right to refuse medication," she retorts.

"No doubt about it," I agree. "However, if you don't take your medications, you are bound to feel sick."

"I don't care," she says.

"This attitude is not conducive to your recovery," I tell her.

"With all these nasty people around, how do you expect me to recover?" she complains.

"Faith, it's not the people; it's your behavior that needs to change."

"Can you ask Dawn not to bother me and let me sleep?" she pleads.

"No," I reply. "You don't even get up for meals. Dawn is tired of bringing your food back to the unit. The only time you get up is for smoke breaks."

"They are paid to help us," she snaps.

"Are you paying them to bring your food to the unit?" I ask.

"They can't keep me hungry," she responds, shrugging.

"That's the problem," I tell her. "You don't do anything to help yourself, but you expect them to help you. I find it really ridiculous."

"They have jobs because I keep using drugs," she rationalizes.

"You don't have to keep using drugs for them to keep their jobs. You don't need to be so generous," I taunt.

"They need behavioral therapy training," she suggests snidely.

"Faith, you keep accusing them instead of taking responsibility for your own behavior. You are showing all the symptoms of relapse, not recovery."

She rationalizes again: "Just because I'm not being compliant with medication doesn't mean I'm going to relapse."

"Faith, you are minimizing. You are more than noncompliant; you are demanding, loud, argumentative, closed-minded, ignorant, stubborn, pompous, and self-centered!"

"You are being fucking rude!" she snaps.

"This is not about being nice," I state. "This is about your life. You have a choice between life and death. Decide now. Decide efore it's too late. If you relapse, you are definitely going to die."

"Do you think I fear death?" She stares at me. "Well, guess what? I don't. I fear nothing."

"You can't face the adversities of daily life, and you are talking about courage," I tell her.

"Others piss when they see death in front of their eyes," she answers.

"That's because they love life. Do you love life?" I ask.

"No," she replies.

"Faith, you need to understand that recovery is a process. Recovery doesn't happen in a day or two. It is a lifelong

process. You need to be committed, sincere, honest, willing to listen, realistic, responsible, open-minded, dedicated,
humble, and devoted, and you need to start loving yourself."

She sneers, "You think all these junkies here are dedicated?"

"No," I reply. "But they are trying."

"Sounds like crap to me," she scoffs.

"That's the problem; everything sounds like crap to you.
You need to work hard to change your attitude. Can you do
that?" I sk.

"No," she answers flatly.

"Faith, give it a try, and see what happens."

The next day early in the morning, Faith declares, "The
nurse is being nasty with me. I am leaving."

"What did she do?" I ask.

"I refused to take my medication, and she says if anything
happens to me, she is not responsible."

"So what's wrong with that? You are non-compliant, and
it will be your responsibility if anything goes wrong."

"I'm tired of attending groups," she says. "I don't want to
do it anymore. I'm leaving ; you are not going to hold me
hostage here."

"Where will you go?"

"I don't know," she replies.

"You have no place to live," I remind her. "You will end
up using again. Leaving here is suicidal for you. Why do you
want to chase your own death?"

"I might use, I might not," she says. "And everybody dies
eventually."

"That is true," I agree. "But it doesn't mean you have to
chase our own death and die prematurely."

"You are also going to die," she snaps.

"No one is immortal, Faith. Take it easy. You will feel more
comfortable as the day progresses."

"I have been here for a few days, and I have not had one

comfortable moment. So how can you say that I will be comfortable?" he demands.

"The use of drugs for a long period of time has messed up your mind and body. It will take some time to heal. You have to bear some pain, but eventually you will feel better."

"I doubt it," she responds. "I am tired!"

"Do you want to change your behavior?" I ask.

"I don't think it's possible." She shakes her head.

"Why not?"

"It sounds unrealistic to me."

"It is your learned behavior, right?" I ask.

"Yes," she answers.

"Are you willing to unlearn it?"

"I don't know," she says. "I'm not even sure what you are saying is possible."

"It's possible. Every learned behavior can be unlearned. The first step is willingness. If you are willing to unlearn your old behavior, then we can go ahead and discuss a further course of action."

"How long will it take?"

"There is no time frame for unlearning old behavior. It all depends on how rigorously you work on changing. You said it took over forty years to reach this stage; it might take equal, less, or more time to unlearn your old behaviors."

"I don't think I have time for that kind of stuff," she says.

"Faith, you had time to get high, so how come you don't have time to learn new behaviors?"

"I can't take care of my issues staying here," she insists.

"Do you really think you will be in a position to take care of your issues when you leave here?"

"Yes," she replies.

"You are going to get high the day you leave."

"I'm not even thinking of getting high." She avoids eye contact. "I'm done with drugs."

"Your history tells a different story," I remind her.

"That is my past," she rationalizes. "I'm no longer dwelling in the past. I want to move forward in life."

"That's the lingo you have learned in various treatment centers."

"Trust me," she says, "I am going to do the right things this ime. I am confident. I know I can do it on my own. I don't need help anymore."

"I seriously doubt it. Everything is messed up around you, you cannot manage your room, and now you are saying you can manage your life."

"I am a little uncomfortable here, but otherwise I am doing well," she responds.

"Faith, you are not doing well enough to take control of your life on your own. If you don't reconsider your decision, you will be committing a grave mistake. You will be right back where you started."

"I don't think so," she replies.

"Just take it a day at a time," I suggest. "Things will improve."

"Whatever," she responds. "I am leaving."

"Faith, leaving treatment and getting high is easy, but staying in treatment and learning to deal with life's issues is difficult. It calls for courage, hard work, perseverance, and a willingness to live life on life's terms."

"I don't want to hear all this crap again," she snaps, and the next thing I hear is the loud bang of the door behind her.

While in the program, she had a roof over her head, three meals a day, clinical and psychiatric help readily available. However, this luxury wasn't enough to keep her. She chose street life with all the uncertainty and danger. What craziness! Whenever I am faced with this kind of situation, my eyes start popping out of my head. It is beyond my understanding. My brain stops working.

* * *

Sabina is a forty year old, homeless woman. She has low self-esteem and poor self image. She lacks insight into her issues and has severe anger issues.

I approach Sabina to complete some paperwork, but she declines, stating that she is tired. "Can't you do it tomorrow?" she yells.

"No," I reply, "tomorrow is Saturday. I don't work the weekends here."

"I need to sleep," she whines.

"Although you have been attending group for the past few days, all you do is sleep or talk about leaving. You need to start working on your issues."

"If I sleep in group, you don't lose your money, do you?" She challenges.

"No," I reply, "we are paid through the insurance company. They spend a good amount of money for you to stay in the program, so please make good use of that money and your valuable time."

"I don't care," she retorts.

"Sabina, what drugs do you use?"

"Cocaine, marijuana, and alcohol."

"Does it affect your sexual desire in any way?"

"Why?" She pauses to think for a bit. "Initially, I wanted more sex. Now when I use cocaine, I don't want to be bothered."

"Do you have children?"

"Six," she volunteers. "They are nineteen, fifteen, fourteen, thirteen, twelve, and four. Two of them live with my pop-pop, two with my sister, one with DHS, and one is on his own."

"Why are they scattered like that?"

"I was doing drugs. My pop-pop and my sister got temporary custody of them." She hesitates. "I am not supposed to see them, but Pop-Pop lets me in. No one can stop me from going to Pop-Pop's."

"Do you have any medical issues?"

"I am HIV positive."

"Do any of your children have health problems?" I ask more gently.

"My fifteen and fourteen year old were born HIV positive," she answers emotionlessly.

Maybe because she has accepted the fact that they are HIV positive and she can't help it, or maybe because she herself has been living with it for the last sixteen years, she seems totally uncaring. I don't know what to say. When I hear about children suffering, I suffer with them and more so if their plight is due to the stupidity of their parents.

"Do they use drugs?"

"I am not sure."

"Sabina, things seem to be really complicated. You need to become strong. You need to stop using drugs. It doesn't do you any good. You need to learn to be a responsible mother."

"I am trying," she responds testily. "I am trying to see whether I can go to see them this coming Sunday."

"Do you think just seeing your children on Sunday will make you a responsible mother?"

"At least they will feel better." She flips her hands through her hair.

"I doubt it. No child likes to see his mother so depressed and lonely."

"But I have been depressed for so long."

"You have to get rid of your depression by being active. You have to involve yourself in activities that interest you. What do you like to do?"

"Drugs."

"Besides drugs?" I urge.

"Sleep."

"Anything more creative?"

"Sex." She smiles for the first time.

"Do you use protection?"

"Sometimes," she answers. "When I'm high, I get careless."

"Sabina, you are already diagnosed with a long-term virus. You need to be careful for your own sake as well as for the health of others. You need to use protection all the time."

"Most of the guys I have sex with are HIV positive already," she rationalizes.

"But it's still a risk to both of you."

"Who cares?"

"Sabina, I don't know who cares, but you better watch out. It's a crime. You must stop doing this. You are risking people's lives. They could sue you. Criminals don't avoid getting caught forever."

"I'm not a criminal!" she shouts.

"Yes, you are! By the way, I have to leave now; I'll see you on Monday. Be active and do something that will help you in your recovery process."

"Can I call my DHS worker?" She picks up the receiver before I can react, calls, speaks for a while, places the receiver back on the hook, and then walks out of my office.

* * *

Monday morning during group, Sabina declares, "I want to leave."

"Why?" I ask.

"I'm ready," she answers.

"You're kidding! Aren't you?"

"No," she says. "I am serious. I feel I am ready."

"How can you possibly say that? What did you do to be ready?

All you did was sleep for the last five or six days," I remind her.

"I don't want to be here," she says.

"Look at your situation," Peter jumps in. "You have no place to live, and you have no money."

"You don't need to tell me that," she snaps. "I know it. You're walking as if you were living in a palace before coming here. You're street dog. People who live in glass houses should not throw stones at others."

"You are so fucked up," Peter snaps. "I am trying to help you stay in the program. Now I don't care if you leave or you stay. It's your problem, you bitch!"

I intervene, "Peter, don't use inappropriate words. Leave her alone. I will deal with her issues later."

"He better stop cursing me, or I'll give him a black eye!" Sabina glares at Peter.

"Sabina, don't forget where you come from. You have a bench warrant out on you, and I don't think you can afford to go to jail," I warn her.

"I'm not leaving," she responds. "I was just sharing my feelings. Can't I share my feelings?"

I nod. "You sure can."

"She's lying," Peter interrupts.

"Peter, stop it!" I warn. "She knows what she's doing ; don't make her business yours. You did the same thing with Kevin."

He apologizes instantly.

"He can't help himself," Sabina snaps.

Mel interjects, "We are wasting time on her; if she wants to stay, she will, and if she wants to leave, she'll leave. I did the same hing nine months ago. Christopher told me not to leave; I left anyway. And now, as you see, here I am again."

Peter shakes his head for a minute, looks at me, and asks, "May I ask you something ?"

"Yes."

"When you were talking about positive mental attitude

the other day, you said a positive mental attitude will make us happy. But what if someone gets happiness only out of negativity?"

"Peter, don't beat around the bush. Are you talking about yourself ?" I maintain eye contact with him.

"Yes." He looks away and continues, "I feel happy when I see others suffering. Sometimes I secretly wish that someone would die; I enjoy imagining someone's house is burning down in front of my eyes. I enjoy seeing others in pain. I am like an arsonist."

"That is abnormal," I tell him.

He laughs strangely and mutters, "He says it's abnormal," and he laughs that strange laugh again.

"It's sadistic," I remark.

"So what would you call me?" he demands.

"A sadist!" I answer.

"No, you wouldn't!" He looks up.

"That's what a person who enjoys seeing others suffer is called," I insist.

"I only feel that way when I get high," he says. "I have been in jail most of my life. I have suffered my entire life, and I guess I enjoy seeing others suffer."

"The explanation is okay, but you would still be called a sadist," I reiterate.

"I don't want to be like that anymore," he tells us. "I don't wish anyone ill fate today. I want to change. That's why I'm here."

"Is that the only reason you are here?" I confront him.

"Yes. I want to stop using drugs," he answers.

"You're lying," I say.

"Why would I lie?"

"You tell me," I reply. "Why are you lying ?"

"I'm not lying," he insists. "You are the one who says I'm lying.

You have to explain it, not me."

"You are here because you wanted to take care of your bench warrants and your welfare card, isn't that right?" I gaze into his yes.

He smiles and then nods.

"At least you are being honest now." I return the smile.

"I like to be honest sometimes," he says, still smiling.

"Why not always?" I ask.

"Sometimes a person has to be dishonest," he answers.

"Why?"

"If I'm not dishonest," he says, "I'll get stuck. I'm on welfare, and I don't get enough money. I have to work under the table."

"That is cheating," I tell him.

"Who cares? We pay taxes, and they use that money for corrupt causes. They fight wars with our money. I say fuck it! I'm not going to work and pay taxes for them to use my money to kill women and children!"

"Peter, if you don't work, you will become useless and rusty."

"I will just work under the table."

"Okay, let's stop working," I joke at the end of the session.

* * *

After a few days, Sabina approaches me in the hallway. "My children are visiting me today."

"Today is not visitor's day," I remind her.

"I spoke with Stanley," she tells me. "He told me to talk to you."

"Did anyone give you permission?"

"No," she replies. "I am asking you for permission now. I am longing to see them."

"What time are they coming ?"

"I don't know," she replies.

"Call them up and find out."

She gets on the phone with her fifteen-year-old son.

"He says they will be here by noon," she relates.

"That's lunchtime," I remind her. "Tell them to come at one and not to be late, because I have to leave at two."

"Okay."

"How many of them are coming ?"

"Four."

I inform Scott, and he responds, "It's okay with me as long as you monitor their visit."

Later, during group, Sabina mentions, "I am so happy because my son is coming and bringing his brothers and sister with him. I m really looking forward to their visit. I can't wait to see them."

After group, Sabina goes to lunch and smokes a cigarette on her way back. At about 1:00 p.m., she comes to my office holding her stomach. "I am going to the ER. I have unbearable pain. If my hildren show up, tell them where I am."

I am about to leave for the day, and there is no sign of her children. Scott sticks his head in my office on his way down the hall.

"They're not going to show up," he predicts.

I feel relieved at the thought. "Who knows?" I respond. "They might pop up at any minute."

Just then, our receptionist buzzes me on the intercom: "Your visitors are here."

In walk four kids and a woman in her late thirties.

I greet them and request that they have a seat. Anna explains that she is their baby-sitter. Three boys and a girl! They are all bubbling and chirping with excitement. The youngest appears very comfortable in the lap of his elder brother. When I ask their names, they can't wait to tell me. They blurt out their names like peas popping out of a pod. Looking at them, no one could possibly have known that two of them were HIV positive. They look healthy physically and mentally, and they share a healthy relationship amongst themselves.

"Kids, I am so sorry, you won't be able to see your mom today. She had to go to the emergency room because she wasn't feeling well." Suddenly, the bubbling and chirping stop. I can see the disppointment on their faces. They didn't come to hear this. They just sit there and look at me.

"They are well-behaved kids," Anna says, smiling affectionately. She writes down the name and address of the hospital and says to the kids, "We will try to contact her there, okay?" They all nod. "We need to go now." She motions for them to get ready to leave.

I don't want them to leave, but there is no reason for them to stay any longer.

"When Sabina comes back, will you try to bring them again?"

I ask her.

"Of course!" she says.

"Good-bye. I enjoyed meeting all of you," I say.

"Bye!" they chorus, waving as they leave.

My mind is full of questions, many, many questions. What must they be thinking about their mother? How do they maintain their cheerfulness and composure? How do they maintain their health? Do they feel depressed? Do they miss their mother every moment? Are they angry with her? Do they believe in God? And if yes, are they angry with their God?

Two days later, Sabina calls the unit to inform us that she is discharged and on her way back. Hours pass, but there is no sign of her. Eboni calls the hospital and is told that she had been gone for several hours.

She leaves treatment on her own accord without any information. She had been talking of leaving from day one. She had no desire to stay in treatment. Some things are beyond my understanding. I keep thinking, how she could abandon her own children? I remember Sabina telling me once that if she contin-ued abusing drugs, her chronic health conditions would worsen and she could ie. Her children would become orphans. But that information and knowledge was not enough to keep her from using. She needs to be awakened.

Chapter 29
Peter Objects to Staff eating Crabs

Early in the morning, next to Peter's name on our communication board in the staff room I read, "Lost all his privileges for three days."

"Peter, what's the matter? What happened last night?" I ask.

"Nothing!" he snaps while settling down in a chair in my office.

"Then why is your name on the board?"

"They are prejudiced against me." He shrugs.

"But three different people have written reports about you in the log book!"

"They're ganging up on me."

"Why?"

"I threatened to write them up."

"Write them up for what?"

"For not doing their job," he answers. "They were eating crabs for five hours. They should be counseling. They shouldn't be sitting there and eating crabs for five hours."

"They don't do counseling," I tell him. "That's not their job."

"Then what is their job?" he demands.

"Their job is to take the clients to the cafeteria for meals," I answer, "and out to smoke. They monitor client activities, facilitate AA and NA meetings, get clients to group, help clients in need, and report back any problems to the director."

"But they also have to counsel us," he insists.

"No," I respond. "They are neither qualified nor trained as counselors. The therapists do the counseling."

"Then I don't want to be monitored by unqualified staff," he responds.

"Peter," I say, "don't even go there. That is not for you to decide."

"I'm done here," he says. "I need to leave this program."

"Peter, you have been talking about leaving since the day your legal issues were taken care of. In the past, you were motivating others to stay in treatment, but the moment your bench warrant got lifted, you changed drastically. It's unbelievable. You were saying exactly what we wanted to hear. So, you were playing a game?"

"Why don't you talk to the staff who sat and ate crabs for five ours?" he retorts.

"The truth is that you wanted them to give you some and they refused. Then you started threatening them, saying that you would report them for not doing their job. Isn't that true?"

"That is real crap!" he shouts. "I was just kidding."

"Then tell me the truth."

"Anne told me that it's her job to eat crabs and get paid. That pissed me off."

"Really!" I look into his eyes. "I was told you were making passes at her and she didn't respond."

"It seems like you don't want to help me either." He starts pacing my office. "You are taking their side. You are partial."

"Peter, for your information, I don't even know those techs. I rarely see them. They work evening shift, and I work days. I know you better than I know any of them. We have no problems between us, do we?"

"No."

"Then why would I be partial?"

"I don't know," he answers. "I don't want to talk to you any more. I fire you as my therapist."

I curb my natural urge to laugh. Instead I manage to say, "Why?"

"Because, you're no good. You are useless." He leaves my office abruptly.

When he leaves, I laugh whole-heartedly. I do not have to worry about being unprofessional or about offending him.

A few minutes later, he's back in my office holding a sheet of paper. "I want you to make a copy for me," he orders.

"No problem," I reply. "Leave it here; when I'm finished, I will make a copy and return it to you."

"When will you be finished?"

"I don't know. But don't worry, I'll make a copy and give it to you."

"No. I want it now!" He slaps my desk.

"That's not going to happen. You have to wait and stop slapping my desk." I warn him.

"Okay, okay." He removes his hand from the desk as if electrically shocked and continues, "When you are free, come and get his paper from me and make me a copy."

"I won't do that, either. If you want me to make a copy, just leave that paper in the tray, and I will make a copy for you after I m done here."

"Fuck it." He slams the door and storms out.

I am relieved. I look at my untidy desk and then think of sorting a pile of papers after I complete my notes, but within a few inutes he storms back into my office. "I want my Certificate of Completion for this program!"

"I can't do that."

"Why not?" he demands, clutching the arm of a chair.

"Because, you haven't completed the program."

"But I'm ready. I don't need to be here any longer."

"Peter, go relax for awhile and we'll talk some more when you are calmer."

"I don't need to calm down," he says, releasing his grip on the hair.

"Let me finish my paperwork," I tell him. "When I'm done, we'll talk."

"You're the last person I want to talk to," he retorts.

I think to myself, 'I will be glad if you don't talk to me'. "Fine," I respond.

"Do you want to read this?" He shoves the paper at me. I tentatively look at it. It is a complaint about two staff members eating crabs for five hours and not doing their jobs. He has also obtained few signatures from other clients.

"I want you to give it to your supervisor," he tells me.

"Okay."

From past experience I know that my supervisor will do nothng about it.

"I want you to give me a copy," he demands, "because I might have a lawsuit against this facility."

I think of telling him "Don't be a fool, you don't have a lawsuit just because they were eating crabs for five hours."

"I will get you a copy later," I tell him.

"Never mind. I will give it to the director myself." He snatches it out of my hand.

I look at him, amazed. "No problem."

"You are against me today."

You seem paranoid. I don't have anything against you. One thing I know is that you need help and I will be glad to help you if you will be receptive to my help. "That's your opinion," I tell him calmly.

"I don't want to attend your group."

"If that's in your best interest, fine with me."

"Your group sucks," he continues.

There are many suckers who attend my group anyway.

"Possibly." I continue my paperwork.

He storms out of my office chanting, "Your group sucks,

your group sucks, it really does."

He is funny and entertains me nonstop. I think he is harmless as long as I don't react to his negativity. However, I don't want to rub him the wrong way.

We discuss Peter in our morning staff meeting. Scott asks, "Is it okay with you if we discharge him on Friday?"

"I guess it would be all right," I respond.

"He's poisoning the whole community," Scott continues.

I nod. "That's true!"

"Did you read the complaint he wrote against the weekend staff?" Scott shuffles through his papers.

"I did. I told him it's not his job."

"He's totally ridiculous." Scott shakes his head.

"Well, I believe he really needs to work seriously on his issues."

"It's not going to happen."

"It's a shame." I shake my head.

Scott instructs Stanley to arrange for Peter's discharge and aftercare placement and then asks, "Where is he going to live?"

"He wants to go to a shelter," I answer.

"Have you spoken with him about housing?"

"Many times. He doesn't want a recovery house because he doesn't want to spend any money."

"Okay, then that's the plan. You may have a tough group today," he warns.

"I hope not," I say.

I am in my office with Peter. I request him to have a seat; he declines my request.

"I need to talk to you," I begin.

"About what? What did I do this time?" he demands.

"Nothing," I reply. "I want to discuss your discharge date with you."

"I'm getting discharged?" His eyes sparkle. "When?"

"This coming Friday."

"Now things are moving! I am so glad that I will be leaving soon. Can I leave tomorrow ?"

I wonder what are you going to do after leaving here. Just go and get high? What have you done different so far besides using drugs? "What's the big hurry?"

"I feel like I am in prison here," he replies.

You are a prisoner of your own thoughts. You are a slave to drugs. This place is much better than your current slavery. "It's only a few more days."

"I guess it's fine with me." He smiles.

I smile back at him.

He happily bounces out the door.

Chapter 30

Brian's Unknown Paradise

During the staff meeting, Scott asks nonchalantly, "Do you mind if I transfer Brian to your group?"

"No problem."

"He will have to sign a Behavioral Contract for threatening Eboni, the doctor, Alana, and other clients," he adds.

As if he cares. Signing a Behavioral Contract won't make any difference. He will continue doing what he intends to do. "Okay," I respond.

"He needs to go," Stanley states flatly. *You are wasting your time Buddy. It's not going to happen. You are a bad businessman. The census is down. We need clients in order to run the business. You know it, don't you?*

"Yes, he needs to leave; he doesn't need to be here anymore," Alana agrees.

I think to myself no one cares about what you think.

"Christopher, do you have a problem working with him?" Scott looks at me.

Do I have an option? I know that you already have made up your mind. I have been working with you for years now. "No," I reply.

"I am afraid of him. He threatened to strangle me." Alana shudders.

Some people will be happy if that happens. Don't you know how any people don't like you here?

"Oh, good grief. He's just a barking dog. He's not going to do anything. You worry too much." Scott slaps his desk.

You say all this because you don't have to deal with him directly.

"I don't believe that," she says. "He appears very dangerous to me."

"Actually, I agree with her," Stanley supports her. *I am surprised. This must be the first time they are together over something.*

"We don't need to be so lenient with him; he really does need to be discharged."

"C'mon guys, he's full of smoke; there's no fire in him," Scott says scornfully. "He's a sick puppy. He just needs help."

Come on, now; you really don't care whether he receives help or not.

"He's threatening other clients, too," Alana adds.

"They could be picking on him," Scott justifies.

"I don't understand why you want to keep him here! He is aggressive, belligerent, and threatening. Everyone on the unit is afraid of him. We can't control him. I know the census is down, but we don't need an incident. Listen to me; he has to go," Stanley insists.

"Christopher, are you all right working with him?" Scott repeats, rolling his eyes.

"No problem," I reply.

"That's it, no more discussion!" Scott decides. "He needs help.

If he does anything crazy again, he's out!" He turns to Stanley.

"Stanley, inform the insurance company about Brian's behavior and our position. Christopher, you talk to him immediately after this meeting, and make it clear that if he continues his threats, he will have to leave."

You could have said that in the first place instead of indulging in a futile discussion. It would have saved us lots of time and we would have got some work done. "I will," I respond.

On my way back from Scott's office, I knock on Brian's door. "Brian, I need to see you, please come to my office."

He follows me to my office. "Sure, Christopher. What's up?"

"I will be your therapist as of today. We need to talk things over before we start working together."

"I'm glad that you are my therapist now." He relaxes his head on a wall behind his chair.

"I shall be happy to work with you." I smile. *But please don't be a pain in the ass.*

"I need help," he admits. "I have a serious anger problem."

I know. I have heard and seen your outbursts multiple times. You are good at it. "Brian, how old are you?"

"Fifty-three. I have been using drugs for forty years."

Great! You should be honored with an award for it. "What is your drug of choice?"

"Cocaine."

"Do you intend to complete this program?"

"Absolutely. I have no place to live."

So you are here just because you are homeless? You are misusing the system. "In that case, you need to follow the rules and regulations of this program."

"I hear you," he says, looking away from me.

"Brian, you have to stop threatening the staff and clients."

"She was a crybaby," he mutters.

I am confused. I don't know what he is talking about. "Who?"

"Alana, my therapist. She has issues. She needs counseling."

"Brian, we are here to talk about you and your behavior. She will no longer be working with you, so leave her alone."

"Okay, I won't talk about her."

"You need to sign a Contract."

"What contract?" he demands to know.

"It's called a Behavioral Contract, restricting your behavior in general and your threats to others in particular. If you breach the terms of the Contract, you will be discharged immediately. I will have it prepared and show it to you. Then you will have to sign it."

"No problem," he says. "I'm not going to threaten anyone."

"Okay," I say. "I will see you in an hour."

When he comes back, he asks, "Are you ready with the Contract?"

"Here it is." I hand it to him. He reads it carefully and signs.

"Brian, if you have any problems with anyone, don't say anything to them. Please come and talk to me. We will handle it together."

"No problem. I'm not going to cause any problems. I'll keep to myself. I'll continue praying."

"Do you believe in a higher power?" I ask.

"Allah," he responds. "Christopher, are you Muslim?"

"Why?"

"I thought you were a Muslim." He shrugs.

"Why?"

"I don't know," he replies. "Maybe because you are so cool."

"I don't think coolness has anything to do with religious beliefs."

"You are wrong," he responds. "Islam promotes peace; we are peace-loving people."

You must be kidding. "Brian, every religion promotes peace, but in reality, it doesn't always happen."

"That's because the followers of other religions don't really want peace in the world," he says.

"Let's not bring religion into therapy. It's a separate topic, and I am not an expert at it. It will be better if we limit our talk to therapy." *If possible, I always would avoid talking about religion, God, politics, and sports to avoid controversies.*

"So, what therapy are you going to give me?" he asks.

"We will talk about your drug use and its impact on your

health, spirituality, finances, family, and social life, and we'll discuss how your life will change if you stop using."

"How would it change my life if I stop using drugs?" he nsorts.

You might start brushing your teeth, taking a shower, wearing washed clothes, and you might stop stinking. On top of it, you will be cleaned and sober. What else do you need? "You will have clarity in your thinking," I explain, "and you will be able to handle your ssues more effectively."

"I don't think that will ever happen."

"Take life one day at a time," I suggest, "and see what happens next."

"That's what I'm doing now," he responds quickly.

"If that's the case, continue doing it, and everything will line up."

"Things never line up neatly for me," he says sadly. "There were times I was clean, but still everything was messed up."

"What was the longest clean time you ever had?" I ask.

"I was in jail for years, and I stayed clean," he replies.

"Did you have clean time besides jail?"

"Yes, actually, I did," he answers. "I was in Alabama, and I was in a relationship. I fathered two kids there. Everything was going smooth until someone crossed me and I relapsed."

"Do you have any contact with your kids in Alabama?"

"No," he says. "I don't know where they are."

You fool, if you don't know the whereabouts of your children, then why did you have them in the first place? "Do you have any ther kids?"

"I do, but I don't want to talk about them."

"No problem," I say.

"I want to stay clean. I'm not crazy, but sometimes people rub me the wrong way and I just snap."

"Brian, we will work on your issues. You will be fine. I'm conducting my morning group in the community room; I'll see you here in a few minutes."

"Sure." He pauses. "Can I shake your hand?"

I extend my hand and notice that he has abnormally long fingers. His hand is chilling cold even though it's a hot day.

Later in group, he observes, "Christopher, it looks like you are only interested in a few clients."

"Why do you say that?" I ask.

"Because only two or three of them are sharing."

"Brian, you are free to participate, but I can't force you to do so"

"What the hell is he talking about?" Jill glares at Brian. "He was sleeping, and now he suddenly wakes up and is spouting nonsense."

"I wasn't sleeping," Brian protests.

"You are so full of shit! You were snoring," she insists.

"It's the meds that I take," he says. "They make me tired."

"Whatever," she says. "We had the best group. Christopher shouldn't have accepted you into our group. We never had any problems before."

"I don't cause problems," he responds.

"You were a nuisance in the other group," she tells him, "and now you are a nuisance here. I'm going to speak to the director.

We don't want you in our group."

"Jill, he will be fine. He needs a little more time to adjust," I say calmly. "He is not saying or doing anything that is caus- ing us any problems."

"Nobody wants him here, except you," Peter interjects.

"He can be our teacher," I state.

"Him, a teacher?" Jill snorts.

"Yes, a teacher," I repeat.

"He has been a total nuisance throughout his stay here! He doesn't need to be here," Peter says.

Peter, you are no better. "I agree that he has a problem

getting along with others," I concede, "and he has been a source of disruption in the community. However, you can use his negativity to learn to deal with it, without causing stress or tension for yourself and others. Moreover, if you are ineffective in dealing with him, it will reveal your weaknesses. In that way, he can be your teacher.

Does that make sense to you?"

Dexter, a new client, speaks up: "It does. We always want to find shortcuts; removing him from the group doesn't seem to be a solution. It's like using drugs to deal with small issues. The real problem remains unaddressed. We feel better for short periods of time, but once the influence of the drugs is gone, we are back to square one, maybe worse."

"Fine, we'll leave him alone," Jill mutters.

"So, are you saying that we can use him as a guinea pig ?" Peter asks.

"We're not doing any experiments here, are we?" I look at him.

"I don't know," he replies. "So, you must be using my negativity too, aren't you?"

I nod. "Yes, I do."

"Didn't I tell you the other day that you were keeping me for experimentation?" Peter's eyes sparkle.

"So?" I continue looking at him.

"I knew it! I knew it!" he chants.

"Peter, you seem to be out of your mind. Your attitude is so negative that you always entertain negative thoughts and nothing else."

"I'm smart." He smiles. "I know how you people work. No one can fool me."

I ignore him and I turn to Brian. "Brian, do you want to share anything ?"

"I want to change my lifestyle," he responds. "But how can I do it when so many grown-up babies are crying all around me?"

"Look who is calling us babies!" Fatima objects. "Don't forget that you are a king baby."

"He sure is." Jill nods.

"Christopher, what is rage?" Brian asks unexpectedly.

"Rage is anger out of control. It takes over our whole being," I answer.

"That is what I am feeling now." He clenches his jaw.

"Why?" I ask.

"This is not about love," he answers. "This is about my life. They are making it difficult for me, moment by moment. They are secretly plotting against me."

"Who is plotting against you?" Jill demands.

"Everyone, including you." He glares at her.

She returns his glare. "We have better things to do, thank you very much."

"Jill, will you please keep quiet? Let him speak!" I reprimand

"I am here. This is no mistake." He shakes his head awkwardly. "Allah doesn't make mistakes. This is no coincidence. I am his messenger. He is with me now, and I will take him with me everywhere I go. I am here only for one reason, and that is to spread love and peace. I believe in his supreme power; I have seen his paradise. It's beautiful, and it will remain beautiful. I will maintain his paradise. I am his angel."

Everyone is bewildered. They look at each other with wide yes.

"Thank you for sharing, Brian. Now, let's close our session with the serenity prayer," I suggest.

"I'm sorry," he responds, "but I can't say the serenity prayer. My faith doesn't permit me to say any other prayers."

"This is not a religious prayer, Brian," I tell him.

"Please, I can't," he pleads.

"No problem," I respond.

"Can I say one more thing before you start the serenity

prayer?"

"Of course, Brian."

"I have been bottling up my feelings for a long time, and it's causing me anger. Now I feel relieved. I am at peace. Thanks for allowing me to share. I never got a chance to share in my other group. I was asked to shut up every time I tried to share my feelings. They thought I was crazy," he blurts out in one breath, then starts sobbing.

"You are," Jill whispers; Brian does not hear her.

* * *

Jill and Fatima go to see Scott the minute group is over.

"Christopher," Scott tells me, "two of your clients came to me complaining about Brian."

"I know. I saw them running to your office immediately after group."

"It looks like we will have to discharge him administratively."

I respond, "He appears disoriented at times, but he will be fine."

"I can't afford to have any more clients leave treatment," he explains. "Two clients left because of him already, and three more are talking about leaving."

"Are you discharging him today?"

"No, maybe tomorrow."

The next day, Scott calls my name from his office as soon as he comes in. "Brian threatened a female client last night. He has to leave today!"

"Can I talk to him?" I patiently wait for his answer.

He takes a deep breath. "There is no point in talking to him.

He's not going to change. Now it's too late. You can tell him to pack his stuff. He's going to a shelter and will attend IOP. We have approval from his health insurance carrier."

Back in my office, I ask, "Brian, what's going on?"

"I have mental health issues. I need help."

"Why are you threatening others?"

"They are getting on my nerves! The girl that I got into an argument with last night is real nuts. She thinks she's smart, but she's not. She is a dumb ass. She doesn't know shit. She needs help."

"Brian, you signed a Behavioral Contract and agreed to abide by its terms and conditions, and still you threatened your peer. Why are you doing this? Don't you want to live in harmony?"

"I really don't know why I do all this. I think I want to be committed. Can you call 911 and commit me?"

"Whatever for?" I ask.

"I want to leave," he responds. "I want to get into another long-term, more structured program. This program isn't doing me any good."

"Brian, if you keep doing what you are doing, I don't think any program will help you. You need to stop being aggressive."

"I need peace of mind," he responds.

"How can you have peace of mind when you are constantly at war with yourself and others?"

He laughs. I have never seen him laugh. He is always sullen and wearing a killer's look.

"Why are you laughing ?" I ask.

"I am laughing because you said I am at war with myself and others as well. It's true." He laughs again. "I dream of paradise and create hell. I know there is so much paradox in my thinking and actions."

"Brian, you said you are here to change your lifestyle, so why don't you do something to change it?"

"I cry like a baby at night. I can't sleep. I'm afraid of the dark. I have hurt people. I have done things you can't even imagine. I have even harmed innocent people. I haven't told anyone; I'm fraid that people will hate me. However, I will talk to you one of these days. I need to get it off my chest. I have been bottling up my feelings inside for so long, and it is causing me anger. I repent my mistakes. I have lost hope. I don't think I can make it now."

"Brian, whatever mistakes you have made in the past, the worst mistake would be to give up in the middle of your present journey."

"What journey?" he scoffs. "A journey of destruction? I am destroying myself every moment!"

"Why don't you stop that destruction?"

"I'm not powerful enough to stop it."

"Of course you are powerful enough to stop it! You need to relieve in yourself and show some courage."

"Courage?" he repeats.

"Yes, the courage to face the challenges of everyday life."

"What is courage?" He looks at me quizzically.

"In spite of difficulties, you stand firm and move forward. In a nutshell, courage is the ability to face the challenges of everyday life without fear, with a hope to do better against all odds."

"I am tired of this program."

"What are your weaknesses, Brian?"

"I have many weaknesses. I don't know where to start. Let's see: fear, jealousy, hatred, anger, greed, revenge, sex, love, life, desire, loyalty, faith, hope, enthusiasm, and many more."

"Enthusiasm?" I ask.

"Sometimes I am overzealous or too enthusiastic, and it lands me in trouble."

I think of asking him about life, loyalty, faith, and hope, too, but I don't, for fear that he will give me some extraordinary answer beyond my comprehension.

"What are your plans to overcome your weaknesses?"

"I have limitations," he answers. "I can't overcome all my

weaknesses."

"What are your limitations?"

"I don't know."

"Brian, do you think you need to know your limitations?"

"I'm not that bright," he answers.

"Is that one of your limitations?" I ask. He looks at me, bewildered.

"People coerce me into situations I don't want to be in," he says.

"How do you cope with it?"

"I snap out." He shrugs.

"You need to assert yourself. Snapping out is not a solution."

"If I don't snap, nothing goes smooth for me, but when I do, then people get frustrated and leave me alone." He sighs. "Everyone responds negatively to me."

"How can you expect positive responses when everything you do is so negative? You have to learn to go with the flow. You have to learn to be friendly."

"People are so screwed up. I just can't be friends with them."

"Why can't you accept people for who they are?"

"I'm tired of people! I'm tired of this program! I'm tired of all our questions! I want to leave." He jumps up, agitated.

"Are you sure that's what you want to do?"

"Yes."

"Brian, you are free to do what you want. I was going to speak with Scott about helping you to stay here for a few more days."

"No." He shakes his head. "I don't want to stay here any longer.

I want to leave."

He collects his Certificate within a few minutes of our discussion and leaves to find paradise. I hope he finds it and tells his story to somebody, someday.

A few days later, Sam, our driver, casually mentions,

"Christopher, did you know that Brian killed three people in his backyard?"

"No," I reply.

"He told me that while I was driving him to see his doctor."

"Did he really say that?"

He nods. "Sure did."

"But he didn't have a backyard," Alana interjects.

"Must be his parents' backyard," Sam says.

"Did you believe him?" I ask.

"Yes. He was serious and didn't appear to be boasting."

"He didn't kill anybody." Alana shakes her head. "He's not a killer."

I think of mentioning that she was the one who thought he was so very dangerous and planning to strangle her. But I hold my ongue.

"He wanted to reveal his dark secret to me, and I always thought it was something to do with child molestation or murder, and that was one of the reasons I wanted him to stay in treatment. His using drugs could be harmful to society. Don't you remember that he was very abusive to his girl-friend's child?" I look at her.

"No, I don't," Alana answers.

"Well, I know. He told me about it, and you had written it in his psychosocial assessment," I tell her.

"Maybe, I don't remember." She shrugs.

Well, I say to myself, I hope he stays sober or is admitted to some mental health institution. He should not be on the streets. In my opinion, he has the potential to be very dangerous. He needs to be committed! Its useless talking about him now; he's already gone; let's hope for the best.

Chapter 31
Jill Contemplates Leaving but Peter is Gone

Jill is a fifty-eight year old homeless woman. She has been in the program for about a month. She started drinking in her mid-thirties and using cocaine in her early forties. She is the only client I know who drinks cocaine after mixing it with alcohol. She has a seizure disorder, and one morning she had a seizure in the hallway. I heard a client shouting, "Help, help!" and I ran out of my office to see her on the floor. It was a scary sight; white froth was coming out of her mouth. Stanley took control of the situation very quickly and asked the other clients to go to their respective rooms, which they did. I ran back to my office, and grabbed some tissue to wipe her mouth, but it kept coming out. Meanwhile, Stanley put on gloves and wiped her face thoroughly. Her seizure stopped and then she had another one, and then, a third. The paramedics arrived, took charge of the situation, and took her to the hospital. She was dischharged from the hospital three days later. She thanked all of s for helping her.

Two days after her return from the hospital, while in my office, she states, "I want to leave."

"Why?" I ask.

"There is a lot of negativity going on here. I can't take it anymore. I had a seizure because of that negativity. I don't want to die."

"Jill, you didn't have seizures because of negativity around you. You have a seizure disorder."

"I know that," she says, "but this episode was a result of the stress that I am going through here."

"When did you last have a seizure?"

"A month ago."

"You weren't here then, were you?"

"No," she admits, looking down.

"But you still had a seizure."

She becomes defensive: "What are you trying to say?"

"That you can be anywhere and still have seizures," I explain.

"But this place is a mess," she insists.

"But it is much safer than being homeless. Jill, if you had been in the street when your seizure started, who knows what would have happened?"

"I don't want to die." She turns her face away.

"You have more chances of dying when you are on the street."

"So, what do you want me to do?"

"Stick and stay."

"But some of the staff here are nasty," she vents.

"Jill, you received immediate and adequate help from the staff when you had the seizures. Stanley kept your head on his lap until he had a pillow to support you. He constantly wiped your face, and now you are sitting here and complaining about the staff."

"Yeah." She takes a deep breath, looks down and then continues, "I was told about it."

"Don't focus on their 'nastiness' Jill. Keep in mind that you have a problem, and that you need help."

"They mistreat people."

"Who did they mistreat?"

"Peter," she answers, without a blink. "You remember the day they were eating crabs?"

"Yes, I do."

"Well, they shouldn't be eating crabs for five hours," she says.

"Jill, that's in the past. You don't need to get into it now. However, you do need to keep away from negative influences. If you don't you might harm your recovery."

"All right, I'll stay away from negativity," she says and we end our session.

* * *

Early morning, Scott calls me into his office, asking, "Can we move Peter out today?"

"Why?" I ask.

"He threatened a female client, and she is scared of him."

"Who?"

"Nikkie."

"Nikkie could be lying. I really hope we are not making the wrong decision."

"We're not," he says confidently.

I give up. "Well, it's okay with me. He needs to be here longer; but he doesn't want to stay, and he's causing problems. It's a shame, really, because he is a natural leader; but, unfortunately, he is using his leadership skills negatively and for the wrong reasons."

"Yeah, we can't help it," Scott agrees. "He has to go. We'll discuss it more in our morning meeting."

During the meeting, I ask, "Scott, do you want me to speak with Peter?"

"No. Stanley can handle it. He'll pull him out of your group and ask him to pack up. How do you think he'll react?"

"It's what he wants." I shrug. "He will welcome it."

Later in the staff room, I ask Stanley, "How did you handle his discharge?"

"Oh, it was real smooth," he replies. "He had no problem with

"I didn't think he would," I remark.

"I said 'Peter,'" he explains, "'I want to discuss your aftercare with you.' He said okay, and I asked if he wanted a shelter. He confirmed that he did, so I gave him the aftercare papers to sign.

After he signed, I told him to pack up. He was surprised and asked about Friday, but I told him there was a communication gap and that he had to sign in with the shelter today. He was fine with it, and he collected his medication, discharge papers, and personal belongings before leaving. He was quite cheerful."

In his excitement about leaving, he forgot to say goodbye to his peers, including Mel, his roommate, who had become Peter's friend by instigating him to act out and create scenes on several occasions. Mel is in his early forties. He has been in many rehab programs and in jail off and on for over ten years. He is intelligent and skill-ful about hiding his background. He is intimidating and wears a hard look. He stares right into your eyes and tears you down. He knows recovery very well and says what he thinks others want to hear. He understands the expectations of others and behaves accordingly. He has left treatment many times claiming, "I know what I have to do to stay clean." This time, he doesn't want to leave because he has a court date coming up and needs his certificate of completion. He constantly tells me that he is ready and wants me to present him with his certificate. When I remind him of his similar statements in the past, he answers, "I wasn't ready then, but this ime it's different. I have hit rock bottom. Something was missing last time. I didn't commit myself 100 percent to the program."

He wants to fool people, but in reality, he is fooling himself. He told me once he wants to be a drug and alcohol counselor. He is gifted and articulate, has enough information, and a sound

knowledge of addiction, but he lacks application of that knowledge to his daily life. He might become a counselor, but he will be a phony. He does not believe that actions speak louder than words. He is averse to setting an example by his behavior. He believes in 'do as I say, not as I do.' Whenever clients have a store run, he persuades Melvina, a gullible woman, to buy cigarettes and other stuff for him. He says pleasing things to her and she gets carried away with it and spends money on him without thinking. He knows how to use her and she fails to see it.

Chapter 32

The Height of Impatience

"I had a bad weekend because of unprofessional staff," Jill says upon entering my office early Monday morning.

"What did they do?" I ask.

"The wrap-up group was extended for fifteen minutes," she replies.

"So?" I look at her quizzically.

"It really upset me. It should have been over by 4:20, but she didn't stop till 4:35."

"A fifteen minute extension upset you?"

"I can't stand negativity," she replies. "My nose was bleeding."

"What!" I exclaim. "Your nose was bleeding ?"

"There weren't any community issues," she goes on. "There was a small issue between Melvina and her roommate, Fatima, and staff addressed that issue in the wrap up. I didn't like it. I had othing to do with it. I didn't want to be a part of it. She held us hostage for fifteen minutes. I was furious, and my nose started leeding. She always harps on issues that are unimportant to us.

She has problems."

"Jill, I think you have a serious problem."

"I don't have a problem," she snaps. "I don't want to be part of negativity."

"You dwell in negativity, so there is no question of you

being a part of someone else's."

"How do you mean?"

"You claim that you were held hostage for fifteen minutes and your nose started bleeding. It wasn't the result of the extra time; it was the result of your negative reaction to what happened."

"She is supposed to be a professional," Jill presses. "She should have spoken with them separately and resolved the issue amicably. There was no need to make their issue a community issue. She was wasting our time. We were waiting to smoke."

"Jill, many times in life we get stranded, and sometimes we are unable to move due to some kind of obstacle; however, we don't react negatively in those situations. We patiently wait or work toward removing those obstacles. In this case, it was just a matter of a few minutes, and still your reaction was negative. You really need to check your attitude."

"But I didn't say anything."

"It doesn't matter whether you said anything or not. What matters is your self-destructive reaction to that incident. You have to remember that you have a seizure disorder and your health is not in good shape. You can't afford to dwell in negativity. Learn to enjoy life even in adversity."

"I'll try." She forces a smile.

"If I tell someone that my client got a nosebleed just because she felt she was being held hostage in a wrap-up meeting, they will seriously doubt my sanity."

She laughs.

"Jill," I continue, "you are almost sixty. Just think how many years you have wasted chasing drugs or doing nothing. I don't think you ever looked at a watch while you were in your active addiction. Nothing mattered to you; now you are letting these petty incidents interfere with your already weak health. Why?"

She smiles and then leaves my office.

The following week Jill enters my office, saying, "Do you have some time? I want to talk to you about something."

"What about?"

"I was in meditation group yesterday, and we were instructed to think about past hurts. I vividly recollected something that my mother did to me."

"What did she do?"

"I was sixteen. My mother hit me hard. See this scar?" She shows me a scar above her left eye.

"It looks like she barely missed your eye."

"She was a bitch!"

"Why did she hit you?"

"I looked like my father."

"Just because you looked like your father, she would hit you?"

"Every time she got angry with my father, she hit me. I guess I was an easy target."

"Did she hit your other siblings?"

"No, just me. She would hit me with a broom."

"That's nuts!" I respond spontaneously.

"My parents never got along."

"Where is your mother now ?" I ask.

"She is dead. I held a grudge against her for a very long time, but when she was dying, I was the one who looked after her. You know I have anger issues; I get mad at the other clients. Now I know the root of my anger. Every time my mother hit me, I used to be angry, and I kept practicing anger. Now I'm fifty-eight, and I still hold a grudge against my mother. I had to let it go. Since yesterday, I am experiencing freedom. I was a prisoner of my own resentment. Now I'm at peace. You see how happy I look today.

I'm smiling all over."

"You have to continue smiling. Jill, when you smile, you

look beautiful."

She cuts me short: "Otherwise I look ugly? You're right; when I'm angry, I do look ugly."

"If just smiling makes you look beautiful, why not continue smiling ?"

She smiles. I return it.

* * *

"I want to leave," Melvina declares early in the morning.

"Why, what happened?" I ask.

"I have a problem with Fatima and Jill," she replies. "They keep talking bad about me."

"How do you know that they are talking bad about you?"

"Fatima says that I'm fat and I eat a lot."

Is it news to you? Don't you know it already? Just accept it and then see the results. "What did Jill say?"

"I'm not sure," she answers, "but I think she was complaining to staff about me."

"Just ignore them."

"No. I can't ignore them. I need to talk to someone. I got up his morning and said hello to Fatima, and she ignored me."

"You can't force people to speak to you."

"That's why I want to leave, Christopher. I have nobody to talk to, especially Fatima. She says I'm too needy and I give her a headache by asking silly questions."

"Melvina, I don't think you should leave just because your roommate refuses to say good morning to you. You are here to work on your issues, not to worry about what she says or doesn't say."

"She calls me fat," she repeats. "She says I have a big tummy."

"Do you think you have a big tummy and are overweight?" I ask her gently.

"Yes." She looks down.

"Then, start paying attention to what you eat. Start taking better care of your health."

"Christopher, I don't like the way she treats me!" She starts crying.

"Melvina, learn to ignore her. We have no control over other people's behavior. Don't respond to her. She will eventually stop bothering you."

"I'll try," she says half-heartedly. "But another thing that bothers me is that whatever I do, they find fault with it."

"They seem to be gifted critics," I tell her. "You can't help it; everyone has issues."

"They do?" she gasps. "I didn't know that!"

Are you kidding me? Melvina is a little slow; it takes time for her to figure things out. Jill and Fatima give the impression that they don't have any issues. So apparently, Melvina thinks they are perfect.

"Melvina, I can't discuss their issues with you, but if they didn't have any, they wouldn't be here."

"I know. They have drug issues, but do they have other issues too?"

"Everyone here has some sort of behavioral issues, Melvina."

"Well," she says, "I will try to be friends with her."

"No. Don't try to do anything about it," I suggest. "Just leave her alone; ignore her as I said."

"But I need someone to talk to," she whines.

"You can talk to the other clients and with the staff."

"No one really talks to me. I talk too much and keep nagging for small things."

"Then stop nagging."

"I'll try."

"Do you want to change rooms?" I ask her since we have beds available.

"Who will be my new roommate?"

"I don't know," I reply. "We have two beds open. You will get a new admission as your roommate."

"No, it's okay," she says. "I'll stay where I am for now."

I talk to Jill and Fatima and tell them to leave Melvina alone and not to bother her or call her names.

* * *

"There was something going on between Melvina and Fatima at lunch," Dawn tells me on her way back from the cafeteria that afternoon.

Immediately after that, Melvina comes into my office. "I want to leave," she states emphatically.

"What happened now ?"

"Fatima is being nasty to me." She sobs, "I wanted to get a juice. I said 'excuse me' to Fatima who was standing in front of me. I asked her to let me grab a juice, and she refused to move. I wasn't being a pain in the ass. I can't stay here with mean and nasty people! She says she has a headache because of me. I don't want to be the cause of her headache. I've decided to leave."

"Melvina, leaving is not the solution. You are not here because of them, you are here because you have problems, and you want help. You shouldn't give them the power to make or break your day."

"But she says I am a pain in the butt, that I'm fat, that I have a big tummy."

"Did she say this while you were in the cafeteria today?" I ask.

"No."

"I told her and Jill not to bother you anymore," I tell her.

"She says I have no manners."

"Don't worry about what she says," I sigh. "*Manners* is a

subjective term and varies by culture."

"What do you mean by that?"

"Let me tell you a story that I heard a few years ago.

"A Guru from India was visiting the United States and living with a friend. His host received a dinner invitation from a friend who requested that he bring the Guru to dinner with him. The hostess prepared many delicious dishes and served them to her guests, expecting the Guru to appreciate every dish. However, he wasn't accustomed to thanking people for everything they did for him. As they were leaving, the hostess called her friend into the corner and complained, 'I am very disappointed in your friend. I worked hard to prepare so many dishes for him, but he was so stingy in appreciation that he thanked me only once at the end of the dinner. I was thinking of inviting him again, but now I'm not so sure.'

"The Guru's friend told him what their hostess had said and advised him to say thank you every time someone did something for him, saying 'If you don't say thank you for everything, you will be considered uncultured and without manners, and we won't receive any more invitations. This is a different culture; people are more sophisticated here, and they believe in manners. You live in caves—it's a different world altogether.'

"'I will keep that in mind,' the Guru replied.

"Several weeks later, they received another dinner invitation, and they accepted. Now the Guru was careful and very conscious of his manners. The hostess gave them water, and he thanked her; she refilled his glass, and he thanked her; after every dish she served, he thanked her. At the end of the evening, she told her friend that she felt very uncomfortable because the Guru was so very formal. She said, 'I felt there was no need to say 'thank you' every time I served him something. I was pleased to have him.

'Thank you' is just a word; his acceptance of our invitation was appreciation enough. Please tell him when he comes next time not to be so formal; that will make me feel more at home, and I will enjoy his presence more.'

"So you see, Melvina, you can't satisfy everyone."

"You are right about that!" she responds emphatically.

"Do you still want to stay in the same room?"

"I'm not sure."

"I will ask Dawn to shift you to another room, but please don't talk about leaving anymore, and try to adjust to your new room-mate when she comes."

"Okay. Thank you! I am feeling better now." She smiles.

* * *

I start group by saying, "Recovery calls for hard work, sincerity, commitment, honesty, devotion, and a willingness to change. Some clients come into the program and don't do anything except sleep, take medication, and smoke. How can they recover?"

"That's true," Fatima responds. "That's exactly what I did in my last recovery attempts. However, this time, I am trying something different. I am sincere this time; enough is enough. I am well and truly done with this shit!"

"What gives you the right to judge?" Nikkie interjects. "Even though you see people sleeping, they might still be getting something out of it; their subconscious might be listening— who knows? You can't judge people like that."

"How is it possible to learn while sleeping ?" Fatima asks pointedly.

"It's not possible," Dexter says, shaking his head. "She doesn't now what she's talking about."

"I know very well what I'm talking about; people may appear to be asleep, but their subconscious mind might absorb what is being said," Nikkie states with superiority.

"I think you are just trying to indulge in a futile discussion," I intervene.

"It's not futile," she insists. "You guys keep making judgments."

"I don't know why you are so defensive." I look at her. "The point I was trying to make, was that recovery calls for hard work. No one can achieve recovery without putting some effort into the process."

"I hear that all the time," she snaps.

"It appears that you hear , but you don't listen. Instead of just hearing, listen, and listen to learn something new, something worthwhile," I suggest.

"I still say people might sleep and still learn," she presses.

"Nikkie," I reply, "you are indulging in mental masturbation. You want to rationalize. Fine, keep yourself busy rationalizing ; you are free to do it. If that's what you want to do, keep doing it."

"But you said we lack commitment and sincerity."

"I said recovery calls for commitment and sincerity. However, it's true that most clients lack sincerity and commitment. For example, Sharita fought with the system to get in this program, but after getting here, all she has done is take her medication, smoke, and sleep! You can ask her yourself if you want. She's leaving tomorrow. Did she learn anything ? No! If she wanted, she could have made good use of the time she had here, but she chose to sleep. If it were possible to achieve recovery by sleeping, then everyone could stay home and sleep. There would be no reason to come to a program like this. It would be a waste of your time and everyone else's!"

"Talk about it; we need to hear that," Lea adds.

Lea is forty-two years old and a very beautiful, soft-spoken woman. She started using mood-altering chemicals at age fifteen. She had thirteen years clean before her relapse four years ago. She is very intelligent. She was seen coming out of a male client's room, but she denied having sex. I remember our conversation.

"Christopher, I just made the mistake of being in a place for a few hours where I wasn't supposed to be," she reluctantly admitted.

Stop lying. "Lea, he confessed having sex with you!"

"Where is the proof? It's his story against mine. He will say anything to get what he wants!"

"But the other day, didn't you more or less agree that you had sex?"

"I didn't say yes or no, Christopher. No one confronted me directly; they just assumed because I was seen leaving his room."

"Lea," I continued, "your roommate was having sex Friday through Sunday, and every time, you went to another room."

"That's not true, Christopher; it is just hearsay, and there is no proof. I had thirteen years clean! I am very honest and spiritual. I don't do wrong things. I am not a prostitute and here for having sex!"

"Just keep your behavior under control."

"I will." She was crying.

"There is always a cause and effect relationship to our behavior," Dexter chimes in. "I always rationalized my behavior, however appropriate or inappropriate it was. I would say, 'Someone made me do it' or 'The situation warranted me acting like that.' This ype of thinking was predominant. However, this tendency has largely diminished since I have embraced the recovery process in earnest."

"Christopher told me to share more," Melvina blurts out. "I started drinking in late 1984 and smoking cocaine in early 1985. I grew up in a very poor family; Mom always struggled to feed us. Most days we had nothing on our table. It was so frustrating. My father was useless. I don't even like calling him 'Father.' He made me have sex with him when I was fourteen. I'm still angry with him. How can I be angry with a dead man? Well, I'm getting better with it now.

"My mom died four years ago, and my addiction worsened.

One of my sisters is also an addict. I have a very close relationship with my grandma. She had ten children. Now only three of them are living. She treats me like her own child. I miss my mom a lot. One day, I asked my grandma how she deals with her death, and she answered, 'I don't think about it; I have accepted the reality that my daughter is dead.' She was just my mother, but she was her child. I am slowly getting better with it. I used to use my mom's death as an excuse to do drugs.

"I have two children, eight and three years old. My sister has partial custody. I have a court date at the end of this month, and if I complete this program, I will get my children back. I have to do it. I'm a slow learner. I have low self-esteem. I ask silly questions. People laugh at me. I feel bad. However, Christopher told me this morning that I shouldn't worry about what other people say, that I am here for me. No one is better than me. I was ashamed to tell people that my children have two different fathers."

She takes a deep breath while she tries to remember their names. She succeeds in remembering one, but not the other. She continues in a rush, "I had many men in my life. I didn't sleep with one or two. I slept with many. I love men. They make me feel good. However, I'm not obsessed with them. If they are there, I enjoy them; if not, I don't care. This time I want to stay clean. I am doing everything Christopher tells me to do. I talk about leaving, but I don't leave. He tells me to stay in treatment, and I stay. It's about my life. If I stay clean, I can get back the custody of my children. They are longing to see their mom. They want their mommy, and I am dying to see them. I have to take care of my health; you know I have hepatitis C? I have severe back pain. I love food. I have to lose some weight. I don't know if I will be able to do it." She pauses, "But I will try. Thank you for allowing me to share."

"You did a good job," Dexter says admiringly.

"Excellent," I agree. "You shared without inhibitions. That kind of sharing helps."

She blushes like a shy child. Her eyes are smiling.

"You know, Christopher, we addicts have acute stinking thinking," Dexter admits.

"What is stinking thinking ?" Melvina leans forward.

"Stinking thinking is basically a negative attitude. Blaming others, sneakiness, and chronic dissatisfaction are some of the characteristics of stinking thinking," Dexter answers. "We always find faults with others; we notice the mole on someone else and fail to see the splinter in our own eye."

"It's very important to check your thinking," I assert. "You have to develop the right attitude to stay sober. It's not your sense of style, intelligence, or money that will keep you sober; it's your attitude. Nothing but a positive attitude will make a difference."

"Yeah, and I have to give up my know-it-all attitude. I rationalize and intellectualize my behavior. I have to stop it because if I don't, I won't be able to get my life back on track," Dexter confesses.

"My problem is that I'm closed-minded. I resist change. I find it hard to accept anything that is new," Fatima states quietly.

"And," Jill adds, "whenever things go wrong and I realize I have a weak defense, I resort to anger to cover it up."

"My other problem is that I am a giver, and other people are takers," Fatima tells us. "I feel sometimes that I am being taken dvantage of."

"Well, in that case, Fatima, simply stop giving," I suggest.

"You don't understand what I am saying," she objects.

"You are saying that you are a giver and others are takers, aren't you?" I ask.

"Yes, that is what I am saying, but I'm not assertive enough," he says. "I don't say no."

"Whenever you give something, you get something in return," says Dexter. "There is no selfless act."

"When I was Melvina's roommate," Fatima says, "I would wake her up to go to breakfast or lunch or group. I wasn't getting anything. It was a selfless act."

"No, it wasn't. You were getting good feelings from your actions, and that should be a sufficient end in itself," I say.

"I don't know what you are talking about," she responds. "I didn't want to do it, and still I kept doing it."

"May I tell a story?" Dexter asks.

"Of course." I smile. "Go ahead."

"Every day, a holy man sees a crippled boy sitting on the steps of a huge playground watching the kids play. The holy man is troubled and thinks that the Creator is too cruel. The boy has every might to play and enjoy life like any other child. 'This is outright injustice, and I must do something about it,' he says to himself.

He starts praying honestly and sincerely, and finally the Creator responds, 'What do you want?'

"'I want you to make that crippled boy normal, able to play like any other child out there.'

"'No. You don't want that. He will be a nuisance.'

"'I don't think so. He must be miserable,' the holy man speculates.

"'He is not miserable. He is perfectly comfortable with his situation,' the Creator assures him calmly.

"'I don't think what you are saying is right.'

"'So what is right according to you?'

"'He must be miserable. I want him to be normal.'

"'He will destroy everything.'

"'I don't believe that.'

"'He's your responsibility.'

"The Creator cures the boy. Now the boy is running wild all over the playground. He sees a bicycle, picks it up, and throws it down a well. He grabs an iron rod and goes on a rampage. He hits every child he can catch. He breaks arms, ribs, and legs.

"The holy man doesn't know what to do. He tries to intervene. He runs toward the boy telling him to stop. The boy turns on the holy man and hits him with his rod, breaking both knees.

The holy man is sobbing in pain and cursing his ill fate when the Creator speaks again.

"'I told you what a nuisance the boy was, but you refused to listen.'

"'Please, please make him a cripple again!' the holy man pleads. 'He broke my knees. I was trying to help him; I had no selfish motive.'

"'You were getting a kick out of doing something noble without knowing the consequences.'

"'I am sorry.'

"Now, the crippled boy and the newly crippled holy man sit side by side on the steps." Dexter looks at Fatima and smiles.

"Fatima, Dexter is correct," I say. "Your act wasn't selfless. You were helping her because you were feeling good. No one forced you to do it. However, I think you were expecting more than good feelings, and that's why you are feeling the way you feel now. Does that make any sense?"

"I'm beginning to understand," she answers, "but I still lack assertiveness."

"Really? I haven't seen anyone as assertive as you are," Dexter states flatly. "In fact, sometimes you are not only assertive, but aggressive."

"Then I don't know what it is," she responds. "I do think I help people even though I don't want to help them."

"If you are feeling bad after helping people, just stop," Dexter suggests.

"It's not that simple," she says. "My parents taught me to

help people. It's hard for me not to try to help."

"We all grew up with that kind of teaching. However, normally we help people because we feel good about it. But you are saying that you feel bad after helping people. In that case, why do you want to borrow trouble?" I ask.

"What do you mean 'borrow trouble'?" She stares at me.

"I mean, if everything is going well for you, and you don't have any problems of your own, and then when you try to help someone, suddenly there are difficulties in your life. This is called borrowing trouble," I explain.

"You don't want to help people at the expense of your recovery. If you want people to be self-reliant, then teach them how to fish rather than giving them fish to eat for a day or two. We have to be careful about what we do and how we help people," Dexter chimes in.

"So, I should just leave people alone?" Fatima responds.

"Yes," I agree. "Let them handle their own issues."

"I lack patience. When people are slow, I can't wait, so I start helping them even though I don't want to help them," Fatima says with a guilty look.

"You know most people lack patience including me. Any-time things don't happen the way I anticipate or desire, I start getting impatient. I start finding shortcuts. I mostly focus on getting my way, on immediate gratification. That is my addictive behavior. I forget that there is always a procedure for everything in life," Dexter adds philosophically.

"Please keep in mind that every problem has a solution," I say at the end of the session.

They all nod.

* * *

Jill knocks and enters my office announcing, "I am very happy today because I am successfully completing my treatment here."

"Congratulations!" I say.

"I just want to thank you for everything you did for me." She sits in a chair across from me.

"I didn't do anything. You did it for yourself."

"You helped me to stay clean."

"You are clean today because you chose to be clean."

"Whatever you say," she says. "But without your help, it would not have been possible."

"Jill, no one can help you stay clean but you. You just have to continue down this path. Be strong, keep doing what you need to do and good results will follow."

"I will continue doing everything that needs to be done," she promises. "This is my first and last program. You can see how happy I am without drugs, and I remember that you said I look ugly when I'm angry. Every time I do drugs, I get angry. I don't want to look ugly; I am going to stay clean. I am too old to do this razy stuff."

She completes her treatment and goes home to live with her daughter. I hope that she really means that she is too old to do the crazy stuff, that she keeps smiling, and that she keeps her anger under control to prevent further relapse.

Chapter 33
Fatal Attraction

Dexter and Fatima are attracted to each other. They don't do any-
thing objectionable; however, their attraction doesn't go unoticed.
Reportedly, after their discharge, they have plans to live together.
They have been telling other clients about their so called plans but
when I confront them, they both deny it. Both of them are intel-
ligent, especially Dexter. They have worked hard to change their
old habits and learn new behaviors. However, it is too early for
them to get into a relationship but they are unwilling to listen.
Both have mental health issues, and have trouble handling rela-
ionships. They need to wait a year or two; if they don't, they will
be inviting trouble sooner than they think. They need to practice
patience.

    Once I asked, "Dexter, do you know the story of Abraham,
Sarah, and Hagar from the Bible?"

    "Yes, why?"

    "Can you tell me that story?"

    "Yes. Abraham was married to Sarah. She had passed child-
bearing age but God had promised them a son. Being impatient,
Sarah urged Abraham to sleep with Hagar, her Egyptian hand-
maid, so that she would provide him with a male heir, which she
did. They named him Ishmael but he was not the promised son.
Meanwhile, Sarah conceived and bore a son, Isaac, who was the
promised son.

    "Ishmael, Hagar's son, had twelve sons and Isaac's son, Jacob,

also had twelve sons.

"The descendants of Ishmael became Muslim and Isaac's descendants became Jewish. Now they are fighting over Israel."

"Very well," I said, "Do you realize how their impatience had repercussions which reverberated down through the generations until our day?"

"But we have nothing going on between us," he had replied.

A few days before Dexter's discharge, he says, "I know I can't afford to be off guard for any reason; one unguarded moment can cause me to relapse. I have been in trouble before because of laxity. I was lethargic; basically, I was off guard."

"You need to develop patience," I tell him.

"I know," he says. "I am well aware of it. It's not that I always make wrong moves. It's just that one wrong move I make, when I'm off guard."

"Dexter, you are intelligent and well read," I say slowly, "but if you don't use that intelligence and knowledge to stay in recovery, it will be a real shame."

"I know there are people who stay clean for years and still don't recover," he responds. "My focus is staying in recovery and not just staying clean. I have learned to listen to myself and to my feelings, which I never did in the past, and things went wrong. I was clean for a couple of years. I was doing very well, and I believed that everything was under control. One day my guard was down, and I gave in to the urge to have a drink, and I relapsed. That one unguarded moment ruined my two years of hard work."

"Do you remember your last run?" I ask.

He thinks for a moment and then begins, "I met this woman. She was charming and very intelligent, and she was in recovery. We always held very interesting discussions. Intelligent women have always been my weakness. Nothing was physical in the beginning. One day after attending an AA meeting, I invited her to my apartment, and she wanted to make love. However, I wasn't feeling confident that day, and I avoided it under some pretext or other. The next day, I went and bought vodka and drank two shots before inviting her to my apartment, and when she came we talked for a while. Then we got into bed, and I performed wonderfully. I felt confident, and from that day on, I always had one or wo shots before making love to her and skillfully avoided letting her know that I was drinking—or at least, I thought I avoided it. But one day, I was drunk and smelling of drink all over; I couldn't do anything about it, and she called it off, saying that she knew from the beginning that I had been drinking. I tried to call her, but I guess she changed her cell phone, and I lost contact with her.

I started getting high again. I didn't realize I needed help until I lost my apartment and everything else."

"Where are you going to live after you are discharged from here?" I ask.

"I don't know," he responds. "I don't want to go to a recovery house. They impose too many restrictions. I don't want to live with my son; I feel as if I keep getting in his way there. However, I am thinking of living with my sister; she lives alone, and she is in recovery."

"Why don't you call her now and confirm whether you can live with her?"

He calls his sister and puts her on the speakerphone. "My counselor wants to know whether I can come and live with you."

"Of course," she replies. "You are welcome as long as you don't drink."

Dexter completes his treatment and goes to live with his sister, and Fatima goes to live with her mother. One of my ex-clients calls and while talking with me he casually mentions that Dexter and Fatima are seeing each other and that they make meetings together. After a few days, I receive another call that Dexter relapsed and had to leave his sister's house. How sad! He didn't use his intelligence and his knowledge for his own good. Dexter is well mannered, polite, friendly, and big-hearted; he deserves a better life. I hope he doesn't give up trying and learns to keep his guard up at all times.

After a year or so, I receive a call from Fatima telling me that she is doing well. She left Dexter when he started getting high, and he is in jail now for drug-related charges. She is working and has her daughter back in her life. She wants a copy of my book. I promise to send her a copy when it is published.

* * *

Melvina enters my office, asking, "When am I leaving ? Fatima, Jill, and Dexter left, and I am still here."

"I'm not sure when you're leaving."

"I want to leave today." She is wringing her hands.

"Why?"

"Nobody likes me here."

"Are you talking about the staff or the clients?"

"Clients," she says.

"Do you like yourself ?"

"No."

"In that case, how do you expect others to like you? I have told you that you are here for yourself and no one else. You need to develop a relationship with yourself and start liking yourself. Just because others reject you, you don't have to reject yourself."

"They call me manipulative," she continues. "Do you think I am manipulative?"

"Yes."

"You too!" Suddenly, her face falls.

Poor soul! She wasn't prepared to hear this from me. I don't know why I felt a need to tell her what I thought of her. I think,

*I thought the truth might help her to see where she goes wrong
and why people don't like her.*

She looks at me dejected and continues, "I know I shouldn't
have gone to Stanley to ask about my leaving."

"You lied to him, Melvina. You told him that I sent you
to ask him."

"I was anxious to know when I'm leaving." She looks down.

"Melvina, you have been focused on leaving since the day
you arrived here. Why don't you invest your energy into doing
something constructive while you are here?"

"He's an asshole."

"Why are you cursing Stanley? You are the one who lied."

"I'm sorry for lying," she says. "Stanley told me I would
be leaving in three days."

"I don't know about that."

"Even Scott said so," she adds.

"The minute I find out your discharge date, I will let you
know."

"When are you going to find out?" she presses.

"Soon."

"How soon?" She starts wringing her hands again.

"You need to stop being so anxious," I tell her.

"Can you go now and find out?" She continues wringing
her hands.

"No," I reply. "However, since Stanley and Scott have both
said that you're being discharged in three days, that means
you must be leaving in three days."

"Good," she says. "Can I go and lie down?"

"Why?"

"I'm not feeling well."

"You look perfectly fine."

"I don't feel like attending group today," she admits.

"Melvina, you need to attend groups. If you only have
three days left here, make good use of your time. You need

to show some enthusiasm and self-discipline. You need to get a grip on our issues."

"I'm doing what needs to be done," she insists.

"You are not doing what needs to be done. You lie, you manipulate, and you have serious problems getting along with others."

"I'll try not to lie," she says.

Two days later, she comes to see me again. "Can I leave today?" Her eyes are darting around my office.

"Why?"

"That new guy threatened me," she replies. "I can't stay in a program where I don't feel safe."

"Why did he threaten you?"

"Someone told him that I called him an asshole," she replies.

"Why did you call him names?"

"I didn't call him names," she answers, avoiding eye contact.

"If you didn't call him names, why would he lie about it?"

"I didn't say anything in his presence," she responds.

Why did you say anything in his absence? Don't you know that is gossip? "So, you admit that you said something behind his back?" I look at her quizzically.

"That bitch shouldn't have told him what I said! He threatned me. I can't stay in a place where others are threatening me."

"I'll take care of it Melvina," I assure her. "But please stop backbiting and cursing people and then trying to appear innocent."

Melvina completes her treatment and goes to live on her own. Considering her mental abilities, she made significant progress; expecting anything more from her would have been unrealistic. Her self-esteem is very low. She finds it difficult to trust people, especially men. How could I expect her to trust men, or anyone else for that matter, when I knew that her own father sexually abused her? She grew up with a confused mind; the man she should have been able to trust the most abused her.

All said and done, I don't think she possesses the skills to live life on life's terms. She has found a place to live, and she has a court date coming up soon regarding the custody of her children. Currently her sister, who is also an active addict, has custody. I don't think Melvina is capable of caring for her children either, but considering the current situation, they are not in safe hands, and I believe a mother is always a mother. Who knows? She might get her act together and become responsible.

Chapter 34

Chester—Mother's Little Doll

Chester, a slender, thirty-six-year-old male, walks into my office for a preliminary talk.

He begins, "I'm glad to be here; at least I have people to talk to. You hit me hard in group with the analogy of crabs being in a pot and struggling to get out and being pulled back down by others. You know, I struggle day and night, but I keep pulling myself down. I don't have enough strength to overcome my own doings, my own weaknesses. I lack courage. When I am on drugs, even my own people don't want to talk to me. I am an outcast. I know I can do it. If others can do it, why can't I? I need some help, and then I'll take it from there."

"Chester, what are those bruises on your face? Did you break your nose?" I am concerned by his appearance.

"My man did it to me." He avoids eye contact.

"What do you mean by 'my man'?"

"That man." He pauses. "You know, the one who dropped off some stuff and twenty dollars for me this morning. I call him my cousin," he pauses again, looks at me intently as if searching for some clues, takes a deep breath and then resumes, " but he's actually my lover."

I look at him confused.

"I am transsexual," he replies. "I have gone through

extensive hormone therapy in the past. I was an escort for many years. I worked for a man who employed prostitutes. I was the only one who was transsexual. He knew I was a man, but he instantly hired me. I had a beautiful face and beautiful legs. I wore high heels and walked with grace. I looked like a model in those days. I escorted visitors in limousines from different states and foreign countries. I charged one-hundred-and-eighty dollars an hour, and my employer made much more than I was making. But that lifestyle destroyed me. I was drinking socially with customers initially, but after a few years, I started drinking regularly and progressed to using cocaine. Now my drug of choice is cocaine.

"I was clean for six months while I was in jail. I had eight counts of prostitution charges against me, and I had a bench warrant years ago that I didn't even know about. One day, the cops stopped to resolve a fight between some teenagers, and they spoted me sitting on the steps of my apartment. They questioned me and ran a scan on their computer. They found my name and immediately handcuffed me and put me behind bars. I was devastated. It was a very bad experience. I said to myself then, that I had made a mess and I had to clean it up myself. Now I don't want to go back to my man." He takes a deep breath and then continues, "He is abusive. He hits me all the time. He is a professional boxer, and he has a short fuse and anger-control issues. He only threw one punch this time, but look, he almost broke my nose. I have decided to leave him alone; I am done with him. My problem is I enjoy masculine men."

"How did you become a transsexual?" I interrupt.

"My mother wanted a girl. She already had two boys, and then he had me. She started dressing me like a baby doll, and I started identifying myself with girls. I was always in fights in school because the kids there teased me about my lifestyle. No one knew I was a boy. People were just speculating about it. I decided to come out of the closet recently. No one but my grandma accepted it whole-heartedly. She is everything to me. I love her to death. I like dressing like a girl, but I'm a man at night, and my partners are women even though they look masculine. It sounds weird, but it's true."

"Then how did you manage with customers when you were working for that man?"

"They just liked going out with a beautiful female," he answers. "I didn't sleep with them. My boss would send someone else to sleep with them if they demanded it."

"Did you do any other work besides being a sex worker?" I ask him cautiously even though I know he was arrested for prostitution eight times in the past.

"I like that term," he says excitedly. "We don't say 'sex worker' here. We say prostitute or whore. Yes, I worked as a dental lab technician. But I got fired for eavesdropping."

"Eavesdropping ?"

"I was hired because I was a minority," he explains. "I had no experience or education in the field. I was paid nine dollars an hour, and it was twenty years ago. It was too good to be true. Something didn't seem right. I was curious. I was given two weeks of job training. I wanted to find out what was going on. I used to cover my mouth while listening to conversations on the telephone, but one day they caught me and fired me on the spot. I want to be dental lab technician again. I want to go back to school after completing this program."

"Sounds good to me. Just take one day at a time and we will plan a course of action for you to achieve your goals.

"It sounds like a plan to me," he says before leaving my office.

* * *

A few days later, at the start of group, Gloria complains, "This place is worse than a jail. I hate being here. I am thinking of leaving. I am on probation, and I know if I leave here, I will wind up in jail, but I don't care. They don't allow me to make enough calls here. I am fed up with these people." The griping seems contagious; many of the other clients start expressing the same feelings.

Then Chester intervenes, saying, "I have been in jail; I have firsthand experience. They beat the shit out of you in jail. We can't compare this place with jail. Jail is jail. No one listens to you. If you do anything nasty, the guards put you in a hole or lock you up in a cell. They treat you nasty there. I don't ever want to go back to jail. I am here to get my act together. I am here with people who are willing to talk to me and help me with my issues. I am with people who have a positive attitude. I also think of leaving here, but not because this place is worse than jail, but because I think of getting high. I know I can't do that. I am done with drugs.

"I am HIV positive. I have cancer and suffer from neuropathy. I know very few people will tell you that they have HIV. But I don't mind saying it; when I say it, I know people respect me for being honest. I know there is more to life than staying clean and sober, but I need to be honest about everything. I can't keep lying, and at the same time, try to get my shit together.

"I am a homosexual. It bothers me, but I am not ashamed of it. Who knows? One day I might start a relationship with a girl and father a child. But that doesn't mean I shouldn't talk about my mistakes. I take responsibility for my past mistakes, and I plan not to repeat those mistakes or make new ones. I want to be careful because I want to lead a normal life. I want to be successful. And I now I can do it."

"I couldn't agree with you more," a client in a wheelchair interrupts. "I was in jail for more than ten years. They treated us like animals. There was no respect for us. They didn't care whether we lived or died. I was badly beaten and had a paralytic attack. I didn't receive immediate help, and both my hips were damaged.

I have had three hip replacement surgeries, and still everything is messed up. You see this?" he says, pointing to his damaged hips.

"You see my condition? This is not the result of drugs. This is the result of the beating I got in a jail."

Gloria, who had started the whole conversation, sat spellbound until the end of the session.

* * *

One afternoon, Chester asks, "Can you mail this letter for me?"

"Who is it to?" I ask.

"My man," he replies shyly.

"Are you sure you want to do this?"

"I do love him." He avoids eye contact. "I need him."

"You told me that he is abusive," I remind him. "He socked you right in your face. So now, why do you want to keep in touch with him? I don't think it's a good idea."

"He'll be all right. He was very humble with me on the phone last night."

"Just be careful. I advise you to think ten times before you take a hasty decision."

Chester writes to his man daily and appears preoccupied with is thoughts. He is always on his visitors list for Sundays. He seeks permission to call his man at all hours of the day. When asked why, he says, "I want to know what he is doing, where he is. I am worried that he is cheating on me." When permission to call his man is denied, he gets disappointed and goes back into his shell. He walks with an attitude. He complains and threatens to call his provider to inform them that he is being mistreated and discriminated against because of his sexual orientation.

After a few days, he walks into my office and declares, "I have a problem with my roomie."

"What happened?"

He pulls a chair, sits across from me, and says, "I am struggling with my homosexuality. I don't want to be homosexual anymore. I am working hard to change myself. You see, I don't even talk like a girl anymore. I don't make it obvious; I'm not hiding it, but I don't want everyone to know my business. I don't want to go there again, and my roomie keeps talking about my business to anyone who will listen. I don't talk about his homosexuality; he's still in the closet. He has a son, but I don't think it's his. He likes dicks. He keeps bragging about how many dicks he has seen and how he enjoys sucking on them. I'm sick and tired of it. You need to do omething!"

"I will talk to him and tell him to leave you alone," I assure him.

"You have to do more than that," he insists.

"Chester, let me talk to him first and see what he has to say."

"You don't understand. That dickhead is threatening to take my man away from me," he whines.

"If he is yours, he will remain yours," I tell him. "No one can snatch your man from you."

"This bastard knows him from the street and claims to have sucked on him twice. I don't trust him. He's a filthy dick-hopper. He is capable of stealing someone's man; that's why I am not putting my man on the visitors list anymore. If you don't handle it in time, I'm going to kick him in his ass like this." He kicks an empty chair next to him.

"I understand your fear," I assure him. "However, I feel it is baseless, and you need to learn to overcome it. Chester, you keep going back and forth. One minute you say you don't want anything to do with your man, and the next minute you talk about how much you want him. You need to stop being so fickle. You also need to leave your roommate alone!"

"I am not doing or saying anything to that silly ass. He needs to stay the fuck out of my life. I am positive in thinking. I am not negative like him."

"Chester, why are you here?"

"I have issues," he answers slowly.

"You came with issues, didn't you?"

He nods.

"Those issues have nothing to do with your roommate, right?"

"Right," he says.

"So don't you think you need to stay focused on your own issues?"

"I understand what you are saying, but I can't concentrate when he is threatening to snatch my man from me." He stands and then starts pacing my office.

"We need to resolve your issues amicably," I tell him.

"How ?" he sits down, biting his nails.

"Chester, I need some time to figure it out. First let me have a talk with him."

"Why don't you just kick him out?" he urges.

"Leave it to me to handle," I say sternly.

"All right," he agrees reluctantly.

"I will get back to you later."

"When?" He is getting ready to leave.

"You aren't going to keep looking at the clock, are you?" I ask him, smiling.

He smiles back.

"Please send your roommate to see me," I request.

"What?" He appears confused.

"I want to see him," I repeat.

"I don't want to talk to him," he retorts.

"Chester, just tell him I want to see him."

"Okay," he says reluctantly. He leaves my office.

When his roommate comes into my office, I ask, "Paul, what's going on between you and Chester?"

He settles into a chair. "He is accusing me of sleeping with his man. I don't need to sleep with his man. He thinks everybody is like him. I don't prostitute like him. He is a male prostitute, and he has trust issues. He is possessive of his man. He feels threatened. I don't want anything to do with his man. He's paranoid."

"But didn't you tell him that you slept with his man in the past, and you are going to snatch him away?"

"He is lying," he insists. "I did say that I knew him from the streets. He didn't like it when I talked to Mark when he was visiting one Sunday, and he felt that Mark was paying more attention to me than to him, so he cooked up that story to tell you. He felt neglected. He has issues. He's a fucking liar. I'm going to get him in here." He throws my door wide open, and to my surprise, I see Chester standing right outside.

"What are you doing out there, Chester?" I ask.

"Waiting for the nurse," he replies, not looking at me as he walks away.

"Shall I call him back?" I ask Paul.

He shakes his head. "No. He is not worth talking to. I have an outside appointment, and I need to leave."

"All right, then, just don't say anything to Chester. If you have any problem with him, come and talk to me instead."

He nods. "Okay."

* * *

Chester's man calls and leaves a message for Chester to call him back.

"Chester, you need to tell Mark that you are not allowed

to receive calls, and no messages will be passed on to you in the future," I inform him.

Chester is on the phone. Without any greeting or preliminary talk, Chester demands, "Where are you now ?"

He goes on: "You don't sound well. Are you trying to hide something from me? Are you with someone? Mark, I know you are with someone. You can't stay away from guys. I know you can't. Are you high? Don't tell me that you love me. You don't. You are lying. I can't trust you. You expect me to trust you? How can I? You cheat on me all the time! I wanted you to be in my life, but now I don't. No means no! You can give your black ass to anyone you want. I don't care. I got to go. My counselor is asking me to get off the phone. All right. I will think it over." He slams the phone down.

"He was with someone, I'm sure of it. I hate him!"

"How do you know ?" I ask.

"He cheats on me," he replies, "and I know that's what he would do. He is unfaithful. I don't trust him. Can I call him again?"

"No."

"I was going to ask him to drop off a few things that I need," he presses.

"But you said you don't want anything to do with him," I remind him.

"That's because I was angry with him." He looks down and then says, "I just want to be friends with him."

"What's wrong with you, Chester?"

"I don't know." He shakes his head hopelessly.

"You need to leave Mark alone," I suggest. "You don't need to be friends with anyone who gets high."

"You are right." He nods. "I need to leave him alone."

"Chester, that's the first time you have said something that makes sense. You have many issues that you need to address. But you are more focused on pursuing your love affair with

Mark. You need to stop this futile indulgence and start taking care of your health."

"You are right," he agrees. "My legs are swollen; fluid is coming out of my toes. It can be dangerous to me as well as others. I have cancer, and my HIV takes a toll on me. From today on, I will do whatever you say."

"Excellent," I respond. "Now go back to your room and relax for a while. I will see you in group."

"Thank you. I'm feeling better now." he says and steps out of my office.

* * *

Two weeks later, Chester is listening to a hostile sharing by Gloria, Nikkie and another female peer. He vents, "I have a difficult time dealing with females. I can't take it any longer."

"What does that mean?" Gloria demands.

"The three of you," he says, pointing to them, "get on my nerves. Day and night you run your mouths like chatterboxes. You give me headaches. I have brain lesions, and I have Kaposi's sarcoma in my leg ; it is a cancer. My nerves are damaged. You don't help anyone here. You are fucking with everyone's recovery. You feel like only the three of you exist in the world. You are very self-centered. The rest of us have problems, too. My problems are worse than yours. No one here has as many problems as I do. I can't even stand for very long. You see this?" He lifts his pants to show his swollen legs. "This is the damage of cancer. There are times I feel like my brain is falling out. I feel like someone is scratching my brain, like this." He moves his fingers near his head above his right ear. "You three are very damaging. I don't think you are ever going to start working on your own issues and stop running your fucking mouths. I want to live. I don't want to die. I need peace. I feel like running away from here. You are intensifying my feelings. I hope you all will stop being so grouchy."

"I haven't done anything to you," Gloria responds. "In fact, I hug you every day, don't I?"

"Yes," he answers, "you do, and I hug you back, don't I? But that is not the point. The point is, you are miserable, and you have a negative attitude and outlook toward life. You are hateful, and you hold grudges against people. You called me a faggot, and you said 'fuck you' to me, didn't you?"

"You know I have a bad mouth," she admits. "I say things I don't really mean."

"That doesn't mean you can go on saying anything you want," he tells her.

"I try hard to keep to myself." She shifts her sides. "That's why I spend most of the day in my room. I'm sick."

"If you are sick, then you should ask for help," he suggests.

"I am trying to stay away from trouble." She shifts her sides gain.

"You are not trying anything ; you are fucking lying!" he houts. "You just keep getting on everyone's nerves."

"I'm not doing anything," she says, darting her eyes around.

"You talk behind people's backs," he says, giving her a stern look. "You are into everyone else's business. You lie. You don't get long with anyone here. You hate all the staff. They are tired of you. They have had enough of you. They don't want anything to do with you. You split people."

"I'm sorry," she says, looking down.

"Chester," I intervene, "why don't you stop taking their inventory and share about yourself ?"

"I'm sorry, Christopher. I had to get that off my chest. It has been bothering me for a while. Now, however, I feel better. Let me share about myself. I grew up with my mother and grandmother. My father wasn't in my life. He was in Puerto Rico. Both my parents are addicts. I have three brothers;

one is in jail for multiple armed robberies. Another was in jail for ten years for robbery, and he has been clean for the last eight years. Being in jail helped him stay clean. Jail did him good. He won't have anything to do with me because, according to him, I am a lowlife. My third brother is an addict and bisexual.

"I have been HIV positive for the last seven years. At one time, I had full-blown AIDS, but a miracle happened. I was in a shelter, and I got unconditional love from the people there. I wasn't stressed. Then I got an apartment. I became hopeful and positive. I cut down on drugs, and my doctor said I don't have full-blown AIDS any longer. Now my HIV is almost non-traceable. I have to maintain cheerfulness and a positive attitude.

"I have two case managers. One of them is coming today to take me to sign the lease papers for my apartment. He has my money. He is supposed to bring money every Sunday, usually seventy-five dollars. I am getting ready to leave here. When I leave here, I want to attend outpatient treatment, and I want to go back to school. I want to go to the gym. I want to be a busy person; that's why I'm being busy while I'm here. I am learning to love myself now.

"I had a bad dream recently. In that dream, my man was beating me up, and he threw away my stuff. He told me to get the fuck out of his life. I'm scared. I think I am holding back on this relationship. I pray a lot. Something or other always keeps popping up. I called my grandma last night, and she told me that my mother received a letter from my probation officer stating that I should contact him. I didn't know I was on probation. I thought I was off probation. I haven't been in touch with him for the last six onths. I saw him once, and he was busy. I said, 'Hi, I am Chester,' and he said, 'Hi.' That's it. I know I'm going to make it. You are going to miss me when I leave." He looks at me. "I leave imprints behind wherever I set my feet. I am not boasting ; I am telling you the truth, nothing but the truth."

"Are you happy about your progress?" I ask.

"I'm doing what I need to do," he replies. "I'm no longer as preoccupied as I used to be. I used to take medication for depression, but I stopped it long ago. When I was depressed, I didn't want to talk to anyone. Basically, I am a loner; I don't allow people in my space. I am no longer depressed. When I am sad and down or angry, I let it out. Letting it out helps me. I take suggestions, and I pray a whole lot. Basically, I am doing pretty well with my recovery. I am being patient. I am staying focused and doing me."

* * *

A few days later, early Friday morning, Chester asks me, "How long am I going to be here?"

"You have been bugging me with that question every day, and I have told you that you are going to be here for about fifty days," I respond.

"But I don't want to be here for more than thirty days," he protests. "I learn fast. I don't need as many days as others do."

"Maybe. But you don't need to rush your recovery. If you leave before your time is up, it will be considered as leaving AMA."

"I don't care," he retorts.

"But the other day, you said you are practicing patience," I remind him, "and that you don't want to rush your recovery."

"Yeah, but now I got a place to live."

"You got an apartment because you are in treatment," I tell im. "Your case manager worked hard to get you that apartment."

"That's his job. He gets paid for helping me," he snaps.

"Whose job is it to stay clean?" I look at him.

"Mine." He looks down at the floor.

"That's why you need to stay in treatment."

"I don't want to live here more than thirty days; I can't wait to get in my own apartment." He is tapping both feet restlessly.

"But you can do that after completing treatment."

"Why do you want me to stay in treatment past thirty days?" he demands.

"For two reasons," I reply. "One, the program requires it, and two, you have several issues which you need to learn to take care of."

"I don't need to be here to take care of my issues!" he shouts. "I always take care of my issues."

"Chester, what you are saying is not true. If you had been able to take care of your issues the way you are saying, you wouldn't have been in the mess that you are in now."

"What mess?" He makes a face.

"You know very well."

"I went for an HIV test last week, and it came back undetectable. My overall health is fine, too," he insists. "There is nothing pressing now."

"How about your addictive behavior, sexual preoccupation, mental health issues, cancer, and brain lesions?"

"I have acquired enough tools and techniques to take care of my issues," he replies. "No, I can't stay here any longer. I want to be home before this weekend is out."

"Well, if you are so adamant, then do whatever you want to do. But I suggest you stay in treatment and don't make a hasty decision."

He left treatment early Saturday morning, stating, "I am leaving because I want to leave."

Chapter 35
Gloria's Confounding Story

Gloria is almost six feet tall. She walks with attitude. No one wants to talk to her. She is furious and agitated. When Dawn tries to talk to her at the end of the day, she says she will only talk with her therapist and no one else. I am busy with another client and am unable to see her immediately.

"Would you like to come to my office?" I ask her when I'm ready.

"Why?" She stares at me.

"You said you wanted to talk to me," I reply, "didn't you?"

"Not now," she says.

"Are you sure?"

"I'm dead sure!" she snaps.

"Then I'll see you tomorrow." I turn to leave.

"On the road?" she asks coyly. "Because I'm not going to stay here. I'll be leaving tonight. I made a mistake coming here."

I half turn to face her. "Gloria, I don't think you made a mistake by coming here. You made the right decision to seek treatment."

"Leaving here will be the right decision," she retorts.

"You seem to be confused. You need some time to relax. Don't rush; take things minute by minute. Once morning comes, you will feel fresh, and all your cloudy thoughts will be gone."

"I'm not staying in this fucking place." She starts toward her room.

"I know you are not going anywhere." I follow her. "You're an adult. You know what's best for you, don't you?"

"You are the therapist. You should know whether I'm grown up or not," she snaps.

"Good night, Gloria." I head back to my office.

Early the next morning, she comes into my office. "I want to talk to someone." She looks sullen, and her eyes are red.

"You might want to talk to me." I smile.

She responds, "Yes, you are the one I want to talk to. I didn't sleep all night. I feel like shit. I need sleeping medication. I didn't get any medication last night. I was tossing and turning all night. If I'm not getting any medication, why should I stay here? I want to leave. I can't take it anymore. My head is hurting. I need to see a doctor. I wasn't sleeping while I was drinking, either. I have had sleeping problem all my life." Now she is sobbing and hitting her head hard. "I'm confused. I don't know what to do. I tried to kill myself twice: once by jumping in front of a car, and another time by trying to get hit by a train. My life is messed up, man! No one nderstands what's going on with me. I am mentally sick, I am tired, and I need medication!"

"Are you on any medication?" I ask.

"No," she answers. "But I want them to give me something to sleep."

"The nurse will be here soon; please talk to her," I suggest.

"She might be able to help you."

"I want to see the doctor," she insists.

"Eboni can tell you what time the doctor will be here. May I ask you for some more information about yourself and your ssues?"

"I am fifty years old. I use cocaine, marijuana, and alcohol. I was clean for seven years. I have a grandchild. My wife died recently." *I sense that she is assuming the role of a man in her lesbian relationships.* "I don't have children. My grandchild is actually my wife's grandchild. My wife's son died. My wife gave her grandchild to me when she died and asked me to take care of her. My mother died before I was twelve. My brother died two years ago, and my dad passed away three years ago. I am devastated. After my mother's death, I moved in with my dad. I had a wonderful relationship with him and spent all my summer vacations with him.

"Later things changed, and he started molesting me. My dad turned me into a homosexual. He was a truck driver. He called me 'baby girl.' He used to tell me, 'It's daddy's and baby girl's little secret.' I ran away from him when I turned eighteen and went to live with my mother's family. There, my uncle tried to molest me. I was in the shower one day, and he came in and tried to have sex with me. When I refused, he tried to put his penis in my mouth. I told my family, but they didn't believe me. When I was twenty-one, six men raped me. Many things have happened in my life, man! I ask my God, why me?" She starts crying again.

"My dad's woman didn't even call me when he died. It hurt me right here in my chest." She points her finger at her chest. "My heart was crying to see him. After all, he was my dad. I was confused about whether I loved him because he was my dad or because he was the first man in my life. I used to wait for him at night all those seven years. I don't like talking about my dad. Even when I ran away to another state, I used to call him on weekends. When I turned twenty-seven, I discovered I was gay. I called him and told him, and he asked what part I played. I told him I am the man, and that I wanted to come home. He said I was welcome, but that I had to change my sexual behavior because his friends would ridicule him. 'They will laugh at me,' he said 'I will be the laughingstock of all my friends.'"

"Why did you consider going to live with a man who molested you for so many years?"

"He was my dad, and I still loved him." There is a sudden change in the tone of her voice. She is angry. "I don't like anybody talking like that about my dad." She pauses, takes a deep breath, then resumes, "I was comfortable having sex with him. It didn't bother me. I didn't want to be with any other man but him. I know it sounds crazy, but I am telling you the truth. I'm not lying. I did like it."

I interrupt, "Did your dad use drugs?"

"Oh no," she answers. "He was a truck driver. He drank white liquor sometimes. I was sneaking from his stock by age thirteen and was an alcoholic by fourteen. He didn't seem to mind." She leans forward and says softly, "I'm sorry for raising my voice at you. You seem to be nice people. You know, I don't like talking about my dad. I'm not angry with you. I am just angry with myself." She is crying again. "I cry a lot. It helps. My current girl-friend is also getting high. I don't want to go back to live with her. She only wants me because I'm on Social Security and get full benefits. I want to find my own place and take my granddaughter with me. I'm approved for section eight. I love children. See these pictures?" She pulls out many pictures of different children and tells me their names

"They look cute."

She smiles.

"Now, tell me, do you have any mental health issues?" I ask.

She shakes her head. "No, but I do feel depressed and lonely, and I cry a lot. That girl with the curly hair was all over me last night. What's her name?" She pauses, "Nikkie. She was trying to hit on me. I told her that I am not here for romance. I don't do things like that, and told her to stay away from me. Some people here are not here for recovery; they are here for the wrong reasons. I don't play games when

I try to get my shit together."

"It's good that you made your intentions clear to her."

"I'm feeling better now." She dries her eyes and leaves my office.

The following morning, Gloria again barges into my office, fuming. "I'm so fucking mad. She is fucking stupid; she has no brains. Look at these pants she dropped off for me yesterday without a belt. I'm thinking of going home and beating the shit out of her. Any fool knows that you can't wear pants like these without belt. I can't keep pulling them up all day. She is using my money, and she can't even get what I asked for? She is so fucking stupid! I can't imagine!" She stops prowling around my office, then reaches or the phone on my desk. "Can I call her?"

"Not now." I wave her toward a chair. "I want you to sit down and relax for a while. We will take it from there."

"I'm all right. I'll be all right." She picks up the phone.

"No! Put that phone down, Gloria," I say firmly, looking straight into her eyes.

"I won't take more than a minute or two," she pleads.

"Gloria—" I raise my voice, "I said, leave that phone alone!" She drops it. "Why the fuck can't I use the phone?"

"Because you are angry, and you are not listening to me."

"All right, what do you want me to do?" She touches the papers on my desk.

"I want you to sit down and listen to me." She reluctantly sits own, but she is restless and uncomfortable. "Now relax. Calm down."

"I can't relax until I talk to that stupid woman," she blurts.

"Just listen to me, close your eyes, and take a deep breath." She is hesitant but does as told. "Do it again." She takes a deep breath.

"Now, do it three more times." I pause. "How do you feel now ?"

"Much better," she replies, her eyes still closed.

"Good," I say. "You can open your eyes now."

She looks at me, wide-eyed. "What next?"

"It's time for group, and we are running late, so let's go." I pick up my laptop and head out the door. She follows me.

"What about my phone call?" she asks on our way to the community room.

"You can make that call when we come back. Is that all right?"

"That will do," she replies.

Entering the community room, she sits on the far left where we usually open our groups.

She begins, "I am Gloria, and I am very angry right now. See this?" She stands up to show everyone her pants falling down round her knees. "That stupid crack head has it in for me. How can anybody be so stupid?" The group chuckles. "She thinks she s my wife; hell no, she is not going to be my wife. I am not going to lick her ass anymore. I am not going to do this to her." She puts her lips together like a pig's mouth. Now everyone is laughing uproariously. She seems encouraged by the response that she is receiving. "I feel like going home and whipping her ass. I'm trying to get better, and she is pulling me down. She doesn't want me to get better because she wants to get my SSI money from me. I will not let that happen. I'm not going to let anyone take advantage of me. I will go home and fuck her real hard." She stands again and shows the others how she will do it. The group is laughing so hard now that they are holding their sides.

"Okay, okay, thank you for sharing, Gloria. Now, let's move on to the next person." She sits down, looking offended. "But I'm not done yet."

"Yes, she's right. She isn't done yet. You shouldn't cut her short," Nikkie says.

"She can start cursing again after everyone has had their

turn," I say.

"But that's how she's feeling!" Nikkie insists.

"Enough. Let's move on." I point to the group member sitting next to Gloria.

Later, we perform a role-playing exercise based on the story of two travelers who set out to relocate themselves, but due to an extremely negative attitude, one traveler ends up being homeless and takes to heavy drinking. The client playing the role of the traveler with a positive attitude performs extremely well. Guess who layed the role of the negative traveler? None other than Gloria!

Everyone has another good belly laugh.

"You know, I'm basically a positive person. I only resort to nastiness when people rub me the wrong way. I like to laugh; didn't I augh when I was in your office?" Gloria asks me.

"Did you?" I look straight into her eyes.

"Yes," she says averting her eyes. "I did."

"When? You were cursing your friend the entire time you were in my office," I remind her.

"That was because she didn't do what I told her to do," she replies.

"She isn't under any obligation to do anything for you," I tell her. "You should be grateful that she even came all the way down here."

"She should have gotten me the right stuff," she insists. "But she is so stupid."

"Gloria, you need to stop expecting so much from people and learn to be happy with whatever they do for you. Your expectations are causing you heartache and relationship conflicts. Whatever someone does for you, you have to take it as a bonus, and be thankful."

"I never thought of it that way." She pauses. "I guess I need to work on my anger issues."

"I'm glad to hear that you are willing to work on your

issues."

Gloria has been constantly complaining about everything. If her blood pressure or pulse is low or high, she talks to the staff as if they are responsible for it. She has a hard time getting along with the other clients, and she fights over trivial things. Every time she gets angry, she says, "I am pissed off, and I want to go out and rink."

Today, however, is a complete turnaround. "I need more time because sixty days are not enough. I feel like I'm in a real program now. I was in an accident six months ago, and my shoulder is killing me. I am full of aches and pains. I have the urge to drink, but I'm not dwelling on it. Satan is all around me. I'm ready to fight him. I am getting stronger physically and mentally.

"I had a sexual relationship with my father. It doesn't bother me, but I don't want to hide it from my peers. They may not respect me, but I don't care. I'm fifty years old; I've got to get honest at gut level. I am here to get myself better. I don't care what you guys think about me. I need to get things off my chest. I need to talk about my issues. How I feel about myself is what matters to me. I think I can do it.

"I am doing it for my grandchild. She is adorable. She needs me. My wife thought I was the most responsible person around her, so I have to prove her right. I can't shy away from my responsibilities. I love children. Thank God I didn't become a child molester because of what happened to me. I am mentally sick, but I'll be all right. If I say something nasty to you guys, please don't mind; I am trying my best to cut down on cursing. It's hard for me not to curse. But some motherfuckers just get on my nerves. I'm sorry. I didn't mean to say that. I have been cursing all my life. I need more time." She has barely taken a breath since she began speaking.

* * *

A few days later, early in the morning, a night shift tech walks into my office, settles down in a chair and begins, "Nikkie was found lying on the floor, naked, in Tim and Joe's room. She had covered her own bed with pillows. Tim and Joe pretended that they were sleeping. However, Nikkie admitted to having sex with Tim and was getting ready to have it with Joe because he demanded it. Before they could get to it, they were found. They suspect he is HIV positive, but I don't think they used protection. I want you to talk to them." She calls Tim, with whom Nikkie claims to have had sex.

"What happened last night?" I ask quietly.

"Nothing. Why?" He answers indifferently.

"Nikkie was found lying naked in your room, and you are saying nothing happened?"

"I saw someone coming into my room. I told her to leave and I went back to sleep."

"She admits she had sex with you."

"She can say anything she wants. I didn't have sex with anyone.

I'm not lying." Tim doesn't meet my eyes.

"Then why was she lying naked in your room?" I press.

"I don't know."

"How many programs have you been in?"

"Fourteen," he shrugs.

"How old are you?"

"Twenty-seven."

"Isn't it time for you to start thinking straight, be honest, and learn to admit your mistakes? Do you think anyone will buy your tory? Stop lying and start taking responsibility for your actions and be ready to face the consequences." I look at him sternly.

"I'm not lying." He still avoids eye contact. "I was asleep. I don't know when she came in or when she left our room."

"C'mon, Tim. Be a man and tell the truth!"

This hits him. He gives in, looking down, he says, "I'm powerless over sex. I am a real nymphomaniac." He looks up. "I like sex because I'm good at it. An orgasm is equivalent to a cocaine high or rush for me. I walk around with an erect penis almost all day. I used to masturbate excessively to feel normal. How do I deal with my sexual appetite and impulses?" He pauses, looks at me, and then says, "I really don't know. I guess I just have to practice more restraint. When I need to release and unload any locked-up cum, I just do it. When I was married, I had sex often, like every other day, and when I was single, I masturbated at will. Maybe I'll grow out of it. I am only twenty-seven, in my sexual prime, and my oats are not sown yet. So I just have to wait it out and maybe my sexual appetite and libido will decrease with age. One day at a time."

He goes back to his room, and next I talk with Joe. "I didn't know until Tim told me this morning. I was sound asleep," he insists.

"Joe, Nikkie said that you demanded to have sex, stating that since Tim had it, you should also get it, and that if she refused, you would inform staff."

"I don't know what she is talking about," he retorts. "I was asleep."

"How come you were so deeply asleep that a couple was having sex in your room and you didn't know it?"

"Trust me, I really didn't know," he asserts.

"You have been constantly complaining about tossing and turning every night, and now you claim that you slept like a dog the night it happened? Unbelievable! Joe, why are you lying ?"

"Why would I lie?" he answers, looking away from me.

"Because you don't want to be asked to leave this program," I reply. "You also have court dates coming up, shortly, and you don't want to go to jail."

But before I get a chance to talk with Nikkie, Scott tells me, "All three of them need to be on Contract. The two who had sex, for two weeks, and the one who didn't, for one week. No phone calls, no store runs, and no family visits."

Joe pleads, "Will you let me make a call on the seventh day? It's my birthday."

"I'll think about it," I say. "But if you do what you are required to do you might be able to make that call."

Nikkie is put on Contract for two weeks, but she doesn't take it well. She is upset because she has two weeks and Joe has only one. "This is outright favoritism," she shouts. "I felt like I was being raped in his room. Joe forced his penis into my mouth. I wasn't willing to have sex with him, but he scared me when he said he'd inform the staff and I would be kicked out. He won't get away with it. I won't let him."

"What do you mean?" I ask.

"I told you, I felt like I was being raped," she repeats.

"Nikkie, you went into their room on your own. What do you expect when you lie naked in a room with men who are starving for sex and who have behavioral issues?"

"I'm leaving," she says.

"Why?"

"Because I'm not allowed family visits, and Joe is on Contract for only a week."

"Don't you think it would be better if you just left Joe alone?" I speak calmly.

"If he hadn't demanded to have sex with me I would have left before they found me out."

"So, basically you are angry because they found you, and you feel Joe is responsible?"

"I want to call my friend," she says, "and tell him that he can't visit me this Sunday, since I'm not allowed to have any visitors."

She calls her friend, but instead of explaining about Sunday, she tells him, "please come pick me up. I will be waiting for you out front."

Later, we are sitting in the side yard, and the clients are complaining about someone who broke the confidentiality of the group. "I don't think anyone broke confidentiality. No one went and told who has HIV or AIDS," Gloria says. "If you all are so concerned, then you shouldn't have bitched so much about Nikkie in her absence. I know who went and told her everything that we said here yesterday. But I don't care, because whatever I said was based on facts. I didn't lie. I didn't gossip. She did try to hit on me. I gave her forty dollars the day she came in. I really liked her big ass; I wanted her pussy. I desperately wanted to have sex with her. She was very seductive, and I was still in my addictive behavior. My focus wasn't on recovery; I wanted sex and nothing else, but after a while, I realized that I'm here to learn different ways of behavior. I have to give up my slimy ways, my old addictive behavior, and my sexual preoccupation. I told myself, 'no more pussy!' I don't want to be stupid anymore. I want to change. They had a threesome last night, but it didn't bother me. That is their shit. I was horny too, but I succeeded in controlling my desires."

"What are you talking about? We didn't have a threesome. I wasn't involved in anything," Joe protests. "I didn't even know that Nikkie was found lying naked in our room; I was sound asleep. I found out about it when my roommate told me this morning, and I am not the one you guys believe breached the confidentiality, either. I grew up in a cultured family. I don't do nasty things like other addicts do. I don't snitch. I'm here to do me. So don't pull me in the middle of anything. I have too much to accomplish while I'm here. I have to go to court twice, I have to go to the welfare office, and I'm homeless, so please spare me. Don't jeopardize my recovery by pulling me into controversy. I'm done. I don't want to share anything more." After this outburst, he walks away from all of us and sits as far away as he can until the end of the session. Meanwhile, Nikkie was gone forever.

Chapter 36

Bob Turns Homosexual

I knock on the door of room 103, but there is no response. I enter the room and am overwhelmed by a strong body odor. Two men are lying in their respective beds. It appears that they haven't showered in days; their dirty clothes are spread all over the floor, including their stinky socks. I desperately want to back out of the room, but I am duty-bound to do my job. I stand there and endure the smell.

"Who is Bob?" I inquire, trying not to breathe.

"Me," says a voice muffled by the covers.

"Bob, my name is Christopher. I will be working with you as your therapist. We need to complete your psychosocial assessment.

Please get out of bed, clean yourself up, and come to my office."

I return to my office and keep the set of papers ready, patiently waiting for him to come, but even after half an hour, there is no sign of him. I jump out of my seat and go back to his room only to find him still in bed.

"Bob, please get up and come into my office so we can complete your paperwork. We need your information so we can call your provider to get you more time if required." This works; he rolls out of bed, and grumbling, follows me to my office.

He has still not showered, and he stinks to high heaven.

"Have seat, Bob. Relax. I am going to ask you some questions; it will not take more than an hour."

"What! You're going to fuck with my brain for an hour?" He frowns.

"Bob, how old are you?"

"Why don't you guys have a better communication system?" he snaps. "I have answered this question no less than three times since I have been here." *The fact is that there is too much repetition of paperwork but that's how the system works. It's pathetic. The focus is more on the paperwork rather than therapy or helping clients with their real issues.*

"How old are you, Bob?" I repeat.

"Fifty-seven." He is reluctant.

"Are you married?"

"What does that have to do with my fucking drinking ?" he shouts, then slowly says, "No, I'm single."

"Bob, why did you decide to seek help?"

"I don't know." He averts his eyes.

"There must be some reason," I press.

"Why don't you understand?" he demands. "I am sick and tired, and you are bombarding me with these silly questions!"

I summon my patience. "Bob, I understand that you are tired and want to rest, but we need to complete this paperwork. Just answer the questions. That will save us a lot of time, and then you can rest."

"And you will get paid," he snaps.

"Listen." I give him a stern look. "You got yourself into this situation, and I'm not getting any pleasure by asking you these questions. If you answer them straight, you can save yourself the unnecessary agony that you are going through." I am struggling not to show my irritation. "Now, let's finish it."

Bob answers a few more questions calmly with a resigned look on his face.

"How do you describe yourself sexually?" I ask.

"Homosexual," he answers, watching the expression on my face.

"How old were you when you had your first sexual experience?"

"What does that have to do with my treatment?" he retorts.

"Everything I am asking has to do with your treatment process," I reply.

"Fourteen," he says. "Do you want me to tell you how I did it?"

I ignore his sarcasm and go ahead with my next question.

"Was it a heterosexual or a homosexual experience?"

"Heterosexual," he answers.

"Was it a good experience?" I ask.

"I loved it," he replies.

"Final question," I say, and he looks relieved. "What are your goals?"

"To get out of this room and never see you again," he snarls.

The next day when Bob comes to see me, he begins apologetically. "Doc, I'm sorry for being so nasty last night. I now I was a pain in the ass. I'm not usually like that, but I was pissed off."

"I'm not a doctor," I correct him. "I work as a therapist; you and just call me by my name."

"Okay, Christopher." He nods. "Do you need more information?"

"Yes, I do," I answer happily. Thereafter, we complete the entire psychosocial assessment without further incident.

"Why were you so agitated last night?" I ask.

"That queen got on my nerves," he sneers.

"Bob, who are you talking about?"

"That fag at the front desk," he replies.

"You should be happy to see another gay man, someone you can relate to."

"No, I don't like his kind. He is feminine, and he is nasty,"

Bob says in the same breath.

"Bob, would you like to share more about yourself ?"

"Nobody loves me," he answers sadly. "My children don't care for me. They have no problem with my drinking, but they don't like the fact that I'm gay. I do drugs because I feel lonely, I just don't know what else to do."

"Bob, sometimes we try to get out of one problem and get sucked into another. We need to be on guard. We need to be on alert all the time. Loneliness is something that we need to understand. It is not something that we can get rid of by using drugs. The use of mood-altering chemicals doesn't help anyone get rid of loneliness." At that very moment, another client knocks on the door to ask if I will conduct the group, since the speakers from Alcoholic Anonymous did not come. Bob and I get up and go with him.

The clients were reading the AA Big Book. I take a seat on the couch between two clients, and Bob settles into a chair opposite me. The president turns the meeting over to me.

I start with a reference to Mark 8:36: "For what shall it profit a man if he shall gain the whole world and lose his own soul?"

"Let me tell you a story I came across a few years ago.

"There is a greedy man who saves the life of a drowning child. Because the child's parents are poor, the man goes to see the king, expecting a reward for his brave act. The greedy man explains the purpose of his visit, and the king, being noble and generous, agrees to reward the man. 'What do you want for a reward?' the king asks.

"'Land,' the greedy man answers happily. 'I want land for a reward.'

"'How much?'

"'As much as you can give me,' the man replies, rubbing his hands together gleefully.

"The king thinks for a minute, then responds, 'Well, start

walking at sunrise, and stop at sunset. The land you cover during your journey will be yours.'

"The greedy man was so happy, he did not even thank the king, but hurriedly left the palace to get some rest before starting his walk the next day.

"The man started walking exactly at sunrise the next day. Being greedy, he forgot that he had a bad heart. He walked and he ran. He fell, he rose, and he ran on repeatedly. He covered more land than he had ever dreamed possible. He was gasping for breath. He was exhausted. He fell again, but rose seeing that it was close to sunset. He decided to run for a last time to gain some more land. He ran faster than ever. He fell for the last time just before sunset and never got up again. He gained acres and acres of land, but lost is life. His greed cost him his life. Therefore, one must learn to be content." I pause.

"Any questions? Does anyone want to share anything ?" I look at the group.

No one speaks. As I get ready to continue, I see a hand raised.

"Go ahead," I say.

A client in his late fifties begins, "I want to ask you something."

I nod. Someone in the group objects, "You have to say who you are."

This pisses off the man. He gestures toward me. "The speaker is not an AA member; he can't speak at this meeting."

"Yeah, that's true," someone mutters.

I hear a lot of whispering and realize I need to handle this issue quickly.

"Attention please!" I get the full attention of the group.

"What is your name?" I ask the client who initially objected to my presence.

"Joseph," he replies.

"Okay, Joseph, what's the problem? Did I say anything bjectionable?"

"No." He shakes his head. "But this is an AA meeting, and you are not a member, so you cannot speak here."

"All right, I will leave." I stand up. "I don't want any contro-ersy involving me; you guys continue your meeting."

"No, we don't want you to leave!" the majority of them protest.

"I don't want you to leave either," Joseph joins in quickly. "I have no objection to you being here. I was pissed off because they asked me to announce my name first as we do in AA meetings."

I see many hands in the air. I allow a few of them to speak. All of them express their anger because Joseph interrupted the session and request that I continue. Then Bob also raises his hand, and I nod.

He sounds frustrated. "What is the fuss all about? The majority of you were half-asleep before Christopher took over the meeting. I've been attending AA meetings daily for the last thirty years; it helps me and thousands of other recovering alcoholics. But I have no objection to him being here. We should be grateful to him for coming here to help us. It doesn't matter who helps as, as long as we get the help we need. I don't need to hear your glorified stories, how you robbed, killed, or prostituted yourself or others, because we have all been there. To me, the messenger doesn't matter—the message does. I want to learn something new, something worthwhile. Moreover, this is not an AA meeting. This s an in-house meeting, and I think most of you agree with me, don't you?" He stops and looks around the room.

All agree with him, Joseph included. Bob smiles.

I am puzzled. I wonder, is this the same man who was so nasty the other night? What changed him? I decide to speak on resistance to change.

"There are five stages of change: pre-contemplation, con-templation, preparation, action and maintenance. You are in the fourth stage of change. You need to learn how to maintain your recovery, and if you don't, then you get into recycling." A few of them ask me to repeat what I said so they can take notes. We end group with a promise to meet again.

Bob was married for seven years. After the birth of his second child, his wife lost interest in sex and told him to get a girlfriend. He messed with his secretary for a while, but the affair did not last long. His neighbor advised him not to mess with girls because "that will break up your marriage." He took Bob to a gay bar and picked up a "Navy guy" who performed oral sex on them in separate rooms. A couple of months later, he started going to the gay bars on his own. Initially, he was uncomfortable, and it took almost three years, but eventually he started having sex with men regularly. However, he could not do it without drinking. Before, he had never been involved in a homosexual relationship, but eventually he became a hardcore homosexual. He recalls, "I slept nude with one of my best friends while I was married, but nothing happened."

He never slept with the same man twice for the first three years. He started going to after-hour drinking clubs with private rooms in he back. There, he and his one-shot partners would have sex without using any protection. Once, he picked up a priest from a gay bar and they had sex for two weeks. He was uncomfortable when asked to wear a cock ring for the first time but eventually came to like it. This behavior ultimately resulted in a divorce that still troubles him. At thirty, Bob got into a relationship with a man six years younger, and it lasted for nine years.

One night Bob came home and found his partner in bed with another man. Despite the infidelity, the relationship lasted for another year, but Bob was devastated and took to heavy drinking. During this period, he was arrested for his first DUI. Six months later, he found another partner. This one was thirteen years his junior. This partnership lasted for eight years and his new lover, a vice president for a telephone company, was physically abusive. Not long after, he was arrested for a second DUI.

At forty-eight, he got into his third steady relationship. This time, Bob was the junior partner. A chief administrator for a nursing home, lover number three, was nine years older. This partnership lasted five years, and his man was a fellow boozer—but not as dysfunctional as Bob.

Bob is a top, and his partners are always bottoms on the lovemaking end of his relationships. Soon into his third relationship he started having erectile dysfunction. His partner started bringing young boys home. Bob became verbally and physically aggressive toward his partner, who had him locked up for two weeks for public intoxication. His partner just wanted him out of the house, so he did not press serious charges. Bob has been in about fifty detox programs and five rehabs so far. His longest clean time was close to two years before his recent relapse.

Bob has passed out at least thirty times due to excessive drinking. At age fifty-two, he's had attacks of blood gushing from his food pipe (esophageal hemorrhage) five times in one year alone; he's been given blood transfusions. In drunken tumbles, he hurt him-self twice by falling down in the street. Once it was so bad that he lmost lost his left leg. Flesh from his left thigh was used as a skin graft on his lower calf. Even after many years, the wound is very scary-looking. His doctor told him that if he drank when he got home, it could cause a bacterial infection, and he could lose his leg. That scared him, and he stayed clean for four months.

Bob is longing for love and affection, and he visits gay bars in search of so called love and affection. The only places he feels comfortable are those gay bars, but at all other joints he feels extremely anxious and like a fish out of a pond.

Once, he asks me to speak on love during a group. I begin, "Self-love is the best love. You have to learn to love yourself. It's unhealthy to depend on other human beings for love. If they refuse to love you, it becomes a cause of heartache and disappointment. If you have an abundance of love for yourself in your own heart, you will be content with it; you will not look for love from others. You will not accept mental slavery just because someone is offering you love. You don't need love from others when you have an abundance of love within yourself."

"You are right! Self-love is the best love," he says. "But I don't now whether I will be able to love myself again. I don't see any hope."

"Bob, trust me, you can do it. Don't give up. Keep trying."

"Okay," he says, half-heartedly. "I'll try."

After completing his treatment, he goes home without an after-care program. He refuses an Intensive Outpatient Program, stating hat he does not have time for it because he has to go back to his part-time job. However, he agrees to attend AA meetings.

Bob calls me the day after his discharge. "This is Bob. How are you doing, Christopher?"

"Fine, thank you. How are you, Bob?"

"Not good."

"What's wrong ?" I inquire.

"I'm having severe shakes," he reports.

"Did you take your medication?"

"Yes." He hesitates. "I did, but not all of it."

"Bob, you must take the medication as prescribed by the doctor."

"Okay, I will."

"Hang in there. Stay strong. It's not easy, but you can do it. It's just a matter of time. Everything will fall into place."

"I have been thinking of drinking since I got home." He pauses, then adds, "I had severe cravings last night."

"Don't do it," I tell him. "It would be suicidal. You might want to reconsider your decision and get readmitted."

"No, I can't. I have to go to work tomorrow."

"Bob, life is more important than work."

"I know," he says. "I will try to get over it. My sponsor offered to hang out with me, but I declined his offer. I guess I can hang in."

He calls me again after three days. "Christopher, I am still going through withdrawal symptoms. Can you find out about these two discharge medicines?"

"Sure, I'll call you right back," I respond. I check with the nurse on duty, who explains that Bentyl is for stomach cramps and the Maalox is for indigestion. I call him back, explain the medicines, and remind him to be compliant with them.

"What else?" I ask.

"I went to a bar last night," he tells me. "I was heartily welcomed by my gay friends. They hugged me; they made me feel good. They really love me there."

"It's unhealthy," I warn him. "You should not go to those bars. They are not for you."

"I know, Christopher, but I feel good there. I feel very comfortable in their company."

"You need to stop going to those bars, they serve alcohol there; it will end up triggering you," I state emphatically.

"Okay, okay, I won't go," he sighs.

"Are you going to work tomorrow ?" I ask.

"No."

"Why not?" I insist.

"I'm shaking," he replies. "I'm tired. I need rest."

"If you go to work, you might feel better," I suggest.

"I'll go the day after," he responds.

He goes to work as he said he would and calls later that afternoon.

"I worked today," he tells me. "I had some physical withdrawal symptoms, but I managed. They were glad to see me. My boss sked me where I was, and I told her that I was in a hospital for mental health issues. I know you told me not to lie. But the way she asked, I didn't dare tell her the truth.

She knows I was in a recovery program before, but if she learns that I relapsed, she would ook at me differently. That's the reason I lied."

* * *

Bob is clean for almost a year. He attends Alcoholics Anonymous meetings three times a week, but goes to Westbury, a gay bar, almost every day. He does not understand that it is not conducive to his recovery. He needs to remember the saying ' if you hang around a barber shop long enough you will end up getting a haircut.' He says, "It helps me to stay clean. If I don't go there, I feel lonely." He goes to a local cinema for oral sex, where he pays $10.00 very visit. The other place he frequents is a sex shop. He feeds coins into a machine. When the coins stop coming, the anonymous mouth stops sucking. He doesn't understand the risk involved. I remember an earlier one-on-one session that I had with him before is discharge.

"How are you doing Bob?" I ask.

"Not so well," he responds. "I'm having cravings."

"I hope you aren't going to act upon them," I say.

"No. Of course not," he replies. "My cravings aren't that strong.

But sometimes they are so strong, I feel helpless."

"Whenever you have an urge to use alcohol, don't give in to it.

"But the distractions are so bad, I can't think about anything but drinking," he mutters.

"Those are the moments that you have to learn to guard gainst," I remind him.

"How ?" he asks.

"Through awareness and control over your desires," I reiterate.

"It's not an easy task."

"I know it's not. But it is your desire. So who should have control over it?"

"Theoretically, me," he answers.

"Not theoretically, but practically, you," I state.

"You haven't been there," he said. "You can't understand my helplessness when I have strong cravings to drink."

"Look, Bob." I lean back in my chair. "I know that your experiences are your experiences; they can't be mine. But you need to understand that I also have cravings or desires; they may not be for using alcohol, but they exist."

"But other cravings aren't as strong as cravings for alcohol."

"Why not?" I ask. "A desire for sex, gambling, or doing something else crazy, can be equally strong."

"I don't think so." He shakes his head.

"You don't think so because apparently you don't have a problem with those types of desires," I continue, "but for someone else, they are equally as powerful as your cravings."

"I do have a problem with controlling my sexual desires," he concedes, "but they don't match my craving for alcohol."

"Bob, it appears to me that you either have to prove your point of view or just want to establish that your pain is bigger than others. Why make comparisons?"

"I'm sorry," he mumbles.

"Bob, what you need is inner motivation to do right things. Follow this up with perseverance, sincerity, and dedication. In spite of those strong cravings, you must remain sincere and devoted to your goals. Leave the cravings to take care of themselves. Finally, yet just as important, you need determination. No matter what, but no alcohol! I would rather die than do drugs. You need that kind of thinking ; you need to tell yourself that. I am glad that you have at least accepted the fact that alcohol is a drug. You had a big problem with that."

He smiles. "Trust me, now I think I have some clarity in my thinking. I am willing to do whatever it takes to stay clean. I am going to make it this time."

"But in your own way." I shake my head at his stubbornness.

"You can't ask me to stop going to those bars," he says. "I love going there."

"I predict that if you continue going to those places, you will definitely relapse."

"No, I won't!" He is getting frustrated.

"Time will prove it," I respond.

"I have a question, Christopher."

"What?" I raise my eyebrows.

"Aren't you getting a lot of information from me for your book?"

"Yes," I admit, "you are right about that."

"Then I want royalties."

"You can have them now," I respond.

"Give."

"Turn your back, and I'll kick your ass."

He laughs on his way out of my office.

* * *

One day, I receive a call. The person at the other end of the phone says, "Hey! How are you doing ?"

"I'm fine," I answer. "Who is this?"

"This is Bob. You forgot me so soon!"

"How are you, Bob? What are you doing these days?"

"I'm hanging in there," he replies. "I go to work. I make meetings. Oh! I also went to that theater I told you about."

"What theater?"

He pauses. "The place I go to get a blowjob."

"That's risky. You shouldn't go there. You are taking a big risk.

You could contract hepatitis, HIV, or other sexually transmitted diseases. You will be adding more problems to your existing problems. You are looking for trouble. This kind of behavior will multiply your issues."

"Yeah, I understand," he responds, "but I need to socialize sometimes."

"Bob, you are out of your mind. You go there for sex, and you are calling that socializing ? That is distorted thinking."

"My sponsor disagrees with you," he rationalizes. "He says I should continue going to those theaters; otherwise, I will be very lonely."

"Bob, don't be stupid; loneliness has nothing to do with the outside world."

"Wouldn't you feel lonely, if you didn't have any friends?" he presses.

"Not necessarily," I reply. "Loneliness is an inner state of mind. It has nothing to do with me having friends or not. I might be amidst a number of friends and still feel lonely. Have you experienced this?"

"Yes," he admits, "many times. I am at those bars with my friends, and I still feel lonely, immensely lonely. I don't even know why!"

"That's the point I am trying to make," I stress. "Your loneliness has nothing to do with the outside world."

"Then how can I get rid of my loneliness?"

"You need to develop more healthy habits," I reply. "Join a library, or go to a bookstore and read something interesting and useful, or join a gymnasium. Develop good eating and sleeping habits."

"But I need to have sex," he insists.

"I'm not against sex," I tell him. "It's healthy to make love. But it has to be with one partner and in an appropriate place. You hink about it!"

Chapter 37

Tracey is Going to be Suicidal Tomorrow

"This client is non-cooperative, and her review is due today. Can you finish her psychosocial assessment, please?" my colleague requests, handing Tracey's chart to me.

"I'll try," I respond looking at a woman sitting in a chair across from him. He gets up, offers me his chair and introduces me to her but she does not even bother to look at me.

I start where he had left off. "Tracey, why did you relapse?"

"I don't know." She shrugs and looks away from me.

"What drugs do you use?"

"I'm really tired," she answers glancing at me. "I don't want to go through this now. I'm in detox. I need to rest. I know my nights. In detox, nobody does any paperwork."

"That's not true," I tell her. "We need your information to prepare your treatment plan, and right now you don't seem to be going through withdrawal symptoms. You look fine."

"Okay, what do you want to know ?" she says reluctantly.

"What drugs do you use?"

"Twenty bags of cocaine, three bottles of gin, and two to three pills of Xanax." She keeps her eyes closed.

"How often?"

"Every day," she replies. "I was clean for nine months and relapsed two weeks back."

"What is your living situation?"

"I'm homeless. I was living in a residential program before my recent relapse."

"Where would you live after discharge from here?"

"My mother's house."

"How is your relationship with your mother?"

She opens her eyes and looks at me closely. "She has control issues. My stepfather tried to rape me when I was fifteen."

"Does your mother know about it?"

"I don't want to talk about it." She turns her face the other way.

"Is your mother still married to your stepfather?"

"No. They separated a few years ago."

"How is your relationship with your boyfriend?"

"I broke up with him." She moves her chair a little closer to my desk. "He has control issues, and he plays a big part in my addiction. We have been together for eight years, but he puts me down. I love him to death in spite of him putting me down. He hurts me. I use drugs to hide my feelings. My love for him is unconditional. I don't expect anything from him. I want nothing from him; I just want him to love me back unconditionally. But in return, what do I get? I get from him a hard dick, heartache, and pain." She chokes on her tears. "He says nasty things to me. It hurts. There are millions of scars on my heart, and he calls me a crack head. He doesn't use drugs, so he doesn't understand. He blames me for sleeping around. He says I am in and out of cars. I was clean for many years. He made me relapse. He can't blame me for what I did in my active addiction. Not everything he says is true. I did sleep with other men, but I did it because I was getting high. What I want from him is just acceptance and unconditional love and nothing else."

"What is unconditional love?"

"Unconditional love is when you love someone without expecting anything in return. You just want to be in the company of that person. You just want that person to love you back unconditionally," she replies.

"That is not unconditional love," I tell her.

"Then what is it?" she demands.

"Unconditional love is when you shower your love onto others without expecting anything, including love, in return. For xample, I love a person, and I don't expect anything from that person. I immensely enjoy the presence of that person, however even if that person is absent, the mere well-being of that person in any corner of the world brings me joy and happiness. Even if that person rejects me, I don't mind. I don't put any conditions on that person. Does that make any sense to you?" I ask.

"I think so," she says, avoiding eye contact.

"Can you think of any other issues that need to be addressed while you are here?" I ask.

"I get frustrated easily," she answers. "I have anger issues."

"Do you have problems following directions?"

"Yes. I am tired of these questions. I want to go and rest." She storms out the door.

* * *

"Tracey has to leave on Sunday," the utilization manager informs me late Friday evening. "She is not getting any rehab days. She came in for detox only; her insurance company wants her to attend IOP and comply with treatment there, and if required, her IOP can refer her back to rehab. Please explain that to her."

I leave my office and go to get Tracey. She was standing in a hallway. "Tracey, please come to my office. I need to speak with you."

"Why?" She does not move.

"I have to speak to you about your discharge."

"What discharge? I only got here yesterday. I'm not going anywhere."

"We have to discharge you on Sunday."

"Why?"

I explain the situation.

"This is absolutely ridiculous!" she exclaims. "I told you that I'm not going anywhere. I want rehab. I want to speak with your upervisor."

"I suggest you speak to the utilization manager before she leaves for the day." I direct her to the utilization manager's office.

Later back in my office, Tracey says, "The utilization manager says I can call my insurance company. May I use your phone?"

I nod. She calls her insurance company, and they tell her to present herself at IOP and take it from there.

The moment she is off the phone, she complains, "I think the utilization manager is trying not to help me."

"But you personally spoke with the reviewer from the insurance company, didn't you?" I look into her eyes.

"Yes," she stammers, "but she could have advocated my case better."

"I'm sure she did everything possible."

"I don't think so. She doesn't seem to be the type."

"Tracey, we have to complete your paperwork. Can we do it now ?"

"Hell no!" she shouts. "I am tired. I need to rest!" She blows out of my office.

The next day, I knock on her door. "Tracey, are you there?"

"What is it?" she shouts.

"We have to complete your discharge paperwork." I assert standing at the door.

"I'm not doing any paperwork!" she yells.

"Tracey, we have to complete this paperwork. Please get

up and come to my office."

"I'm not going anywhere!" she shouts.

"That's not an option. Please come to my office, and we will discuss this matter again." I return to my office and leave the door open, hoping she will come.

Within a few minutes, I overhear a female complaining in a loud voice, "How can staff come in our room without knocking ?"

I come out of my office to see who is complaining. I see a woman walking back toward her room.

"What did she say?" I ask a heavy-set tech who is about six-feet-five inches tall.

"She says you walked in her room without knocking," he answers.

"I didn't go to her room at all," I clarify. "I knocked on Tracey's door."

"They are roommates," he tells me in his chirpy voice. "She wants to create problems. She wants what she wants."

A few minutes later, Tracey approaches the tech. "Are you a supervisor?"

"Yes," he says, even though he isn't.

"I want to talk to you about something," she says. "How can someone just knock and enter our room?"

"Tracey," I intervene, "what are you talking about? I knocked on your door and called out your name. I never set a foot in your room."

She says nothing, staring down at the floor. I walk back to my office, and she follows me.

"What do you want now ?" she asks.

"I need some information to complete your discharge paper-work," I reply gently.

"I'm not in the mood." She makes a face.

"I am trying to help you with your aftercare planning," I explain.

"Fuck it." She stamps her foot. "I don't need your fucking aftercare."

"Tracey, if you cooperate, it will not take more than fifteen or twenty minutes."

"Why should I cooperate with you? What did you or anyone else do for me here?" she retorts. "Nobody advocated my case. No fucking staff wants me to stay here."

"Tracey, you are forgetting that this is a business. Your stay here is our survival. We need patients. Help comes second; money comes first. If we don't have clients, how will we get paid? Your insurance company is not covering your stay here. It is not our fault. What you need to do is comply with your aftercare, and if you still feel you need rehab, your IOP can refer you to one."

"I don't want IOP." She stomps her foot again.

"Forget what you want to do, and do what you need to do," I reply calmly. "If you do what is required, you will not ruin your chances for future treatment."

"Okay," she mutters. "What do you want from me?" She sits own.

"Where are you going from here?" I ask patiently.

"I have no place to go," she says.

"But you must be going somewhere," I sigh.

"My mom's," she says. "Can I call her?"

"Yes, and ask her whether you can live there."

On the phone, she says, "Mom, I need cigarettes, clothes, and money. Thank you, Mom." She is off the phone in a few seconds.

"Tracey, you are leaving tomorrow. Why did you ask for all that stuff ?"

"I need it," she snaps.

"Why didn't you ask your mother whether you can go there or not?"

"I know she will be all right with it," she replies casually.

"May I have the address and phone number there?" I am trying to be patient.

"There is no phone number." She avoids eye contact.

"But didn't you just speak with your mother on the phone?"

"I don't want to give you the phone number."

"Where is your IOP?"

"Chinatown," she answers.

"Any contact number for them?"

"I don't know."

"Who was your counselor?"

"I don't remember." She avoids eye contact.

"When did you see your counselor last?"

"Three weeks ago. Can I call the director of the long-term residential aftercare program that I was in before my recent relapse? I want to see whether I can go back there."

"But you just said you can go to your mother's. Don't you want to call and ask her?"

"No," she responds. "I can always go back there. Can I call the director?"

She calls and leaves a message for the director of that program to call her back.

"I am going to be suicidal tomorrow," she says, looking at a spot on the wall behind me.

"What do you mean?"

"I know what to do to stay here," she responds. "Lots of people say they are suicidal, and they are allowed to stay."

"No, you don't want to do that."

She rolls her eyes. "Why not?"

"Because we will have to commit you and transfer you to a psychiatric unit," I explain.

"I don't care," she says. "That unit is on the second floor of this building, I know. At least I will be able to stay a few days more."

"Tracey, you don't want to play that kind of game. You

may be ble to stay here for one or two days more, but what about your conscience?"

"I don't care," she repeats.

"One of these days, your insurance company will find out about your game. When people tell lies to stay in treatment, they aren't helping themselves. You need to be honest. You don't want to establish your foundation on lies, do you?"

"I don't know." She looks away from me.

"Tracey, you know recovery calls for honesty, sincerity, commitment, open-mindedness, and hard work. You have to give up our deceptive behaviors."

She gives in. "All right. I won't say that I'm suicidal. But I want to go and rest now. I am tired. If she calls back, please let me know."

"Are you sure you don't want to wait?"

"I'm sure," she replies. "I'm sorry for trying to cause you a problem this morning. I was angry. I didn't want to be bothered. I wanted to sleep."

"It's over," I tell her. "But please don't repeat that kind of behavior; it can take an ugly turn."

"I really am sorry." She walks out, leaving my door wide open.

A few minutes later, her roommate, Lisa, a blonde, walks in.

"Tracey says I can make a call from your office. I want to call my mom. I want to inform her that I am here."

On the phone, she pleads, "Mom, I'm trying, Mom. I am trying to get better. Why are you being so nasty, Mom?"

She is sobbing, and the other line rings. "Lisa you have to get off the phone. I need to answer that line; I will let you call again."

"May I speak with Tracey?" the caller asks. "She just left me a message to call her back."

"Lisa," I say, "please get Tracey. Tell her there is a call for her."

"Sure," she says, leaving the office.

Lisa comes back. "Tracey said to take a message for her."

"Any message for Tracey?" I ask.

"I was returning her call," the woman at the other end tells me.

"She can call me back if she has anything to say to me."

I hang up. "Lisa, why didn't Tracey come to the phone?"

"She's nasty," she replies. "She wants to sleep. She keeps bitching all day long. She's giving me a hard time in that room. She goaded me this morning to complain about staff coming in the room."

"Did you see anybody come in the room?"

She shakes her head. "No. They just keep coming and knocking on the door all the time. They don't let us sleep."

"She complained about me this morning, and you did, too," I tell her.

"I'm sorry. I didn't know it was you," she says, looking down at the floor. "She really is nasty."

She gets back on the phone, telling her mother that this program is not like the other program she was in recently. "This rogram is scary. It sucks, the staff here is very unprofessional, and they don't allow us to rest. I am trying, Mom. I am trying.

Why don't you understand? What else do you want me to do? I shouldn't have called you. I wasted my one call talking to you. You always feel I don't do anything for my recovery, and that I always complain. But you would be scared if you came to this program.

"You don't need to tell me that you have never done drugs; I know you don't need to come to a program, but I am just saying it. You don't understand, Mom. I want to leave now. I don't know where I'll go; I thought I could stay with you… You are being unreasonable. I don't want to go for rehab. No, I'm not thinking of using drugs. Mom, you don't understand.

I am sick as a dog, and you want me to stay here. Mom, I'm not going to a recovery house, I would rather go to jail. I am not going, Mom! I said I'm not going!

"Mom, you know I have no place to go. You at least have a home and a husband to go to after work. I have nobody. I've got to go, Mom; you just don't understand. Do you want to speak with my counselor?" She pauses, then continues, "I can't talk with you anymore; you are nasty, Mom. That's it, I'm outta here!" She slams the receiver down, crying And then she looks at me. "Can I talk to you for a minute?" She blows her nose, then continues, "I now why I do drugs."

"Why?"

"Are you my counselor?"

"Yes," I reply. "Monday through Friday."

She smiles. "I do drugs because of depression. I am not depressed because of drugs. I was depressed first, and then I started using drugs. I was in a beautiful relationship for eight years with a man named James. Everything was going very well, and then we started getting high together. He's a beautiful person, inside and out. He made me feel good about myself. He used to tell me how beautiful I was. He always appreciated my beauty. I like to hear good things about me. His parents are millionaires. He is their only son, but since he started using drugs, they disowned him.

He's not going to get anything from them now.

"I broke up with him, and he started doing more and more drugs. He was devastated. After our break up, I started dating another guy. I was pregnant. My doctor said it had to be James's child. I was still seeing James off and on. Seeing his apartment in a mess was heartbreaking. His family loved me like their own daughter. My son, Jim, is almost two years old now. His parents loved their grandson.

"I'm not a whore. I have only slept with seven guys in my entire life. Are those too many to sleep with? I am twenty-eight now. My cousins, though younger than me, have slept with more than fifty guys each. They used to call me the little virgin.

"Anyway, James's family took my son for a DNA test and found that he was not James's. They cut off all ties with us. James started hating me. I am devastated. Now my son is without a father. I'm a single mom. What will I tell him if he asks who his ather is? You know how difficult it is to be a single mom, don't you? I love my son. I want to get better. I had a great upbringing. I need to go home. I can't stay here." She is crying non-stop.

I interrupt, "Why can't you stay here?"

"I have to take care of my son." She avoids looking at me.

"Isn't your mother helping you with your son?"

"My mother works." She continues looking down.

"But I heard your mother say that you should complete this program, and you said you weren't going anywhere. Did you leave other programs before?"

"I didn't leave. I was asked to leave because they found me using a cell phone." She hiccups. "I was using a cell phone to call my son. I wasn't calling my boyfriend. I was missing my son. He's my life, and he's all I have."

"If you really love him, then you must concentrate on your treatment," I suggest. "Get your act together and learn to be a responsible and loving mother."

"I have always been a responsible mother," she retorts.

"A responsible mother does not continue using drugs."

"I'm depressed."

"Using drugs is not going to make your depression any better," I say. "In fact, it will make it worse."

"Then how do I get rid of depression?"

"You don't have to do anything special," I reply. "Just stop using drugs. Don't think about your past, and start living in the present with the hope for a bright future. You also need to spend quality time with your son. When you start doing this, time will take care of your depression."

"I told you that I never neglect my son," she insists.

"Your life is unmanageable," I remind her. "You are engrossed n your depression and relationship conflicts, and you think your problems are the biggest problems in the world. You are here, and you still keep saying that you are a responsible mother, when all the facts are saying something different. Stop lying to yourself, and start doing what needs to be done."

"My son goes for physical therapy because he is almost two and still doesn't walk."

"Your son needs you. He needs his mom healthy, physically and mentally. You will not be a responsible mother if you keep going in and out of treatment facilities."

"Now I feel so relieved . Can I hug you?" She moves forward.

"I am sorry." I move backward. "I'm not allowed to hug clients."

"I understand." She nods. "Thank you again. I really feel much etter. I'll see you later."

Lisa comes to see me again after a couple of days. "Do you think a long-term program will help me?"

"What do you think?"

"I really don't know," she answers. "I am always preoccupied with my past relationships, and I have serious anger issues. I lack patience and tolerance. People hurt me by saying nasty stuff. I feel depressed and lonely. I don't feel good about myself. I'm kind of disconnected from myself. I worry about my son's and my future all the time."

"Lisa, considering what you are saying, you do need a long-term program."

"But I don't think I will be able to concentrate, because I will keep worrying about my son," she responds.

"Just worrying doesn't resolve problems," I tell her. "You have to do something constructive to help your situation."

She nods. "I know you're right. But I keep thinking about what others think about me. I like when others appreciate things about me, and I can't stand it when they criticize me. I have low self-esteem."

"In that case, you need to be open-minded," I suggest.

"You know, I'm curious," she says. "I want to ask you something, but I don't know whether I should or shouldn't."

"If you think you will learn something by asking, then you should go ahead and ask. Otherwise, let it go," I say.

"Don't you hate me for trying to cause you a problem the other day?" She looks at me intently.

"No," I reply.

"I can't believe that you aren't angry," she says.

"It's in the past now," I say. "Bygones are bygones. I am not doing you a favor by letting it go. I am helping myself to have peace of mind. If I hate you, I will be very uncomfortable in your presence, and I can't afford that."

"I lack enlightenment," she responds. "I have a difficult time forgiving and forgetting people."

"Don't worry about being enlightened now," I suggest. "Just take one day at a time to get through the current mess that you're in."

"How about when you are pure, and people still blame you for impurity?" she asks.

"If I am pure and my conscience is clear, I wouldn't worry about what others think about me," I reply. "I am answerable to myself and not to anyone else."

"Really?" Her voice holds disbelief.

"Of course. Let me tell you a beautiful story from the East.

"A master and his student were on their way back to their cave. The river was running high and fast, and the master saw someone thrashing in the current. He immediately jumped into the water determined to save the life of this drowning person. The student saw his master dive into the raging river and start swimming. Suddenly, he realized that the master was about to save a beautiful girl.

"'Master!' he shouted, 'You can't touch that beautiful girl; our sect doesn't allow us to touch females. We are prohibited from doing so.'

"The master ignored him and stayed focused on his goal. How could he possibly fail when he had such devotion and sincerity? He succeeded! He swam the girl to the bank of the river and revived her by performing CPR.

"'You should not have touched her,' reprimanded his student.

'It is not permitted.'

"The master remained silent and kept journeying on.

"Later, the student asked, 'Master, how did you feel when you touched that girl?'

"The master ignored him and kept walking.

"However, the student couldn't forget the incident. Therefore, he asked again, 'Did you get any sexual feelings when you touched that beautiful girl?'

"The master sighed. 'Let me tell you that no sexual thought ever crossed my mind at all. When I jumped in the river, I didn't now whether I was swimming toward a man or a woman. And when I saved her, I didn't even expect a word of thanks from her. In fact, I forgot the incident then and there. She went her way, and I'm going on mine. For me, saving a life is a million times more important than those religious rules. And, by the way, who performed CPR on her?'

"'You did.'

"'Who thought of sex?'

"'I did.'

"'So, what do you think possibly happened?'

"'I was sexually preoccupied.'

"'Do you think you need to do some work?'

"'Yes. I need to clean my mind. I need purified thinking to move toward the path of enlightenment.'

"'Well, let me tell you, the path toward enlightenment is very rough. It calls for devotion, sincerity, hard work, honesty, willingness to change, and open-mindedness. If you keep this in mind and do your part, nothing can prevent you from being enlightened.'"

"Wow! That's a beautiful story," she exclaims. "I will stay focused on being enlightened."

"Lisa, first things first. Today, your focus should be on getting yourself together and starting to think straight. If you learn to go with your conscience, you will be on the path of enlightenment without a doubt."

She leaves all smiles.

* * *

Later, I am with Gary, another client. He is trying to contact his stepdaughter. He dials the number and gets a busy signal. He dials it repeatedly with no success. Now he is restless, pacing my ffice.

Gary is in his mid-fifties and appears physically healthy and is well built. He has been using cocaine for the past thirty years. "Do you have any health issues?" I had asked him when I was completing his psychosocial assessment.

"No," he answered.

"Do you have any physical, emotional, or sexual abuse history?"

"No."

"Have you abused anybody physically, emotionally, or sexually?"

"No."

"Can I try again?" he asks.

"Sure," I reply.

He dials the number two or three times more but still can't

get hrough. He slams the receiver down. "Fucking bitch," he mutters. "I'm going to kill that whore."

"Gary, what's wrong ?" I ask quietly.

He looks at me with tears in his eyes. He wants to say something but appears apprehensive.

"Gary, take a deep breath, and try to calm down," I suggest.

"Okay, okay. I know you are right. I shouldn't act like this, but I am so disheartened." He blinks fast, trying to hide his tears.

I knew something was wrong when I heard him cursing his stepdaughter.

"Gary, tell me what is going on," I urge him.

"I've never told anyone what I am going to tell you today." He takes a deep breath and mumbles, "I don't even know how to tell you." He looks away from me.

"Gary, if you are not comfortable telling me, you don't have to."

"Thanks for being so considerate, but I need to tell you," he murmurs. "I feel comfortable talking to you."

"Well, then, go ahead," I say.

"I sleep with my stepdaughter," he mumbles, staring at the floor.

I am speechless. What does he expect from me?

"It started ten years ago," he continues looking down.

"Are you still married to her mother?" I ask.

"We're separated." He lifts his head.

"Does she know about your affair with your stepdaughter?"

"No."

"How old was your stepdaughter when you started having sex with her?"

"Twenty."

"How old was she when you first met her?"

"Six."

"So, you're telling me you didn't do anything with her until he turned twenty?"

"Yes," he replies, looking straight into my eyes.

"How did you look at her when she was growing up in your house as a child?"

"I never had any bad intentions when she was growing up."

"I'm not convinced." I look at him intently.

"I didn't try to seduce her," he insists. "In fact, when she turned fifteen, she started trying to seduce me. I ignored her."

"So it was her fault?" I snort sarcastically.

"No," he mutters, "I am not saying that."

"Then what are you saying ?"

"I am trying to tell you that I am heartbroken." He clasps his hands tightly together. "She doesn't find me attractive anymore.

She has found someone younger than me. But I can't live without her!"

"Don't you think what you are doing is wrong ?"

"We are both adults," he justifies, "and we started our relationship with mutual consent."

"Mutual consent doesn't make a wrong into a right," I tell him.

"What should I do?" His voice is husky.

"First," I say, "stop thinking of her as a sex partner and sever all ties with her. Second, maintain your recovery. Don't use drugs no matter what. Third, you have to recognize that what you are doing is unhealthy, emotionally, morally, and spiritually."

"I know, but I can't forget her," he mumbles.

"Why not?" I ask.

"I just can't," he says. "She is the best girl in bed I have ever met."

"So what? Stop thinking of her as a sex object. You talk as though you are proud of your immoral act." I shake my head.

"I am neither proud nor ashamed," he says carelessly.

"You say your ex-wife doesn't know about your illicit relationship with your stepdaughter; how is that possible?"

"Because she would be mad at us," he whispers.

"Do you and your stepdaughter live together as husband and wife or as boyfriend and girlfriend?"

"No," he replies. "No one knows about our relationship. We don't want anyone else to know about it."

"Gary, you are hiding this relationship because you are ashamed of it. It is unacceptable in society's eyes, and you know it!"

"I have no reason to be ashamed of it, and I don't care."

"You do care, or you wouldn't be hiding it!"

"What can I say now ?" He stares at the floor.

"You don't have to say anything." I take a deep breath. "You've said enough. You can start listening now. Gary, you need to stop hearing and start listening, and listen from your heart. It will help you understand the futility of your indulgence in an illicit relationship with your stepdaughter, and in turn, it might help you to stop this indulgence. You might wake up. You might just become conscious."

"I am conscious. I'm awake, always have been," he boasts.

"No, you're not," I counter. "You consciously don't feel anything wrong in what you are doing."

"So, you think I am wicked?" He stares at me.

"What I think doesn't matter; what you think matters."

"So, what do you want me to do?"

"You have to do what your conscience permits," I answer.

"But what are people going to think?"

"What you think matters," I repeat. "What others think doesn't matter."

"I don't feel guilty," he asserts.

"Gary, you are in denial! You do feel guilty, but you don't want to admit it and do anything about your guilty feelings."

"Why do you say that?"

"You are hiding this illicit relationship from others. You said that I am the first person you've told about this. You told me your story not because I am your therapist, but because you feel guilty. And," I continue, "you wanted someone to listen to you because you are feeling overwhelmed, uncomfortable, and heartbroken."

"I am still heartbroken." He rubs his eyes.

"It's a matter of time," I state. "Time heals all wounds. You have to let time take its course. Be patient."

"Patience! How will patience help me with this?" He drops his head into his hands.

"Patience helps in every situation," I say. "Just be committed and sincere in your efforts."

"I am committed to my treatment." He looks up.

I look at him sternly. "If you are really committed to your recovery, you will do whatever you need to do to stay in a recovery process."

"I said I am doing everything possible." He shifts in his seat.

"No, you are not! You are lying to yourself. If you were doing everything necessary, you wouldn't pick and choose what to work on."

"I'm seeking help," he whines.

"Well, you are seeking help, but in your own way."

"What do you mean?"

"I mean," I continue, "you are here seeking help, but you are unwilling to discontinue this ongoing immoral relationship. You have reservations, don't you?"

"Kind of," he admits.

I look at my watch and start to get up. "Gary, I have to go now. Relax, put your worries aside, and get some sleep. Just take things one day at a time."

"But I'm so restless, I can't relax." He is up pacing the floor again.

I sit back in my chair. "When did you first realize that you had a drug problem?"

He thinks for a minute. "Well, for the first ten to fifteen years, I didn't think there was a problem. It was only when I started spending a lot of money on drugs that I realized something was wrong."

"It took fifteen years for you to realize that you had a problem. So, surely, you realize that you can't fix your problem in a day or wo. There is no quick fix."

"I want to get out of this mess," he pleads.

"Of course you do, no doubt about it." I nod. "But you have to have the right approach. We'll discuss it some more tomorrow, okay?"

He mumbles, "See you tomorrow," and leaves my office, looking unconvinced.

But tomorrow never came. He was gone much before I resumed my duty the next day. I shake my head and think, you can lead a horse to water, but you can't make him drink. How sad!

Chapter 38

A Crack head

Margaret claims that she does drugs because people get on her nerves. She does not feel that she plays any part in it. She is unwilling to change because she thinks her addictive behavior is a part of her personality. She hates her parents for being strict with her. She claims, "I am helpless. I have no choice but to do drugs because people push me into it."

"Are you talking about people in general?" I ask.

"No. I'm talking about my parents. They get on my last nerve."

"I understand your frustration, but—"

She cuts me off. "You don't!"

"Margaret," I respond politely, "you are here to receive help, so first of all, stop blaming others. I understand that your parents might have played a role in your addictive behavior. But it's unfair to blame it entirely on them. If you are willing to change, you might be able to see different results. But to do this, you need to be flexible, open-minded and willing to see the part you play in our predicament."

"But they didn't love me," she whines. "They were always so strict. I couldn't stand them. They were a pain in the ass. They always had that cop mentality, even at home."

"Maybe they were just trying to discipline you. Can you give me some examples of their extreme strictness?"

She thinks for a while. "Well, they wouldn't allow me to

attend late-night parties even when I turned fourteen."

"I don't think there is anything wrong or unusual with that," I state.

"All my friends were enjoying freedom, but I couldn't, because of those two—especially my father."

"Why, what would he do?" I inquire.

"He would drop me off at school and then pick me up after. He kept track of my friends, and my friends called me a 'sissy.'" She looks away from me.

"Margaret, you are lucky to have such a protective and caring father."

"Bullshit!" she snaps.

I explain, "Here in this country, everyone is so busy; no one has time for their kids. Most parents work, or are so busy doing drugs that they have no time for anything else. In your case, your parents managed some time for you from their busy schedule. Trust me, you were blessed!"

"If you like my parents so much," she retorts, "why don't you adopt them?"

"Not a bad idea," I chuckle. "I don't have American parents, and I guess I will get a package deal, too, won't I?"

"What package deal?" She appears confused.

"A sister along with parents." I grin at her.

She laughs wholeheartedly. "You are funny. I am so lucky to have you as my therapist."

"Don't come to that conclusion so fast," I warn her.

"I really mean it," she insists.

"Then you are lucky for two things." I smile at her.

"What two things?"

"One, you say you are lucky to have me as your therapist, and two, you have very caring and protective parents."

"You are so stupid," she snarls.

"Correct." I smile. "I was born stupid. Now my stupidity is growing into insanity."

"You are funny." She smiles. "You make me laugh."

"Thanks! By the way, it's not me who is making you laugh," I explain. "It's natural to laugh. You just need to think right and do the right things, and everything will change for the better."

"Okay," she says calmly. "I'll listen to you and do whatever you say."

"Good." I grin at her mischievously. "I like that spirit. Now, jump out this window."

She laughs.

"What?" I ask, pretending to be serious.

"Nothing," she responds.

"I am serious about jumping," I assert.

She looks at me, confused.

"I need a monkey. I'll twist his tail, and he'll jump the way I want him to jump. Isn't that a good idea?" I ask.

She laughs again, and I think she understands.

"Okay, Margaret, I have to see another client, so I will see you again when I am free." She leaves my office happily.

I don't have time to see her again that day, but I meet with her first thing the following morning.

"How are you today?" I ask.

"Fine," she replies.

"What did you do last night?"

"We ordered out for supper," she answers, "and guess what? I met another girl, and you'll be surprised to know that her parents are cops, too. We're friends now."

I know she is referring to Ronnie, and her story is not much like Margaret's. There are a few similarities: both girls are addicts, and their parents are cops. Both girls are young and beautiful. However, Ronnie's story is that her parents were busy working and getting high. They never had time for her. Now Ronnie is twenty-five and a mother. In fact, Ronnie became a mother when she was sixteen. She believed that she had been a bad daughter and that even if her parents had no time for her, she should have been good. Now she is an irresponsible mother. Ronnie's daughter, who is nine, lives with her parents. Since they never had time for their own daughter when she was growing up, I doubt they have much time for their granddaughter, considering that they are still in their progressive addictions. Ronnie is soft-spoken, ready to help others, and apparently very well mannered. She has been in several treatment programs but has not stayed clean. Every time she leaves treatment, he picks up drugs on her first day after discharge.

Surprisingly, she has no bitterness toward her parents. "I'm grateful to my parents for taking care of my daughter," she told me while I was completing her psychosocial assessment. "I know they aren't good parents, but you can see what I'm doing. Am I a good parent? No! I am busy getting high all the time. I haven't been with my child one day clean. I don't even know what she likes or dislikes. For that matter, I don't know anything about her. I am so ashamed of myself. I don't deserve to be a mother. You don't know how much I want to be a good mother. I want to give her love and affection. I suffered, but I don't want her to suffer. But the fact is I'm messed up. I have to get myself together. I haven't figured out how; the only thing I know is that I've got to do it." she said, tears rolling down her cheeks.

"Margaret," I continue, "tell me more about your life."

"There is nothing worth telling," she responds.

"Then tell me something that is worthless," I insist.

"All right," she says haltingly. "I'm a crack head. I love heroin. I love pills. I was raped at fifteen. I hate my parents. Oh, sorry, you wouldn't like me saying that, because they are going to be your parents, too."

"You are right about that." We both laugh so hard she bursts into tears. "Okay, tell me about getting raped," I say gently. "How did it happen?"

"I went to a block party."

"What is a block party?" I ask.

"Parties arranged for the whole block and the street is closed off for traffic," she explains.

"Was it at night?"

"Yes."

"Did you tell your parents that you were going to the party?"

"No." She pauses. "I sneaked out without their knowledge."

"Why did you do that?"

"You know how screwed up they are," she rationalizes. "They wouldn't have allowed me to go."

"Do you think if you had listened to them, you probably would have avoided that painful incident?"

"I don't believe in ifs and buts," she states. "Whatever happens as to happen, anyway."

"That doesn't mean you make yourself vulnerable, and then suffer the consequences your entire life."

"I didn't make myself vulnerable. I just wanted to enjoy the party." She breaks eye contact.

"At what cost?" I ask.

She starts crying again, and after a few minutes, she admits, "I put myself into a bad situation. I could have avoided that fateful incident."

"You never told me," I chuckle.

"What?" she asks anxiously.

"About the spring of water that you have somewhere behind your eyes."

"I'm sorry." She gulps. "I forgot to tell you about that." She is laughing and crying at the same time.

"You know you are good at two things?"

"What two things?"

"One is crying," I reply, "and the other is laughing."

She laughs again, and this time she laughs for a long time.

"Do you want to call your parents?" I ask.

"They must be at work now."

"Don't they have cell phones?"

"My dad does."

"Why don't you call him?"

"He is going on vacation day after tomorrow," she tells me. "He dropped me off here yesterday."

"So what? Call him," I insist, "and just tell him that you are doing fine."

"He won't believe that," she says. "He's probably thinking I've already left."

"But the fact is, you haven't left, and he will be glad to hear that."

"Then he'll ask me if I'm calling my boyfriend." She sits motionless.

"Doesn't he like your boyfriend?"

"No."

"Why?"

"We used to get high together," she admits.

"Are you still in touch with him?"

She hesitates, then says, "Not really."

"What does 'not really' mean?"

"I call him sometimes." She avoids eye contact.

"Okay, let's call your father," I persist.

She calls him. "Dad, can you drop me off some cigarettes and money?"

"Why don't you say something more?" I suggest.

"What?" She waves her hand questioningly.

Tell him you are doing fine, I write on a piece of paper, and *you love him.*

"I am doing fine, Dad. I like being here." She smiles. "Thank you, Dad. I love you too." She hangs up.

"How do you feel now ?"

"I'm glad I called him, and I am happy because he is going to drop off some things tonight!"

"Good," I respond. "I'll see you later." She leaves my office delighted. One call to her dad made her day. Dads are wonderful, aren't they?

* * *

Margaret walks into my office again later that day. "May I come in?"

"You're already in, so you don't need any permission," I respond. "What's up?"

"Nothing much. I was bored, so I thought I would come see you."

"So you see me to pass the time?" I joke.

"No." she blushes. "How are you doing, Christopher?"

"I was doing great, but now I don't know," I chuckle.

"Why?"

"Because you are here," I reply.

"You are a mess." She smiles at me.

"Birds of a feather flock together." I return the smile.

"I want to call my dad again." She reaches for the phone.

"Why?"

"I just want to find out what time he is coming," she answers.

I give her the phone.

"Hi, Dad, what time are you coming ? Did you say 8:30 in the evening? Dad, my counselor is very good. His name is Christopher." She covers the receiver with her hand. "What country are you from?" She looks at me. "I know you told me some country."

"India," I reply.

She removes her hand from the receiver. "He's from India, Dad. Would you like to speak with him?" She hands me the receiver.

"Hi, Mr. Christopher, how are you?"

"I'm fine, Mr. Smith. How are you?"

"I'm good," he responds.

"You have a beautiful daughter!" I tell him.

"Beautiful, but real messed up." He laughs.

"She is willing to make amends," I state.

"She is a great manipulator." I hear harshness in his tone.

"I don't know about that, but one thing I do know is that she needs her parents," I stress. "She needs you."

"I'll be there tonight around 8:30," he says. "How long are you going to be there?"

"I'm leaving shortly," I reply. "But I would be happy to meet with you for a family session."

"We are going to Mexico on vacation," he continues. "We are leaving the day after tomorrow."

"I'm working tomorrow. Instead of coming today, why don't you come tomorrow?" I suggest.

"Let me talk to my wife and call you back." He hangs up.

"Why did you ask him to come tomorrow?" Margaret demands.

"I want to speak with him," I tell her calmly. "I want to find out more about you. I want to see how he can support you in your recovery process."

"What about my cigarettes?" she asks anxiously.

"You will have to wait," I answer. "By the way, tell me what kind of support you want from your parents."

"My mother is a darling," she says. "I love her. The problem is Dad."

"Why do you say that?"

"He calls me a junky," she replies.

"What else?"

"He never allows me to speak with my boyfriend."

"Why should he allow you to speak with your boyfriend if he is an active addict?"

"But I am a grown-up," she says, pride in her voice.

"You are grown up in age," I tell her, "but you are still immature mentally."

The phone rings.

"Christopher, this is Smith. I spoke with my wife, and she feels it is a good idea to meet you tomorrow. Is it okay with you?"

"It will be my pleasure," I respond.

"What time?"

"How about 1:30 p.m.?" I suggest.

There is a long pause. Finally, he says, "Okay, that's fine."

"Done," I say.

The security guard calls the next day when the Smiths arrive. Margaret and I walk over to the front entrance. I can't tell whether he is happy or not. She appears unenthusiastic.

"Hi, Mom. Hi, Dad," she greets them.

"Hello, Margaret." They smile tentatively.

"You are Mr. Christopher?" Mr. Smith asks. He is tall, well built, elegantly dressed, and he appears to be in his mid-fifties.

"Yes," I respond. "How are you doing, Mr. Smith?"

"I'm fine." He smiles.

"Mrs. Smith, it's nice to meet you. How are you today?" I ask.

"Good," she says, her expression blank.

I lead them to an empty room, and we all pull our chairs into a circle.

"Mrs. and Mr. Smith, I am glad that you came in." I look at both of them respectively.

"We appreciate your time," Mr. Smith responds.

"It's a part of my job, and I'm hopeful our meeting will help Margaret," I state.

"We have heard a lot about you," Mrs. Smith adds.

"Nothing bad, I hope," I say, pretending to be concerned. We all laugh.

"Mr. and Mrs. Smith, we all need to be on the same page.

We know that Margaret has been using a significant amount of moodaltering chemicals, and she has behavioral problems. She needs our support. I know you have been very supportive parents, but still—"

Before I can finish my sentence, Mr. Smith cuts in. "Did she tell you that we aren't supportive?"

"No, she didn't," I reply. "If I gave you that impression, I am sorry. In fact, she told me that you are very protective. She loves both of you, especially her mother. She told me how you would drop her off wherever she needed to go. She also talked about all the beautiful vacations you took together. She did say, however, that she has some issues with you."

"What kind of issues?" Mr. Smith demands.

I look at Margaret. "Why don't you tell your dad how you feel?"

"Dad," she hesitates, takes a long breath, looks at him, then continues, "I don't like it when you call me a junky."

"Okay." He shrugs. "I won't call you a junky. I'll call you an addict. Is that better?" He stares at her.

Margaret looks to me for support.

"Mr. Smith, you should avoid calling her a junky," I suggest.

"Whether I call her a junky or an addict," he replies dismissively, "it's one and the same."

"Mr. Smith, please don't call her junky anymore," I request.

"Fine. I will refer to her as an addict."

Mrs. Smith speaks up. "There have always been problems between the two of them. They never got along."

"What sorts of problems?" I ask, looking at Mrs. Smith.

"My husband has a temper." She smiles at him.

"How do you handle his temper?" I ask.

"I ignore him. I just don't react. He is hot one minute and cold the next." She looks at him lovingly.

"You are a smart lady," I respond.

She smiles.

"Any other problems?" I ask.

"I don't think he understands that she is still a girl in many ways." Mrs. Smith looks at Margaret. "He keeps nagging at her, and then she reacts negatively because she doesn't know how to handle his anger, and she also has a temper."

"I do have an anger issue," Mr. Smith admits.

"Mr. Smith, are you willing to support your daughter in her recovery process?" I look at him.

"I have been supporting her her whole life," he replies. "To be frank with you, I am tired of supporting her. I don't want to do it anymore."

"You don't really mean that, do you?" I meet his eyes.

"No. He doesn't mean it," Mrs. Smith cuts in. "He loves her beyond belief. He simply wants her to stop using drugs. He is saying that because he is angry with her right now."

"So, Mr. Smith, you would provide her with the necessary support, wouldn't you?" I press.

He nods somewhat reluctantly.

"Margaret, are you willing to do your part?" I turn to her.

"Yes," she answers half-heartedly.

"What will you do to stay clean?" I ask.

"I will make meetings," she replies. "NA meetings help me to stay clean."

"But NA meetings alone aren't enough, Margaret." I gaze at her.

"Ask her about her boyfriend," her father prompts.

"Margaret, The Twelve Steps of Recovery, having a sponsor to talk to when needed, and going back to school, might help you in our recovery process," I say.

"I don't know about that," she sighs.

"See, that's how she answers," her father states, a touch of annoyance in his voice.

"It's okay if you don't know. You just need to try. These things have worked for other people in recovery, and they might work for you, too. Are you willing to listen?" I respond patiently.

"Yes," she answers quietly.

"Are you willing to do what is required to stay in a recovery process?" I push for a commitment.

"Yes," she answers. "I will do anything and everything that needs to be done to stay clean."

"She says this kind of stuff, but she always does what she wants to do," her father sighs.

"Mr. Smith, we need to forget her past and move forward," I assert. "I understand your frustration with her. She needs to stop repeating the same mistakes. Margaret, this might be your last chance, so be mindful of it. Even your own family won't put up with you if you don't stop using drugs and learn to stand on your wn."

"I'm going to make it this time," she states confidently. "But the doctor needs to lower my methadone dose."

"That's between you and the doctor," I tell her. "However, I will have a word with her. By the way what dose are you on?"

"Ninety milligrams," she says quickly.

"But you were only using two-to-three bags at the most." Her mother appears somewhat surprised.

"I was also using Benzos," Margaret admits.

"You never told me that!" her mother says, shocked.

"Well, I am telling you now," Margaret says without hesitation.

"How many pills were you using ?" her mother presses.

"One or two," she answers, avoiding her mother's eyes.

I sense something isn't right. I know the doctor wouldn't put her on ninety milligrams of methadone for the amount of drugs she claims to have been using for such a short period of time. I excuse myself and go check her chart. I discover that she has admitted to using eight to twelve bags of heroin and eight to ten pills daily. I return to the meeting.

"Margaret, you can speak with the doctor about your methadone dose," I suggest, "but you need to be honest with her. You have every right to discuss your treatment and decide what treatment you want."

"She thinks of herself as an expert on treatment. She is a master at using drugs. But by using drugs, you don't become an expert on treatment." Her father stares at her.

"How do you manage with your husband?" I ask his wife, smiling.

"I know he has a temper," she repeats. "I handle it by saying nothing."

"She keeps me under control." He looks at her appreciatively. "She keeps me together."

"Well, I ask that both of you continue giving Margaret the support she needs, and show some faith in her."

"All right, we will," Mr. Smith replies, "but this will be the last ime."

"He really does love her," her mother chimes in.

"Margaret," I say, "please use this beautiful opportunity. Very few people get a second chance in life. You are lucky, so please be focused and committed."

"I will," she promises.

"And don't be on the phone with that addict friend of yours," her father commands.

"No problem. Dad, can you drop off some more cigarettes, some cosmetics, and some money before you leave tomorrow ?"

"Why do you need money?" he demands.

"For order out," she replies. "On Fridays, we are allowed to order food from outside."

He gives in. "Okay, sure."

"Mr. Smith, just get her the basics," I suggest. "She doesn't need cosmetics. She is here for treatment, not for decorating herself."

Her mother nods. "I agree."

"But I need them," Margaret whines.

"It's not a basic necessity," I tell her. "You may want them, but you don't need them."

She shrugs and drops the subject.

"Mrs. and Mr. Smith, I need to go." I smile. "But I promise to see you again when you come back from your vacation. It was a pleasure meeting you. Have a wonderful trip."

"Thank you for conducting this family session. See you soon."

They kiss their daughter and leave.

Margaret's father dropped off money, cigarettes, and a long-distance calling card on his way to the airport, but no cosmetics

I see Margaret on the pay phone.

"Margaret, did you call your parents in Mexico?" I ask.

"No," she responds. "I'm leaving them alone. They are on vacation, and I don't want to bother them."

I am impressed, but at the same time, I say to myself, "look who's talking." A girl who is inflicting pain on herself as well as her loved ones is being so considerate of her parent's privacy. However, I say nothing to her about what I am thinking.

I tell her, "I saw you on the phone several times. Who did you all?"

"My friend." She looks down at the floor.

"The one your father told you not to call?"

She rolls her eyes. "My dad simply doesn't like him."

"You are on black out," I remind her. "You are not supposed to take calls."

"But staff gave me permission," she says huffily.

"Stop calling your friend; he is an addict. You will end up in trouble. The staff on duty might not have realized that you are on a seven-day black out, but when they do, they will hold you responsible for breaking the rules."

"But they gave me permission," she whines.

"That doesn't matter," I say. "You also need to take responsibility for your part in it."

"But—"

I cut her off. "Stop the ifs and buts. I don't want to discuss it. You are not going to make any more calls. However, if you want to call your parents, you can call them from my office. Do you nderstand?"

"Okay, okay," she sighs.

I don't see her on the pay phone anymore, and she doesn't come to my office to call her parents. She progresses to the next level of care, and I am no longer her therapist. I become busy and don't know if she completes her treatment or not. I have an uneasy feeling that she left. I don't know why I feel that way, but the truth is, I do. I never hear from her or her parents again. I have her father's cell phone number and consider calling him several times to find out how she is doing, but I don't, and eventually I misplace the number.

To my pleasant surprise, after almost three years, when I was going through my old papers I find her father's cell phone number so I call him. He informs me that Margaret is clean. In addition, she is working on her bachelor's degree in criminal psychology and has a part time job. Isn't that wonderful? I wanted to ask him whether she left our program against medical advice or what, but then a better sense prevailed upon me, "How does it matter?" What matters is that she is still in recovery, don't you think?

Chapter 39

Lust Mistaken For Love

Julie is a twenty-five-year-old, stylish young woman. She uses drugs every day. Even though her uncle knows she is using, he gives her money to support her habit.

She tells me that her uncle does not do drugs. So I ask, "Then why does he give you money to buy drugs?"

She shrugs. "He doesn't want me to go to others and ask for money."

"What about your parents?" I ask.

"They don't talk to me." She hesitates and avoids eye contact.

"They don't talk to me because I live with my uncle."

"Why don't your parents want you to live with your uncle?"

"I don't know." She fidgets uneasily.

"What does your uncle do for living ?"

"He's a cop," she says, looking away from me.

"He's a cop, and he gives you drug money?" I exclaim. *I suspect that something is wrong.*

"Yes. Why do you want to know about my uncle?" She becomes irritated.

"Julie, you live with him, he supports you financially, he is playing an active role in your addiction, and he is your enabler. Therefore he could play a significant role in your recovery!"

"You're not going to tell him to stop giving me money, are ou?" Her voice shakes.

I shake my head. "No, but I think it will be beneficial if we have a family session with him. What do you think?"

"I don't think that's a good idea." She starts wringing her hands.

"Why not?"

"He won't come," she declares. "I know him."

"Okay," I say, "but there is no harm in trying."

"NO!" she shouts. "I don't want you to try."

"It appears you don't want him involved in your recovery process, is that right?"

"Uh-huh," she mumbles. "I don't want him involved."

"Do you intend to go back to live with him?" I ask gently.

"I'm not sure." She hesitates. "He cares for me, he brought me cigarettes and money today; but-" Another pause, and then he blurts out, "He gives me a hundred dollars every day and then makes love to me. I hate him."

"Oh, I see. How long has this been going on?"

"Three years." She looks guilty.

"Is he married?"

"No," she replies. "He is a widower. My parents know about us, and my father is very angry. He doesn't want me to live with im. He says I can come home if I stop using, but I don't want to stop."

"That would be the right thing to do," I tell her. "Why complicate your life?"

"It's already complicated." She looks helpless.

"Exactly. So why complicate it more?"

"Oh, I don't know!" She sighs wearily. "Maybe there is no other way of living life."

"Let it go for the time being. When we meet next, we will discuss this and try to find the best way out," I reassure her.

She walks out of my office a bit more relaxed.

Two days later, she comes to see me again. "I want to call my uncle," she announces.

"First, stop calling him uncle," I snap. "Second, why do you want to call him?"

She shrugs casually. "I just want to know how he's doing."

"What?" I ask, shocked.

"I want to know how he is doing," she repeats.

"Julie, that is a bad idea." She sits silently. I ask her again, "Do you intend to go back and live with him?"

"Not sure," she responds.

"Is there a possibility that you might?"

"He's a good person," she replies.

"Are you in love with him?"

"No."

"He is your uncle. He is having an illicit relationship with you. He gives you one hundred dollars a day, knowing that you will spend that money on drugs. Two days ago, you said that you hate him, and now you want to call him to find out how he is doing. Nothing seems to be right. There are a lot of gaps in your thinking."

She answers, "He gives me money because he is afraid that I will find someone younger; he is fifty-six. He is basically a nice uy."

"A nice guy wouldn't give his niece money to buy drugs," I sigh, "and then have sex with her. But it looks like you do want to continue your relationship with him, don't you?"

"I'm not sure." She looks down.

"This is insane!" I remark.

"I know," she says, "but I can't help it. I just don't know."

"You know what?" I say. "You need to stop waffling and make a decision."

"I just don't know," she repeats.

"You are blundering about because of your stupid behavior."

"Are you calling me stupid?" she demands.

"Well," I reply, "what do you expect? Should I call you smart?"

"You have no right to call me stupid!" She stamps her foot.

"I don't think I called you stupid. I said what you are doing is stupid."

"You are arrogant," she hisses. "I don't want to listen to you. I don't appreciate the way you talk to me."

"Julie, I don't need you to appreciate what I say. I am not here to please you. I have to tell you what is in your best interests and what is not. Don't expect me to tell you what you want to hear. I will tell you what you need to hear; it's your option to listen to me or not."

"I'm a grownup. I know what is best for me." She glares at me.

"Evidently, you don't. You refuse to listen because you don't want to change."

"I do want to change," she insists. "If I didn't want to change, I wouldn't have come here in the first place."

"Julie, I'm glad you are here. But you didn't come here because you wanted to change. You came because you needed relief. You had severe aches and pains; you were throwing up and had stomach cramps. You couldn't stand it anymore. You had no alternative but to get admitted. Now, you have an opportunity, and you can make use of it by staying focused and committed."

"You don't understand how much I miss him." She looks away from me.

"If you get in touch with reality and develop a relationship with yourself, you won't miss him."

She rolls her eyes. "How do I get in touch with myself?"

"Through observation," I reply. "If you observe what's happening within and around you, it will help to reveal yourself to you. It will make you aware of the wandering of your mind."

"I think I need to get some sleep," she yawns.

"No. That's not the best thing to do now. If you sleep during the day, you won't be able to sleep at night. You have to consider some other options."

"I don't know of any other options," she whines.

"Well," I say, "here's a suggestion: go and attend the group that is being conducted on this unit. You might gain some knowledge about addiction."

"Fine." She leaves.

She comes back a few hours later, declaring enthusiastically, "I'm leaving. My uncle is coming to pick me up."

"How do you know that your so-called uncle is coming to pick you up?"

"I just know it." She avoids eye contact.

Although the clients are not supposed to have access to the pay phone on this unit for their first seven days, I suspect she found a way to use it.

"Julie, I don't think you are making the right decision."

"I know. But I'm still leaving."

"You will feel sick." I hope my concern shows in my expression and my voice.

"No," she responds, "I won't."

"How can you be so sure?"

"I am not feeling sick now."

"Julie, you are not feeling sick because all the drugs are out of your system, and you are getting enough medication to manage your withdrawal symptoms. You need to give yourself a chance. You need to show some patience."

"I can't stay in here any longer. I'm suffocating. I feel caged in. Everything is so controlled."

"What about your life? Don't drugs control your life? That's the real prison!"

She looks away from me. "That was a bad choice, but I am not going to do it anymore."

"I don't see any truth in what you are saying." I look straight into her eyes.

"But I am telling the truth." She averts her eyes.

"You are just talking the talk," I respond.

"Whatever," she snaps.

"Julie, don't leave. Stay. Give it a try."

"Nothing will happen," she says.

"You never know," I counter optimistically. "Everything might fall into place. Sometimes, miracles happen."

"I don't believe in miracles," she retorts.

"If you stay in treatment and do your part, you will most certainly have amazing results," I reassure her.

"Well, I don't know about that."

"Julie, just wait and see. Be patient. And if you expect the best, most of the time, you will get it. If you expect the worst, most of the time, the worst is what you'll get ."

She gives in. "Okay. I'll stay and see what 'miracle' is going to happen." She calls her so-called uncle and tells him not to come because she is tapering down methadone and she might have withdrawal symptoms if she does not receive the prescribed dose.

* * *

"Good morning, Julie." I smile at her when I see her two days later. "How are you doing today?"

"Well, I can't say I am doing great, but I am doing better than before. I was tossing and turning all night though. I miss him," she mumbles, looking down.

I take a deep breath; I don't know what to say. After a pause, I say, "Julie, you are young and beautiful; you can always have boyfriends. What you need to do now is concentrate on your recovery. Don't waste your valuable time thinking about him. Leave him alone. He should be in your past. You have to take care of the issues at hand."

"Have you ever been in love?" she asks, avoiding eye contact.

"Don't tell me you are in love with this man."

"I really don't know," she says wearily.

"It's not love. It's lust. He is using you." I insist.

"I know that." She looks up for the first time.

"If you know it, then why do you want to continue your relationship with him?"

"I don't know." She looks away from me.

"You are not thinking straight," I say. "You aren't using your head."

She starts crying.

"Julie, crying is not a solution. You have to start thinking. It will help you to realize the irrationality in your thinking and actions."

"Fear makes me run away." She is still crying.

"Fear of what?"

"I don't know. I'm just afraid." After a long pause, she resumes,

"I'm kind of lost. Everything is so cloudy."

"You are not lost. It's just a matter of time. You need to be firm and make well-informed decisions. Everything you see is cloudy and murky because you are fighting internal conflicts and temptations, but as you keep going, the clouds will disappear, and you will be fine."

She looks uncertain. "I hope so. I'm happy that I didn't leave the other day."

"You did the right thing by not leaving," I assure her.

"I'm thinking of going to a recovery house from here," she adds.

"That's a good plan." I nod. "By the way, you will be stepping down tomorrow."

"What does that mean?" She gives me a confused look.

"Don't you remember," I remind her, "you requested a rehab program? This is a detox program. Starting tomorrow, you'll be transferred to rehab. You will have a different counselor, and you will be able to go to the cafeteria for meals."

"Oh," she responds excitedly, "that will be great! I have been longing to go to the cafeteria with everyone else."

"Julie, I'll see you tomorrow, before you are transferred."

"What time tomorrow ?"

"In the afternoon."

She leaves my office all smiles.

* * *

The following day, as soon as I walk in, I am told by my colleague that Julie left.

"She left?" I am taken aback.

"She had some visitor, and she left with him," he states.

I didn't say anything, but I thought I knew who the visitor was. She was just learning to smile, but what can be done if she just wanted to smile for one day and cry the rest of her life? Some people love misery. She refused help, and she couldn't resist temptation. She apparently didn't know that it is easier to divert stream of water than a river, and that temptation is best resisted at the thought level. Her focus was on immediate gratification. She wanted sex and drugs. She refused to see the futility of her indulgences. All said and done, her so-called uncle does know how to keep using her to satisfy his lust.

Chapter 40
Is This Fate?

I see a man at the table having dinner, and he looks familiar. I walk closer, and I recognize him. It's Bill, my ex–client who left treatment because he was afraid to hear the results of his biopsy. He is disheveled and looks very tired. His skin is hanging under his chin and arms. He has many more tattoos on his arms and all over his body than he had before. He was in good physical health when he left treatment last time.

"Hey, Bill, how are you doing ?" I ask.

"I'm sick." He looks up. He can't close his mouth when he sees me. His mouth is open for so long I worry that his jaw is locked. He gathers himself together and asks, "What are you doing here?"

"I work here," I reply.

"Aren't you working at the other place anymore?"

"I work there, too. Bill, when did you relapse?"

"The same night I left treatment. I shouldn't have left in the first place. I should have listened to the staff. They asked me to get the biopsy done, and I just couldn't handle it."

"Did you ever get the biopsy report?" I ask.

"I recently found out that it was negative."

"So you were worrying for no reason?"

"I guess you are right." He looks guilty. "Can you be my therapist here?"

"No."

417

"Why not?" He sounds offended.

"I work for detox, and you are in rehab," I explain.

"Are you angry with me because I left treatment last time?"

"Bill, we all make mistakes. We have to learn from our past mistakes and move on."

"I'm really messed up this time," he says sadly. "I have five more charges pending against me."

"If you keep relapsing like this, it's bound to happen," I tell him.

"I really don't know what to do," he says hopelessly. "I'm not getting any help here, and this place is a mess. I'm on a sixty-five milligram dose, but it's not enough. I was doing a bundle a day. I need at least ninety milligrams. Can you help me get more methadone?"

"No," I reply, "I can't. You have to speak with the doctor."

"These doctors don't listen, and the nurse is very unsympathetic. She tells me, 'I didn't tell you to do drugs. You did it on our own; now you have to face the consequences. If you want recovery, then you have to bear some pain. I have my own problems, and I deal with them without using drugs. Why can't you? Don't bother me again; I can't give you anything more than what is written in the order.' She is crazy talking to a patient like that. I don't now who the fuck made her a nurse. Trust me, she is an absolute asshole. They should administer a drug test on her."

"Bill, you have to understand that she has no authority to give you any extra, even if she wanted to."

"I'm trying to get help," he responds. "I'm trying to get better, and these fucking people are giving me a hard time."

"Bill, I don't think anyone is trying to give you a hard time. You just don't want to accept the fact that you focus on immediate gratification. You always want what you want, when you want it, and how you want it."

"That other place was a thousand times better than this

one," he tells me.

"You hated that place so much you didn't want to stay there for one more day when you left," I remind him.

"Christopher, I was pissed off."

"You're always pissed off. It seems to be your birthright. Look at you. Aren't you pissed off now ?"

"These people here are inhuman. I am going through so much pain, but they show no concern."

"Bill, you have to stop blaming others."

"How can I get recovery when there is no support?" he whines.

"All said and done," I state, "your recovery is always in your hands."

"I get fed up with all this, and then I leave," he rationalizes.

"That is escapism," I explain. "You always want to escape from reality because you lack the courage to face it. You are a coward."

"I don't mind anything you say," he tells me, "because I respect you."

"Bill, you need to start respecting yourself and be serious about recovery. It's high time you accept responsibility for your situation. You need to show some patience, and things will turn the way you want them to."

"You know very well that I lack patience," he mutters.

"Impatience will get you nowhere. You have to practice patience."

"Can you be my counselor again?" he asks slowly.

"No, I told you that earlier. However, you may be able to attend my group."

"That would be good." He smiles halfheartedly.

"Bill, I need to get back to my office. I'll see you later, okay?"

"Sure." He shrugs. "See you around."

When Bill runs into me three or four days later, he is whining again: "Christopher, I don't know whether I can survive one more day here."

"Why, what happened now ?"

"Everything," he replies.

"Everything ?" I look at him quizzically.

"Well," he complains, "the food is bad, nobody cares, I am not allowed to make calls, I haven't seen my therapist for all these days, and I don't get enough medication."

"Bill, you know what? You have become a chronic complainer. You have to stop complaining about petty matters. You have to invest your time and energy into something more important and constructive."

"There is nothing constructive to do in these fucking prorams," he sniffs.

"What could be more important in your life than your recovery?"

"I doubt that I can get any recovery here," he replies.

"Whether you get it or not," I say, "don't worry about it now. Just start working, and you will be amazed by the results."

"I'll give it a shot," he says.

"That's the spirit." I smile.

"By the way, Christopher, did you see Jack?"

"Yes," I answer.

"He's avoiding me."

"He must be feeling ashamed of what he did to you last time," I tell him.

"I bet he is."

Jack is the one who allegedly put the plastic bag of feces under Bill's mattress when Jack left treatment last time. Jack is capable of doing it, but so is Bill. He has an absolute jail mentality. Who knows? He might have done it himself just to make Jack look bad.

"Hi, Jack, what happened?" I ask him while he's in my office.

"I relapsed, duh."

"Why did you pick up drugs again?"

"I don't know. I was clean for eight months and then I just started; they were there."

"Jack, stop lying. You didn't stay clean for eight months."

"Actually, I was clean for a few months," he insists.

"No, that's not true either. Why are you lying? You relapsed in a few days. You know that we make follow up calls when clients leave treatment, don't you?"

"I'm sorry." He looks down, starts playing with a pen in his and, and continues, "Everybody was using drugs in the recovery house where I lived."

"Jack, look at me and listen. You need to be honest if you want to stay clean. When you tell the truth, you feel good about yourself, and you don't have to remember what you said earlier. And we'll find you another place to live where they don't allow people to stay who use drugs."

"That will be good," he says. "But I don't want to leave now. I need a long-term program. How long can I stay here?"

"It depends," I answer. "I'll have to find out what level of care you are eligible for and how many days your insurance company is willing to give you."

"When can you tell me? I was told that once I complete detox, I will have to leave."

"I can tell you in a few minutes."

I go see the utilization manager, who tells me, "He's not getting rehab; he has been in twenty programs, and he doesn't follow up with IOP. I told him that, and he called his insurance company on his own. So, why is he involving you?"

"He is anxious," I reply.

"He has to leave on Monday, but if he wants to appeal the decision, he can," she says. "Do you want me to talk to him?"

"No, I'll handle it." I walk away.

The moment Jack sees me, he asks, "What happened?"

"Jack, your insurance company is declining rehab, and you

are being discharged on Monday. You can attend IOP if you want."

"But I need long-term rehab," he pleads. "Why don't you call my insurance company?"

"You have already spoken with them," I reply.

"They told me that I can call them on my last day of coverage," he says.

"Your last day of coverage is Sunday," I tell him, "so you can call them then."

"But no one will be there on Sunday," he says.

"They work seven days a week, so you can make the call from my office on Sunday."

He gives in. "Fine. I'll call them on Sunday. Thank you."

On Sunday, my colleague tells me, "Jack is claiming that you promised to get him more days in treatment."

"I didn't promise him anything." I shake my head.

"Can you talk to him?" he asks.

"Sure."

He returns with Jack.

"Jack, what's the problem now ?" I ask.

"I want methadone maintenance. Can you help me?"

"No," I reply.

"Can I see a doctor today?" he asks.

"I doubt it. This being Sunday, the staff doctors are not here," I explain, "and the on-call doctors only come in case of an emergency."

"Can I call my insurance company?"

"Of course you can," I reply. "But why did you say that I promised to get you more days?"

"I'm sorry." He looks away from me. "It was a slip of the tongue."

"No, it wasn't," I say firmly. "When you saw another therapist working in my office, you thought I was not working today, and you felt that you could get away with a lie."

"I said I'm sorry!" He continues looking away from me.

"How many times do you say 'sorry' in one day?"

"I don't know," he says carelessly.

"If you really don't know, try to figure it out," I tell him. "You will be amazed."

"If I don't get any more days here, I will definitely use drugs. I need help!" He looks up for the first time.

"Jack, if you really need help, then stop splitting the staff, stop lying, stop manipulating, and give up your slimy behavior. And you don't have to use drugs just because you are not getting any more days here, but it's up to you."

"You mean to say even if I pick up drugs again, you guys don't care?"

"Whether we care or not isn't important. What is important is whether you care!" I decide to change the subject. "By the way, did you meet Bill?"

"Yes, I did."

"Did you speak with him?"

"No. I don't want to talk to him. He's a pimp."

I consider asking him whether he defecated in the plastic bag aound in Bill's bed at the other treatment facility, but I resist the thought. It really doesn't matter now. If we dig into it, he might ask Bill about it, and that could cause serious problems between them. In addition, I didn't want the other therapist to know about it. Therefore, I let it go.

"Jack, do you want to call your insurance company now ?"

"No, I'll call them later," he replies.

In the end, he did not call his insurance company. I think he accepted the fact that he was not going to get any more time in treatment. Jack was discharged to another recovery house. I hope he takes responsibility for his behavior and becomes an active agent in his recovery process.

* * *

A few months later, Jack is back. He looks like a malnourished teenager even though he is close to fifty. He is frail, almost vanishing. Last time when he left, he had put some weight back on.

"I am back," he declares the moment he sees me.

"I see that, Jack. How are you doing ?"

"I can't say I am doing fine since I am back here. So many things happened, and I couldn't handle them. I screwed up everything. You know that I work as a fundraiser, but I couldn't do it this time because of my ill health. You see how much weight I've lost." He pulls up the sleeves of his shirt and shows me his weak forearms. "Do you know how I lost so much weight?"

"No," I reply. "You haven't told me yet."

He smiles. "I was missing rehab food." He laughs.

This time, he is lively. He has a changed personality. He is getting along with his peers very well. However, in the last few days, he appears sedated, and I think something isn't right. He is scheduled to be discharged on Saturday because, according to a prescription written in his chart, he was going to get his last dose of methadone on Saturday. His aftercare was set up with his consent. But the day he is being discharged, the nurse asks him the name of the clinic he was going to use to get his daily methadone, and he didn't know.

Now he is in my office. "Christopher, do you know which clinic I am going to?"

"You aren't going to any clinic. You are not on methadone maintenance," I answer.

"Of course I am," he insists.

"Jack, are you out of your head? You received a five milligram dose today, didn't you?"

"No," he denies, "I received fifty milligrams today."

"Jack, look at this." I show him the doctor's order in his chart. "This is what you were receiving daily. There is no other order in our chart. Your reviews were also done based on this prescription; that's why your last covered day was yesterday. You have to leave. I have to complete my remaining reviews. And you know that your insurance company declined you methadone maintenance. Please don't try to play games with me. I am busy. We will speak on the phone occasionally."

"I am serious," he pleads. "I am not lying. The nurse who gave me the morning dose is out to lunch, but you can ask him when he comes back."

"Jack, I can't keep you in that room any longer. You have to vacate now."

He collects his stuff and leaves the unit. Later, the shift supervisor is in my office. "Christopher, how can you discharge a client on methadone maintenance without setting up a clinic for him to receive his daily dose?"

"Jack is not on methadone maintenance," I tell him. "Look here."

He reluctantly looks into his chart and nods. "You are right, but he claims that he got fifty milligrams today."

"You need to talk with the nurse." I go back to work.

He calls out to the nurse. "Of course he is on methadone maintenance," the nurse says firmly.

"No, he is not. Look here." The shift supervisor shows him the order in the chart.

"Oh, shit!" The nurse almost jumps out of his skin and suddenly looks worried. "I think I made a mistake. I gave him the wrong dose. I don't know how I did that. I might have taken off some other client's order for him." He pauses and then continues, "But he knew he wasn't on methadone maintenance; he should have told me. He seems to be dishonest. I had too many new admissions that day. I was flooded

with orders. Let me find out those orders I took off for him."
The nurse hurries back to his ffice.

"What are you going to do about Jack?" The shift supervisor looks at me.

"You need to call a doctor," I reply, "and see what can be one."

The shift supervisor gets hold of a doctor and explains the whole situation to him. We decide to get Jack back on the unit and assign him to his previous room. The nurse writes down the phone order, but the next day, the order is changed again because the doctor decides to taper him down more rapidly.

"You know, Christopher, I have a case," Jack says when being discharged the second time. "But I won't do anything about it, because I have decided to do the right things in life."

"Jack, did you put a plastic bag full of shit under Bill's bed when you left last time?" I ask him since Bill isn't around and Jack seems to have changed.

"Yes, I did," he chuckles.

"Why did you do that?"

"He deserved it. But I wouldn't do it now; I want to change. I want to be a man. I want to walk the talk."

Jack is clean for almost two years now, and I feel that he is learning to walk the talk. Isn't that wonderful?

Insanity
I am in a search.
But I don't know what I am searching for.
Am I searching for peace of mind?
Happiness?
Name?
Fame?
Money?
I am going round and round and round.
I don't know how long this circle will go on.
I don't see any end to it.
And I am killing myself bit by bit.
Is it worth it?
The inner voice says
No. It is worthless.
And I see the futility of it
And still I am going after it.
Things are right in front of my eyes
And I am still fighting for it.
Isn't that insanity?
It sure is.
Insanity– Beyond Undestanding

Bajeerao Patil was born in rural Maharashtra, India. He acquired both his bachelor's degree in social work and master's degree in human resources from Bombay University, India. He is currently working in the field of addiction as a therapist. For the last nineteen years, he has worked with school dropouts, slum dwellers, sex workers, people with HIV and AIDS, and other less privileged sections of society in different capacities. He enjoys conversing with friends, playing chess, writing, working out at the gym, traveling and exploring forests. He is married to Dipti for the last ten years and his greatest pleasure is to spend time with their three young children, Adwaita, Aditya and Arohi.

www.ingramcontent.com/pod-product-compliance
Lightning Source LLC
Chambersburg PA
CBHW072104270326
41931CB00010B/1458